Capital without Borders

Capital without Borders

Wealth Managers and the One Percent

BROOKE HARRINGTON

Harvard University Press

Cambridge, Massachusetts, & London, England

First Harvard University Press paperback edition, 2020
First Printing

Library of Congress Cataloging-in-Publication Data
Names: Harrington, Brooke, 1968– author.
Title: Capital without borders : wealth managers and the one percent /
Brooke Harrington.
Description: Cambridge, Massachusetts : Harvard University Press, 2016. |
Includes bibliographical references and index.
Identifiers: LCCN 2016010534 | ISBN 9780674743809 (cloth : alk. paper) |
ISBN 9780674244771 (pbk.)
Subjects: LCSH: Financial planners. | Globalization—Economic aspects. |
Wealth. | Wealth—Moral and ethical aspects. | Income distribution. |
International finance.
Classification: LCC HG179.5 .H576 2016 | DDC 332.6—dc23
LC record available at http://lccn.loc.gov/2016010534

To ACH with love

Contents

Capital without Borders

Introduction

"HE IS SURROUNDED BY A MYSTERIOUS HALO OF FAMILY CONFI-
dences, of which he is known to be the silent depository."[1]
With these words, Charles Dickens introduces one of his most
memorable characters: Mr. Tulkinghorn, the villain of *Bleak
House*. Tulkinghorn is a lawyer specializing in trusts and
estates, making him privy to the private lives of Britain's nobility.
A master of legal intricacies, Tulkinghorn's emotionless, un-
readable façade gives him a reputation much prized by his
clients for protecting their secrets, as well as their fortunes.

Though he is their employee, Tulkinghorn wields a power
that quietly controls the lives of his clients. This distinguishes
him from the legion of other professionals and servants in the
novel: unlike the family physicians, butlers, and governesses
who serve the nobles, Tulkinghorn's knowledge of the families' innermost workings makes him *their* master. Such "inside
outsiders" deserve more scrutiny than they have received,
given their role in managing large capital flows at the boundary
of private family life and the public worlds of law and the
market.[2] This is a gap in knowledge that I aspire to fill here.

In a sense, *Bleak House* can be read as a story of the triumph of professionals over nobles, and of knowledge over wealth. Dickens' description of Tulkinghorn as the "master of the mysteries of great houses" is reminiscent of what Max Weber once wrote of the court accountants of the Persian shah: they "made a secret doctrine of their budgetary art and even use a secret script" to consolidate their power and ensure the shah's dependence upon them through obfuscation.[3] This is one way of characterizing elite professional work, particularly in the domain now known as "wealth management"—the business of deploying legal and financial expertise to defend the fortunes of high-net-worth individuals and families. These are the contemporary successors to Mr. Tulkinghorn.

Wealth managers will be the focus of this book because their work constitutes what the French anthropologist Marcel Mauss called *un fait total social*—that is, "a total social act," bringing together all the major institutions of a society.[4] Their remit is both technical and social, touching on finance and the family as well as on the role of the state and organizations.[5] It also affects many issues of contemporary debate, such as inequality, taxation, and globalization. One observer has described it as "the most complex role in any field of financial or political life."[6]

The profession and its origins

Wealth management is "a professional milieu coming together and in the process of being organized."[7] Recognition of its professional status did not begin until the era of *Bleak*

House, in the mid-nineteenth century. The profession's main representative body—the London-based Society of Trust and Estate Practitioners (STEP)—was not founded until 1991. Until recently it has not been possible to get a university degree or any other credential in wealth management.[8] As a result, the labor pool for the profession draws from other fields. Many contemporary practitioners are, like Tulkinghorn, lawyers by training; another major group comes from accountancy.[9] Still others come from backgrounds as diverse as academia and environmental activism. From an organizational perspective, wealth managers may be employed in a wide range of contexts, from private banks and trust companies to family offices and sole proprietorships.[10]

Because wealth management has only recently been professionalized, some basic issues are still being worked out, such as how to define the boundaries of the field and what name to adopt for practitioners. While the few studies of the profession acknowledge that "there is no generally accepted standard definition of wealth management," there is widespread agreement among scholars and practitioners that "a basic definition would be financial services provided to wealthy clients, mainly individuals and their families."[11] In choosing a name, the founders of the professional society elected to emphasize their historical connection to the feudal practice of trusteeship by calling themselves "trust and estate practitioners."[12] Yet that label seems increasingly inadequate to the complexity of the profession's activities. Now that STEP represents more than twenty thousand members in ninety-five countries, contemporary practice often involves not only trusteeship but also oversight of family businesses, coordination of many different types of assets around the world, and the ever-important consideration of the tax consequences of ownership and trading.

Attempts to capture the full complexity of professional activity have included the fanciful ("fiscal alchemists"), the utilitarian ("transaction planners"), and the politically pointed ("income defense providers").[13] However, consensus seems to be developing around the term "wealth managers," even among many STEP members.[14] Indeed, a much-discussed article in the *STEP Journal* claimed that STEP practitioners—unlike lawyers, bankers, or other competing professional groups—are "the true wealth managers," because their domain comprises "the whole spectrum of the client's assets and other financial affairs. Wealth management is seen as the overarching role pulling together the advice of various investment, tax, and other experts into a coherent plan."[15] Thus "wealth managers" is the term I will use in this book.

That the professionalization of trust and estate planning remains incomplete owes something to the changing nature of wealth itself. Historically, land ownership has been the primary source of great fortunes globally; this remains true in many parts of the world, particularly in Africa and Latin America.[16] In that context, family wealth could be defended without the intervention of professionals, through practices such as intermarriage, primogeniture, and entail.[17] In cases where those strategies were unavailable or impractical—as when knights of medieval Europe departed for the Crusades, leaving their lands vulnerable to seizure by the church, the state, or rival noblemen—some adopted the practice of putting their assets in trust. This involved transferring legal ownership of the property to a trusted kinsman or friend for the benefit of a third party, usually the original owner's wife and children, who had no legal standing to own property themselves and were thus left vulnerable to dispossession. This separation of legal ownership from the beneficial use of property, along with the use of volunteer trustees, proved a highly effective and versatile means of preserving wealth.[18] Until well into the nineteenth century, class solidarity sufficed to hold the system together without the intervention of professionals.

The professionalization of trust and estate planning ostensibly began with the *Harvard College v. Amory* decision of 1830, in which the Supreme Court of Massachusetts first acknowledged trustees as a professional class.[19] This coincided with the development of a new kind of wealth, characteristic of the New World. The largest family fortunes native to the United States grew through global trade—particularly in whaling, furs, and textiles—rather than agriculture. These businesses generated immense sums of cash, along with the need for investment opportunities and advice. As wealth took on new forms, moving from material property to merchant capital, the need for expert assistance in managing wealth increased as well. In other words, professional wealth management began to emerge with the transformation of capitalism itself.

A second catalyst for the professionalization of trust and estate planning was the development of offshore finance and the loosening of international currency restrictions—a process that unfolded from the 1960s through the 1980s.[20] These changes released many of the limits on the cross-border flow of capital. From a financial point of view, the boundaries of the nation-state became much more permeable, freeing wealthy families and individuals to shop around for the most favorable tax, regulatory, and political conditions for their assets. These conditions continue to change as states compete to attract private wealth to their jurisdictions. This makes finding the best bargain a complex task, usually outsourced to wealth managers. They are charged with deciding what kinds of legal, organizational, and financial structures are best suited to contain assets, and where to base those assets geographically. These decisions depend on the type of asset in question (is it a yacht, an art collection, or a stock portfolio?) as well as on the goals of the client.

What wealth managers do

As a practical matter, wealth managers' daily practice is somewhat like that of architects, in that they design complex, multifunction structures. Indeed, the Nobel Prize–winning economist Robert Shiller recently defined finance as "the science of goal architecture—of the structuring of the economic arrangements necessary to achieve a set of goals and the stewardship of the assets needed for that achievement."[21] From this perspective, wealth management is a profession operating at the very core of finance.

The financial architecture created by wealth managers contains assets rather than people; instead of bricks and mortar, the structures are composed of linked organizational entities, such as trusts, corporations, and foundations. The structures often serve multiple ends, commonly including tax reduction, avoidance of regulation, control of a family business, inheritance and succession planning, investment, and charitable giving. Legally binding documents, such as a will or a trust instrument, serve as the blueprints for these designs. Unlike architects, wealth managers also maintain the structures they create. As laws, financial conditions, and political climates change, so do the strategies needed to manage clients' assets. Keeping up with all this requires a complex skill set; this is why many wealthy people who have made or inherited fortunes find it impractical to manage the assets themselves. Instead they hire wealth managers, who must be—as one STEP training manual puts it—"part lawyer, part tax adviser, part accountant and part investment adviser all rolled into one."[22] While some professionals are able to master all these forms of expertise for a single jurisdiction, international transactions require wealth managers to assemble and coordinate a team of advisors. In this sense, wealth managers are more like general contractors than architects: responsible for executing the client's strategic plan, but relying on a team of subcontractors for highly specialized parts of the job.

Though the precise configurations of such complex structures are rarely made public, we can get a sense of them from professional publications. The following is a typical client scenario from one of STEP's training manuals:

The proposed settlor is a Brazilian national, but has been living in Canada for the last 15 years where he considers his permanent home to be. The trustees are to be a trust institution in the Cayman Islands with a professional protector situated in the Bahamas. It is intended that the trust assets will comprise shares in two underlying companies: the holding company of the settlor's Latin American business empire is incorporated as an exempt company in Bermuda; and an IBC [International Business Corporation] incorporated in BVI holding a portfolio of stocks and shares. The discretionary beneficiaries comprise a class of persons who reside throughout Europe and South America.[23]

Three aspects of this scenario are worth noting to illustrate the complexity of wealth management. The first is the international scope of the client's situation: six countries and their respective laws are implicated in this asset-holding structure, not including the various states in Europe and South America where the beneficiaries (the people who will benefit financially from this wealth management plan) reside. The wealth manager must coordinate with experts in each of those jurisdictions to keep abreast of changes in tax laws and other regulations. The wealth manager must also be prepared to move the assets from any of the jurisdictions at any time, should conditions become unfavorable to the client's interests (e.g., through nationalization of industries or a significant rise in inflation or taxation). Second, there is a complex cast of characters involved, including not just professionals—such as the trustees in the Cayman Islands and the directors of the International Business Corporation in Bermuda—but also the client (the settlor) and the beneficiaries.

Third and finally, there is the mix of structures, with a trust holding shares in multiple underlying corporations. This trust-corporation configuration—which I will explain in Chapter 4—allows assets to be transferred back and forth in

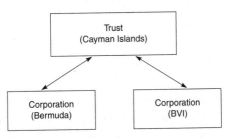

Figure 1.1. An asset-holding structure combining a trust with underlying corporations.

what has been characterized as a "shell game extraordinaire."[24] The game's objectives include the avoidance of taxes, creditors, and inheritance laws. A simple illustration showing the relationship among the substructures is found in Figure 1.1.

Keeping assets circulating among structures and across jurisdictions allows them to move through the regulatory apparatus of nation-states in a nearly frictionless manner. "Friction" here refers mainly to the activities of tax authorities, courts, and other governance bodies. Thwarting the aims of the state without breaking any laws has been described by legal scholars as a set of "tricks" for "manipulating facets of ownership."[25] Through wealth managers' skillful use of tools such as trusts, foundations, and corporations, the game of "now you see it, now you don't" can go on almost indefinitely, leaving clients' wealth to grow untouched by tax authorities, creditors, heirs, and anyone else who might want a piece of the fortune.

Major themes of the book

This study seeks to shed light not just on what wealth managers do but also on why it matters. Thus I examine the profession's impact on key social structures, as well as what wealth management can tell us about changes in of institutional and private life. Topics will include:

Economic inequality. From their origins in medieval England, the practices on which wealth management is based have served two related ends: the protection of family fortunes and the reproduction of elites. By identifying the central role of wealth managers in these processes, this book addresses a major theoretical challenge in the study of stratification: "to ascertain *who* makes things endure and *how*."[26] While other research has posited a link between professions and inequality, I look specifically at a new group of actors who are "crucial" and "irreplaceable" to global stratification processes, along with the techniques they use to defend the wealth of their clients.[27]

The impact of the profession hinges on its deep historical connections to dynastic wealth, dating back to feudal Europe, coupled with its use of innovative legal and financial techniques, putting it at the forefront of contemporary global finance. Ordinarily, wealth managers are employed by clients who have already accumulated their fortunes, so the professional's job is less to increase the value of those assets than to protect them from dissipation at the hands of tax authorities, creditors, and heirs. This defensive orientation gives the profession an unusual position within the finance industry, which is otherwise associated with aggressive profit seeking.[28]

A century ago wealth managers' clients were known collectively as "the leisure class," a group that probably numbered in the low four figures, concentrated in North America and

Europe.[29] These days the clients are far more diverse, since "the world is becoming more wealthy, and much of this wealth is global rather than in traditionally wealthy countries."[30] Thus the contemporary client base includes the world's 167,669 "ultra-high-net-worth individuals," defined as those with at least $30 million in investable assets.[31] Unlike their predecessors, these elites are widely distributed around the globe, and—thanks in part to the expert interventions of wealth managers—they constitute "the hegemonic fraction of capital worldwide."[32]

As world wealth has grown to record levels in recent years— to an estimated $241 trillion—inequality has also grown, with 0.7 percent of the global population owning 41 percent of the assets.[33] This is coupled with lowered wealth mobility, meaning that to an increasing extent, the rich stay rich and the poor stay poor, generation after generation.[34] This is important because, despite recent attention to income inequality, the distribution of wealth is actually far more unequal, and far more consequential.[35] While income fluctuates, wealth stabilizes, affecting access to opportunities in virtually every domain, from education to the labor market, marriage, property ownership, and political power.[36]

Through facilitating tax avoidance—including the intergenerational transfer of family fortunes free of inheritance tax—wealth managers have contributed to this pattern of increasing global inequality. As one recent study observed, "These professionals are crucial: as far as we can tell, they were present at each and every legislative innovation designed to avoid tax and regulation."[37] In concrete terms, wealth managers are estimated to direct the flows of up to $21 trillion in private wealth, resulting in about $200 billion in lost tax revenues globally each year.[38] In effect, these professionals detach assets from the states that wish to tax and regulate them, creating a form of capital that is, like its owners, "transnational" and "hypermobile."[39] By "artificially manipulating paper trails of money across borders," wealth managers are creating not just asset-holding and tax-avoidance structures but a new body of transnational institutions, which are expanding outside of any democratic process of checks and balances.[40] STEP's publications acknowledge this aspect of its members' work, framing it as a defense of capitalists against the depredations of "confiscatory" states.[41]

Professions' role in society. Much of what wealth managers do as part of their day-to-day practice occurs in an "ethical gray area"—a realm of activity that is formally legal but socially illegitimate.[42] This includes not only tax avoidance but also the use of trusts, offshore corporations, and other tools to help clients avoid paying their creditors and to exclude family members from their legally mandated share of an inheritance.[43] Such tactics, many of which are also used by corporations to avoid taxation and regulation, are attracting increasing public attention and condemnation, posing a threat to the profession and putting it "on a collision course with civil society."[44]

Indeed, the profession has been singled out for blame by government agencies concerned with tax evasion, money laundering, and growing worldwide wealth inequality. For example, in its 2006 Seoul Declaration, the Organisation for Economic Co-operation and Development (OECD) initiated new legal sanctions on tax avoidance practices and made special mention of the roles played by "law and accounting firms, other tax advisors and financial institutions in relation to non-compliance" with international laws.[45] U.S. senator Carl Levin has complained about the asset-holding structures created by wealth managers to obscure their clients' assets: "Most are so complex that they are MEGOs, 'My Eyes Glaze Over' type of schemes. Those who cook up these concoctions count on their complexity to escape scrutiny and public ire."[46]

As an example, consider the Pritzker family of Chicago, whose $15 billion fortune has made them one of the wealthiest families in the United States. Their assets are held in 60 companies and 2,500 trusts, using structures and strategies that *Forbes* magazine—normally a cheerleader for wealthy elites—describes with an unusual hint of moral distaste as "shadowy . . . constructed to discourage outside inquiry—and brilliantly exploitive of loopholes in the tax code."[47] This complex asset-holding structure was created not by the Pritzker family itself but by its lawyers, accountants, tax specialists, and investment advisors. These professionals not only shelter wealth from taxation but serve to "obscure concentrations of economic power," using entities such as shell corporations and trusts that make it difficult (if not impossible) to identify the true owners of wealth.[48] The use of trusts is particularly common because most jurisdictions do not require them to be registered, and even in the few places where registration of trustees is required, the identities of settlors and beneficiaries remain secret. The use of corporate structures, on the other hand, does require public registration in many jurisdictions, but ownership can be readily disguised using nominee shareholders and directors—third parties hired expressly to create a

"It's snappy, it's today — I like it."

Figure 1.2. Wealth management has a negative public image in some quarters. *Source:* www.CartoonStock.com.

buffer between those with the legal responsibility for wealth and those who actually benefit from it.

As a result, what was once a low-profile profession with an impeccable reputation—epitomized by Tulkinghorn—has acquired a very negative public image, as lampooned in Figure 1.2. Wealth managers combat this threat to their reputation at multiple levels, including individual interactions with clients, firm-based efforts to build and preserve a reputation as honest brokers, and the work of the professional society (STEP) to influence perceptions by the media, politicians, and the public. These efforts are crucial to the survival of wealth management, because reputation provides access to clients, markets, and opportunities to expand professional jurisdiction. As one study put it, "Reputational capital [is] at the apex of selling complex products in professional markets."[49]

In contrast, failure to maintain a professional reputation can result in blacklisting, crippling financial penalties, and the loss of jurisdictional territory to competitors. Maintaining a reputation for ethical as well as formally legal conduct is particularly vital for a recently recognized profession, because practitioners are still obliged to justify themselves and "the special importance of their work for society and the common weal."[50] While STEP approaches this problem through lobbying government bodies and carrying on an active public relations campaign in the media, firms and practitioners must address the issue one client at a time, navigating the competing demands to deliver a luxury service to ultra-high-net-worth individuals while staying within the patchwork of laws and social norms surrounding their work.[51]

The institutional triad: families, states, markets. The original purpose of wealth management was to ensure the smooth transfer of landed estates—free of taxation and legal encumbrances—from one generation to the next. Creating asset-holding structures to transfer large fortunes within families remains the bread-and-butter work of most wealth managers today: hence the inclusion of the term "estate practitioners" in the name of the professional society. This practice, which C. Wright Mills called the "pass[ing] on to children of strategic positions in the apparatus of appropriation," affects far more than the private wealth and interpersonal relationships of individual families.[52] By consolidating resources over generations, it creates *dynastic* wealth, which in turn fuels a political power elite—a new aristocracy, symbolized by people such as Mitt Romney and George Bush, whose inheritances and multiple trust funds were factors in their ability to run for the U.S. presidency.[53] In ensuring that those family assets are not for sale to others—and the wealth not redistributed through taxation—wealth managers deprive markets of liquidity, hindering their development.[54]

Families, states, and markets are among society's key institutions.[55] The work of wealth managers spans these domains, bringing them together in ways that are at times conflicting, at other times mutually reinforcing. For example, the transmission of inheritances is regarded by a wide range of social scientists—from archaeologists examining Neolithic tribes to economists studying modern parent-child relationships—as an essential component in the maintenance of family solidarity and identity.[56] By ensuring that assets remain under the ownership of a single family across generations, wealth managers contribute to the stability of those families and of the larger social structure.

On the other hand, wealth managers may also find themselves presiding over the erosion of solidarity, in which inheritance—in the words of Marx and Engels—"reduce[s] the family relation to a mere money relation."[57] In some cases, the fortune that holds the family together may also destroy it. For example, the Pritzkers (mentioned above) lost a sizable part of their fortune in a ruinously expensive lawsuit when one heir accused the family's wealth managers of apportioning the benefits unfairly.[58] The frequency with which such intrafamily disputes occur is suggested by the multiple forms of support and training the wealth management professional society offers its members on this subject: for example, STEP has a special-interest group for "Contentious Trusts and Estates," and it offers advanced certificates in both "Trust Disputes" and "Mediation." A recent *STEP Journal* article noted that in addition to the threats that creditors and tax authorities pose to a family's wealth, "the 'enemy within' needs to be considered. Putting it bluntly: how can you stop the family from pushing the self-destruct button?"[59] Professionals may not be able to stop this self-destruction, since they are legally obligated to adhere to the terms of the wills and trust documents on which the structures they create and administer are based. This obligation sometimes makes the wealth manager the living representative of long-deceased patriarchs (rarely matriarchs), whose restrictions on the right of inheritance (requiring, for example, an unequal division of property among siblings) can breed bitter resentment among later generations.[60]

Wealth managers find themselves in a similarly conflicted position with regard to nation-states. On the one hand, they are state-builders in some domains, writing the key laws of offshore financial centers and consulting to onshore legislatures (such as the U.K. Parliament) on matters of professional jurisdiction.[61] On the other hand, their work radically undermines the economic basis and legal authority of the modern tax state.[62] "Professional subversion" is their stock in trade.[63] This consists in finding and exploiting loopholes and "regulatory voids," as well as arbitraging conflicts of laws across multiple jurisdictions, all in the service of helping their clients escape the bounds of state power.[64] In this undermining of the state, alliances among elites may be more complicated than wealth managers versus regulators. As recent research has shown, political, economic, and professional elites in some nations (notably the United States) collude to create a highly complex tax system that keeps wealth managers in business and their clients wealthy enough to contribute to the political campaigns of the lawmakers. Though the state loses billions in tax revenues, the intermediation of the wealth managers maintains a "delicate balance" among elite interests, often at the expense of democratic participation and popular sovereignty.[65]

With regard to the market, tying up family fortunes over multiple generations—and, increasingly, in perpetuity—puts wealth managers in conflict with the dynamics of capitalism.[66] Over time, family fortunes generally dissipate on their own, a phenomenon summed up in an adage found in multiple cultures and languages worldwide: "shirtsleeves to shirtsleeves in three generations."[67] Wealth managers seek to arrest this process. But capitalism, as Schumpeter observed, depends on change rather than stability.[68] As early as the Enlightenment, recognition of the need for wealth to circulate freely in order for markets to develop created opposition to trusts, entail, and other "market-independent form[s] of allocation of capital."[69] With the growth of global commerce through the nineteenth century, philosophers such as John Stuart Mill noted that "the 'dead hand' of the past had hampered the growth of a free economy."[70] Such critiques continue into the present day with the movement by wealthy individuals such as Warren Buffett to ensure that inheritance taxation continues, so that at least some family wealth gets redistributed into the economy.[71]

Finally, while their intent may be conservative, the *methods* wealth managers have innovated to achieve stability in their clients' fortunes can have a profoundly disruptive impact on markets. For example, many of the financial and legal tools they refined to protect clients' assets also formed the organizational structure of the subprime mortgage crisis. This is particularly clear in the case of "special-purpose vehicles," which are like the fireproof safes of offshore finance: asset-holding structures designed for the sole purpose of insulating their contents from risk. Put a corporate subsidiary into a special-purpose vehicle, and it is protected from bankruptcy, creditors, and litigants. The entangling of many contemporary private fortunes with corporate wealth meant that putting assets into special-purpose vehicles created new risks for the financial system as a whole, moving an enormous volume of wealth off corporate balance sheets, out of the sight of regulators and auditors.[72]

The plan of the book

The remainder of the book will proceed as follows:

> Chapter 2 reviews the origins and evolution of wealth management as a profession. The historical trajectory of the profession is unusual in two respects: first, because of its independence from state control, and second, because for centuries wealth management was an amateur undertaking conducted by elites for elites. The late establishment of formal institutions within wealth management—such as a credentialing program—is indicative of a larger pattern of class-based resistance to or ambivalence about professionalization, as well as of the entry of commercial norms into transactions among gentlemen. How wealth management navigated this

transition and how this developmental history continues to shape the profession in contemporary practice will be the subject of this chapter.

> Chapter 3 is devoted to client relations and the insights of wealth managers about their elite clientele. Distinct from other contemporary professionals, wealth managers enjoy an extraordinary degree of intimacy with their clients, delving into virtually all aspects of clients' lives. Once such relationships are established, they often endure a lifetime, or over several generations of service to a single family. But in order to get there, practitioners must first gain the trust of individuals who are deeply suspicious and wary of being exploited—often with good reason. In a globalized economy, this feat of building trust must be achieved across barriers of culture, language, and religion. How wealth managers gain and keep clients under these challenging circumstances is the subject of this chapter.

> Chapter 4 offers an in-depth look at the financial and legal innovations through which the profession achieves its aims of wealth defense. It reviews the basic tools of the profession—trusts, corporations, and foundations—and shows how they are deployed to solve common problems that clients bring to wealth managers. These problems go far beyond tax avoidance: depending on the client's country of origin, he or she may also need help protecting the family fortune from corrupt government officials, kidnappers, or frivolous lawsuits. Other clients may wish simply to avoid paying their debts. The role of offshore financial centers in wealth defense and law avoidance is reviewed in detail, and an appendix offers a primer on the basic legal-financial structures in use.

> Chapter 5 takes up the subject of inequality in detail, examining the economic and political impact of wealth

managers' work, not just for their clients but for larger patterns of socioeconomic organization as well. It offers an analysis of wealth inequality and its significance in comparison to the better-known form of stratification, income inequality. The chapter also provides a model to illustrate the three processes by which wealth managers contribute to inequality, through techniques that can turn one individual's surplus income into a "perpetual-motion machine" of wealth reproduction. A final theme of this chapter will be practitioners' reflections on their role in deepening economic inequality globally, and how they respond to the reputational challenges this poses to the profession.

> Chapter 6 will review the complex relationship between wealth managers and nation-states, including the neocolonial dynamics of the offshore financial centers. The profession's independence from state authority—discussed in Chapter 2—gives it a distinct position in contemporary practice. On the one hand, wealth management undermines the state in many respects, by depriving it of tax revenue and by helping clients avoid laws they find inconvenient. On the other hand, these practices are possible only because of state sovereignty, without which there would be no laws (or loopholes, or conflicts of laws) for wealth managers to exploit. Thus, wealth management professionals sometimes take the opportunity to write (or rewrite) the laws of certain jurisdictions themselves; at the same time, their profes-sional society, STEP, takes an active role in lobbying legislatures. The multifaceted relationship of wealth managers to states really comes to the fore in the offshore financial centers, which are essential to the global capital flows the profession manages. How wealth management is a state-building force in some respects and a state-

destroying force in others—and with what consequences—is the subject of this chapter.

> Chapter 7 concludes the book with implications for
policy and research, as well as observations on the future
of the profession.

APPENDIX

How this study was conducted

As members of a relatively new profession, bridging financial-
legal innovation with the rarely examined world of large private fortunes, wealth managers make a compelling subject for
research. Given their influence on law, politics, and vast global
capital flows, one would expect them to have been the subject
of a robust research literature. But the profession is virtually
unknown to scholars, outside of a few recent articles and portions of a book now more than twenty years old.[73] This is due
not to a lack of interest but to the difficulty of obtaining information. In the remainder of this chapter I will say more about
this difficulty and the unusual steps I took to overcome it.

Barriers to access. The wealthy and powerful are notoriously
difficult to study.[74] Because of a variety of factors, including
privacy concerns, geographic remoteness, and a formidable
array of gatekeepers protecting them from outsiders, elites
are "out of reach on a number of planes: they don't want to be
studied."[75] Within this domain, wealth management presents
additional barriers to access for researchers due to the norms

and technical characteristics of the profession. The work itself, like that of the shah's accountants, depends on complexity and secrecy for its effectiveness.[76] There is also the professionals' commitment to fiduciary discretion: a code of conduct that requires them to maintain strict privacy around their clients' wealth and the means used to preserve it.[77] As a result, the professionals themselves have kept a low profile publicly. In recent years these tendencies have been accentuated by the perception that the profession is under attack by entities such as the OECD, which has portrayed wealth managers as agents of money laundering and tax evasion.[78] These public characterizations have generated considerable resentment and suspicion of outsiders among some professionals.

Because of the unusual access strategy I designed—in which I undertook the full training program to become certified as a wealth manager, as explained in greater detail below—this suspicion did not present a significant problem for my data gathering until very late in the study, when the first two papers based on this research were published. Until then, professionals who didn't wish to speak with me either ignored or politely refused my requests for interviews. Only once my findings started to be published, about six years into the project, did anyone treat me with open hostility. It is worth mentioning one case in particular, because it vividly illustrates the sense of grievance some wealth managers feel regarding their profession's public reputation, along with their reluctance to discuss their work with anyone inquiring into the consequences of their professional activity.

In August 2013 I conducted a prearranged interview in the British Virgin Islands (BVI) with a white male in his sixties, a banker by training and a native of Great Britain. He greeted me by saying that he had read my two recently published papers from the project and found my work to be "left-leaning" and "disapproving of what the [wealth management] industry and wealthy people are doing." He added, "The whole STEP community in BVI are wondering what you're doing here." Although he graciously answered my interview questions, he wasn't done with the subject of my "agenda." At the conclusion of the interview, he crossed his arms, leaned back in his chair, and expressed his resentment that wealth managers and their clients had been "vilified" as being "immoral for not paying as much tax as some people think they should." He added that "a member of the STEP community" in BVI suggested that "you should be thrown off the island based on your writings" about the profession.

I was so taken aback by this statement, and the hostility with which it was delivered, that I went into the default politeness-and-deference mode that many women learn as a means to defuse threatening situations.[79] So instead of responding with more scholarly inquiry, I thanked the man for his time, shook his hand, and walked back to the bar at my hotel to have a drink. I was unaware then of a highly relevant precedent: just two years previously, another tax haven (the Channel Island of Jersey) had detained, deported, and ultimately banned a reporter from *Newsweek* magazine for investigating claims of illegal activity there. Even though the story had no connection to financial services, it was expected to bring negative publicity to the island, threatening its reputation as a quiet, off-the-radar place for elites to park their fortunes. Remarkably, the financial authorities on the island were so well connected that they managed to bar the reporter not only from reentering Jersey but also from entering the United Kingdom as a whole.[80] Learning of this story made me view the conversation with the BVI banker in a new light: I realized it was consistent with a larger pattern of enmeshment between the wealth management profession and state authority, at least offshore. This crystallized some of the analysis found in Chapter 6, on wealth management and the state.

From a practical point of view, this experience also underscored the value of taking the "full immersion" route to conducting the study.[81] I suspect that I would have experienced much more hostility and suspicion had I not first invested two years in the wealth management training program, which made me less of an outsider than I would have been otherwise. Immersion—while not a common strategy in contemporary social science because of the high costs in time, effort, and money—is nonetheless a classic approach for studying groups that are otherwise too secretive, defensive, or marginalized to grant access to outsiders. In taking this approach, I was inspired by classic studies, such as those by William Whyte and John van Maanen.[82]

Van Maanen set a particularly good example, because—like me—he wanted to conduct research on an occupational group that was particularly suspicious of "left-leaning" academics. For him, the subject was police departments, and his timing made the work particularly difficult. Van Maanen undertook his project at the height of the antiauthoritarian 1970s, not long after the Watts riots shook Southern California.[83] His initial requests to study police departments in the region yielded more than twenty rejection letters. But instead of reorienting his research to a more practically feasible subject, van Maanen interpreted the rejections as all the more reason to push for access. He made the most of his freedom as a doctoral student by enrolling in the police academy and undergoing the full training process to become an officer— ultimately even going out on patrol. Only through this means did he win enough trust and cooperation to conduct his groundbreaking research.

Like van Maanen, I started my research by going back to school. In November 2007 I enrolled in a two-year wealth management training program leading to a credential that is now the accepted global standard for practitioners: the TEP, or Trust and Estate Planning certification. Earning the credential is contingent upon passing five courses in key domains of technical competence: trust law, corporate law, investments, finance, and accounting. During these courses, which I attended in Switzerland and Liechtenstein, I had three objectives: educating myself about the field from the inside and developing an informed interview strategy; collecting thickly descriptive data on the professionals, interactions, and settings I observed; and recruiting wealth managers to participate in extended interviews.[84]

Although I never used the credential I earned to practice wealth management, completing the program with honors made me just enough of an insider to overcome the profession's formidable barriers to access. This was a question of both legitimacy and practicality: holding the wealth management credential, or being enrolled in a credentialing course, was a formal prerequisite for attending the professional society meetings where I ultimately recruited most of the participants in this study. Without the credential, it would have been difficult or impossible for me to conduct the interviews that form the basis for this book. The investment of time and money involved in pursuing such an access strategy was significant—and a common barrier to access in the study of elites.[85] Unlike van Maanen (and Whyte), I was no longer a doctoral student with time aplenty. But I was fortunate to have the support of research fellowships from the Max Planck Institute for the Study of Societies and the Alexander von Humboldt Foundation, which gave me the resources to undergo this costly training process. I was also helpful that, like the majority of wealth managers, I am white, a native English-speaker, and possessed of an upper-middle-class habitus.[86] The necessity of having the right "tone," the right "gestures," and "appropriate language" when studying elites has been well documented, and these (along with the credential) assisted me in accessing this profession.[87]

Why ethnography? Because of the many barriers to access presented by elites, and the additional challenges associated with research on wealth managers, ethnography was one of the only practical methods for studying these professionals. Survey research was impractical, since the dearth of previous research on the profession and the lack of up-to-date information on their practices made it impossible to create a valid questionnaire. Use of archival data and public records, such as tax filings and corporate registrations, would be of limited value, since careful analysis shows that they are often misleading, sometimes intentionally so.[88] Wealth management in particular produces a paper trail that is of limited value for researchers: the use of trusts (whose existence and beneficiaries are not publicly registered) and corporations (which employ nominee directors and shareholders to disguise their true ownership) create formidable barriers to data-gathering efforts.

Finally, this study's approach is grounded in a distinct philosophy of science derived from the work of Max Weber, who defined sociology as "a science concerning itself with the interpretive understanding [*Verstehen*] of social action."[89] This focus on interpretation, which is shared by disciplines such as history and anthropology, stands in distinction to the approach of natural sciences such as physics or chemistry on explanation [*Erklären*]. While explanation-oriented research seeks to define universally valid laws of causality, the objective of studies oriented to interpretive understanding is to create historically contextualized typologies of action. From these differing goals stem different approaches to research design: "the emphasis on *verstehen* encourages more inductive research designs and demands that developments at the macro-level are explained with reference to their micro-foundations."[90] In order to achieve these goals, it was necessary to undertake an ethnographic study.

While there is disagreement among scholars as to what constitutes an ethnography, such a study is typically grounded in data gathered from interviews, observation (participant or nonparticipant), and material culture, including documents and objects of significance to those being studied.[91] Analytically, the focus is on meaning, interpretation, and interaction. The interactional aspect of the study is particularly significant, because dominant perspectives on globalization, such as the "world polity" approach or theories that privilege structural relationships among states and classes, overlook the negotiated encounters that make up the bulk of professional activity on a day-to-day basis.[92] As a result, they can tell us little about how those interactions are connected to global norms, policies, and practices in the professions.[93]

In contrast, ethnography assumes a concrete, relational, actor-centered perspective. Beyond the information gathered through interviews and observation, the trust and rapport established in face-to-face settings can open doors to new and valuable data sources, from introductions to other informants to the provision of documents otherwise unobtainable or previously unknown. In this sense, ethnography can access "information not recorded elsewhere, or not yet available (if ever) for public release."[94] The method offers insights into the rarely glimpsed "back stages" of elite professional work, which "are carefully protected from outsiders and . . . only known to insiders."[95] These are particularly useful characteristics for the purposes of this study, given that the majority of what wealth managers do lies in that protected backstage zone, along with most information about the fortunes of their elite clients.

Why STEP? While STEP is not the only professional society to which wealth managers may belong, it is has virtually no competition. Bar associations have long offered special-interest groups for trust and estate practitioners, but these have not produced the kinds of professional coherence or institutions (such as credentialing programs) we find embodied in STEP. The entity most similar to STEP in terms of its ambitions to represent a distinct professional domain around wealth management is the American College of Trust and Estate Counsel (ACTEC). Founded in 1949, ACTEC is much older than STEP, but its membership and purpose are far more restricted, comprising only lawyers in North America. In consequence, its membership base includes just 2,600 individuals, compared to the 20,000 who belong to STEP.

Other organizations offer credentials that cover similar intellectual territory as STEP's program but do not claim to represent the profession as a whole. Thus the College for Financial Planning provides training to become an Accredited Wealth Management Advisor; the Institute of Business and Finance offers the Certified Estate and Trust Specialist designation; and the American Academy of Financial Management has a training program leading to certification as a Chartered Trust and Estate Planner.[96] None of these has achieved the industry-standard status of STEP's Trust and Estate Planner (TEP) credential.[97] By intent, STEP represents wealth management globally, and it has established the organizational structure to achieve this. Along with its huge membership, this gives STEP a position of dominance in the field, and makes it the best site from which to conduct a study of the profession.

Participant observation. The coursework to earn the wealth management credential was quite rigorous and challenging. Each of the five courses took about two months to complete: after several weeks of self-study focused on a course book of 300 to 400 pages, the twelve to twenty people enrolled would meet for a weeklong classroom session culminating in an exam. The intense effort created a kind of camaraderie that facilitated my research strategy. As students, we were all working so hard to pass the courses that we spent considerable time together over meals, during breaks, and after class. Conferring about the course material led to sharing "war stories" from the profession, including insights on cultural differences among high-net-worth clients from different regions of the globe, as well as tales of career trajectories and the latest techniques for evading regulators. Observing the racial and gender composition of the student groups, as well as their self-presentation norms, also became valuable data, feeding into the design of the interviews I conducted later.

During the participant observation phase of the study, the other students knew who I was and what I was doing there. It was not necessary to "go undercover," nor to entice wealth managers into breaching their duties of confidentiality, both of which would have violated sociological research ethics in any case.[98] I registered for every course and event with my real name and institutional affiliation. My badge provoked questions about my identity and reasons for being in the course, which turned out to be a useful icebreaker. I found that disclosure of my academic position and purposes encouraged some participants to talk with me, because—they said—they knew I was neither in professional competition with them nor part of the rarified social milieu of their wealthy clients. This, combined with the anonymity I guaranteed, made it unlikely that anything they told me would affect their professional reputation or their monopoly on expert knowledge.

A final reason for these professionals' cooperation may simply have been the ready availability of an informed but nonthreatening listener. Many people in technically complex professions don't have many opportunities to vent about their work lives with anyone: their family and friends are unlikely to understand the nature of the work, and with professional peers, there are often concerns about exposing proprietary information. I didn't pose any of those risks, but did have the advantage of understanding the profession well enough to follow along when practitioners told their stories. For wealth managers, talking with me may have been similar to travelers sharing stories on a long flight: a means of venting or of relating achievements that made them feel proud, or embarassed or ambivalent, secure in the knowledge that both parties would walk away from the conversation and never cross paths again.

Semistructured interviews. Between 2008 and 2015 I conducted sixty-five interviews in English with wealth managers in eighteen countries.[99] The interview sites included many of the most significant financial centers in the world, such as Switzerland, Liechtenstein, Hong Kong, Singapore, Mauritius, and the following British crown dependencies and overseas territories: Guernsey, Jersey, the British Virgin Islands, and the Cayman Islands. I also conducted interviews in the newer, up-and-coming financial centers, particularly those serving the growing wealth in Asia, such as the Seychelles. Figure 1.3 shows the geographical distribution of the data gathering.

Interviews typically lasted ninety minutes, with a range of twenty minutes to more than three hours. In more than 80 percent of cases, I was able to capture participants' responses by typing directly into a word-processing program; when this was not possible, I took handwritten notes that were transcribed within twenty-four hours. The interview questions focused on client relations, varying cultural attitudes about

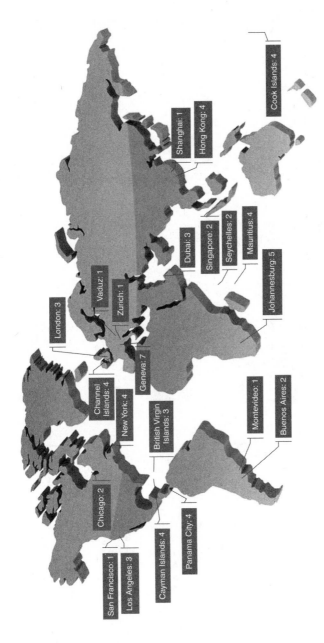

Figure 1.3. Quantity and location of wealth manager interviews.

Cook Islands: 4

Shanghai: 1
Hong Kong: 4

Dubai: 3
Singapore: 2
Seychelles: 2
Mauritius: 4
Johannesburg: 5

Vaduz: 1
Zurich: 1
London: 3
Geneva: 7

Channel Islands: 4
New York: 4
British Virgin Islands: 3

Montevideo: 1
Buenos Aires: 2

Chicago: 2

San Francisco: 1
Los Angeles: 3
Cayman Islands: 4
Panama City: 4

Table 1.1. Demographic composition of interview sample

Characteristic	Count	Percentage
Gender		
Women	19	29
Men	46	71
Age Group		
20s	1	2
30s	21	32
40s	21	32
50s	13	20
60s	9	14
*Race/Ethnicity**		
White	46	70
Black	6	9
Indian or Pakistani	5	8
East Asian	3	5
Latino/a	5	8
Professional Background		
Law	25	39
Private Banking	20	31
Corporate Finance	6	9
Accountancy	6	9
Other	8	12
STEP Membership		
Yes	44	68
No	21	32

* This study acknowledges that is it problematic to classify people by race and ethnicity. For example, the category "black" in this context includes people who identify as African American, Afro-Caribbean, Seychellois, Mauritian, and bi- or multiracial. In this sense, racial-ethnic groupings are bound to be inaccurate and reductive. However, within the context of the broader demographic picture presented here, information about race and ethnicity may be helpful—particularly since a majority of interview participants mentioned that culture and identification play a significant role in the establishment of trust between professionals and their clients. The importance of perceived racial and ethnic similarity between professionals and clients has also been documented in recent research. See in particular Becky Hsu, Conrad Hackett, and Leslie Hinkson, "The Importance of Race and Religion in Social-Service Providers," *Social Science Quarterly* 95 (2014): 393–410.

wealth, financial and legal techniques for protecting clients' assets, and key factors for success in the profession. Table 1.1 shows the demographic composition of the sample. The interview participants were fairly diverse, representing nineteen nationalities and ranging in age from late twenties to late sixties. Like other domains of professional service, however, there was little diversity in gender or race/ethnicity.[100] The majority of participants—71 percent—were male, and 70 percent were of white European origins. These figures are roughly consistent with those published by the U.K. Bar Council and the American Bar Association, which track the demographics of the legal profession—a useful comparison, since the majority of wealth managers are lawyers by training.[101]

Within the text, participants are identified by pseudonyms and the location where they practice. When necessary to contextualize their remarks, they are also identified by nationality. I considered creating a table of pseudonyms showing the age, nationality, ethnicity, and other demographic characteristics of individual participants in this study, but had to abandon the idea when it became clear that it would make them too easily identifiable. This was a particular concern for the participants working in small jurisdictions with few practitioners, in which two or three characteristics would suffice to distinguish individuals.

⋖ 2 ⋗

Wealth Management as a Profession

THIS CHAPTER EXPLORES HOW A SET OF PRACTICES THAT FOR centuries were carried out by amateurs evolved into a profession that impacts contemporary global politics and finance. As early as the 1930s, professions were recognized as a force that would change the world. Talcott Parsons, one of the major sociologists of the twentieth century, identified these knowledge-bearing occupations as a new way of organizing social life, distinct from both families and bureaucracies.[1] In this early, optimistic view, professions were seen as fundamentally progressive, essential to the smooth functioning of modern societies. Neither management nor labor, unpropertied but armed with formidable expertise, these actors were thought to be endowed with benevolent transformative power in organizations, markets, and politics.[2]

A generation later, more critical perspectives began to emerge, arguing that professionals had morphed from the role of "social trustees"—guardians of the public interest—to profit-seekers.[3] In many ways, the trajectory and public reputation of wealth management exemplifies this pattern. But the findings of this study suggest that social trusteeship has not been supplanted by the pursuit of profit; rather, the two orientations coexist in uneasy tension with one another, giving a distinctive shape to contemporary professional practice.

Tracing the emergence of wealth management as a profession reveals several continuities between medieval and modern conditions. This is congruent with insights about contemporary elite professions, which note that "their function has been not unlike those of the medieval guilds."[4] The guilds arose in the late 1300s and early 1400s—around the same time as trusts and trusteeship, from which the modern wealth management profession emerged. This is not coincidental: both trusts and guilds, as self-organizing and self-governing institutions, challenged state power.[5] In addition, some have noted that the impact of wealth management—its success in protecting wealth from taxation and regulation—"is taking us back in time, back to the values and society of the feudal world."[6] Still others have observed that many of the microstates that have become leading global centers of wealth management activity are a "feudal remnant," their territories and sovereignty created from duchies and principalities predating the Westphalian political order by centuries. These include the Channel Islands of Jersey and Guernsey—the last sovereign fragments of the Duchy of Normandy, once held by William the Conqueror—along with Luxembourg, Liechtenstein, and Malta, among others.[7] The most important of these feudal holdovers is undoubtedly the City of London, the self-governing square mile enclosed by but distinct from London, the national capital. An estimated $1.1 trillion in personal wealth originating outside the United Kingdom—11 percent of the private offshore finance business worldwide—passes through the 1,000-year-old City, making it literally "a medieval commune representing capital."[8]

My point, while related to these, is more specific to the practices and norms that define the work of contemporary wealth management. Many of the practitioners I interviewed see their work as governed by an ethic reminiscent of medieval knighthood: an aristocratic code based on service, loyalty, and honor, dedicated to the cause of defending large concentrations of wealth from attack by outsiders. In the past, large fortunes consisted primarily of land and were defended by force of arms. Today the fortunes are primarily financial, and wealth managers use legal and organizational tools as their weapons of choice. But the objectives and results of their activities remain remarkably consistent: the maintenance of a highly stratified social structure through the preservation of large private accumulations of wealth.

The process through which wealth protection became a profession occurred in two main phases. First, as wealth became more fungible, the work of protecting it changed from a passive activity—holding title to land—to an active one. This development was made possible by legislative changes that acknowledged the emergence of a "putative professional class," allowing wealth managers (then known as trustees) to be compensated for their work and to exercise increasing discretion in the investment of clients' assets.[9] The second phase, which is still under way, has been characterized by collective action on the part of these professionals, including institution-building—such as the formation of STEP and the establishment of university degree programs in wealth management—as well as lobbying to define and protect jurisdictional boundaries.[10]

Kinsmen and volunteers

As mentioned in Chapter 1, contemporary wealth management is a direct outgrowth of the English feudal custom of trusteeship—a practice that has spread to become an indispensable tool of global finance. During the fourteenth century, landowners faced several problems that put their family fortunes at risk. The threat of land seizure during the owner's military service, particularly during the Crusades, has been mentioned. But landowners of that period also faced two problems that persist to the present day: taxes and inheritance. In an era when land transfers were subject to onerous duties and wills were not recognized as a valid means of conveying land, a family's estate could vanish upon the death of the paterfamilias.[11] Putting assets into trust, by transferring title to an adult male friend or relative while the original landowner was still alive, solved all these problems at once. For one thing, there would be no tax due as long as the title holder remained living, whether that was the trustee or the heirs to whom he was to transfer the property. Second, if the original landowner had no adult male heirs, the trustee could hold the property for the benefit of the widow, daughters, or minor sons until a solution (such as marriage) could be found to keep the property within the family. This innovative strategy of applying

two forms of ownership—legal and beneficial—simultaneously to a single property makes trusts "the most distinctive
achievement of Anglo-American law."[12]

The trust also created the unique cultural and social position of the trustee, which was intimately tied to feudal customs.
For example, the central constitutive act of becoming a trustee
lay not in the property transfer but in making a promise: the
pledge to own land without appropriating it for one's own
benefit, and to honor the wishes of the settlor after his death.
This practice was derived from the ceremony of vassalage, in
which a knight pledged loyal service to a lord in exchange for
protection. Vassalage ceremonies involved an exchange of
oaths, often made in the presence of sacred objects such as
saintly relics, which made promises permanent, irrevocable,
and secured by divine authority.[13]

Similarly, medieval property transfers were executed orally,
with little or no reliance on written documents.[14] Transmission
of land and other valuables were made through "performative
conveyances," in which a property owner would state his wishes
aloud in front of a group of specially designated witnesses.[15]
This format gave his speech the force of law. Trusts arose in
this context, and thus spoken promises were sufficient to
enact them and make them binding. Becoming a trustee of
land, then, was one of several "speech acts" through which
medieval life was transacted—another example being the quin-
tessential feudal utterance, "I dub thee knight."[16]

Like the oath of vassalage, the pledge to hold assets in trust
was considered sacred in a religious sense. Thus for centuries,
conflicts surrounding trusts were adjudicated not in law tribunals but in the ecclesiastical courts.[17] Trusts, like the practice

Figure 2.1. Segment of the eleventh-century Bayeux Tapestry showing Harold Godwinson—at right, hands laid on sacred reliquaries—pledging an oath to William of Normandy. © Reading Museum (Reading Borough Council). All rights reserved.

of knighthood, were essential components of the "web of oaths" that structured medieval society and linked it to the spiritual realm.[18] As one historian of the period has observed, "The act of entrusting oneself was thus critical to feudalism."[19]

Of course, oaths were violated—sometimes famously so, as in the case of Harold Godwinson (shown in Figure 2.1), who allegedly broke his pledge of fealty to William of Normandy, leading to the Battle of Hastings in 1066.[20] Complaints against "faithless feoffees"—trustees who broke their pledge and appropriated for their own use land that had been entrusted to them—are recorded as early as 1390.[21] But the system held together nonetheless, backed not only by the formal authority of the ecclesiastical courts but also by the informal power of norms and values, enforced by shame and dishonor. To a significant extent, those who put land into trust "had to depend on literal trust and community opinion to ensure that the trustees discharged their duties."[22] Remarkably, this custom worked well enough to preserve many great fortunes in England, America, and other common-law countries until well into the nineteenth century.[23]

Class solidarity also contributed to the robustness of this honor system. The individuals who took on the role of trustee shared a common enemy with the landowners who requested their service: laws that threatened to dissipate dynastic wealth. Trustees were often "friends and relatives of the same social class" as the settlor and beneficiaries.[24] Indeed, "almost every well-to-do-man was a trustee," even well into the twentieth century.[25] Of particular concern to these elites were feudal incidents (a series of taxes, many related to land transfer, that lords could impose on their knights and vassals) and primogeniture. The former were onerous enough to threaten the family fortune, and the latter meant that on the death of a landowner all but the eldest male in a family would be dispossessed (a catastrophe dramatized in novels such as Jane Austen's *Pride and Prejudice*). The institutionalization of the trust represented a type of collective action effected through evasion rather than direct, violent confrontation. As one authority on the history of trusts summed up the class solidarity argument: "Trustees of old were unpaid amateurs, that is, family and community statesmen who lent their names and their honor to a conveyancing [land transfer] dodge."[26]

The impact, then as now, was to assert the property rights of elites against governing authorities. In medieval England, knights were instrumental in creating a society in which landowners appropriated nearly all the wealth and "became more powerful than any central institution."[27] They protected the interests of landed elites at a time when one's position in the social structure was dependent upon property ownership. Trustees helped their peers deprive the Crown of taxes and of its jurisdiction over land, which had formerly been absolute.[28]

Contemporary wealth managers stand in much the same relation to the present-day distribution of financial wealth: preserving the concentration of assets and the socioeconomic status of an elite seeking to assert their autonomy from governance institutions. But these institutions now include state bureaucracies and transnational bodies such as the OECD, and the field of battle now spans the world.[29] For this profession, "their 'raw material' is capital . . . and their theater of operations is the globe."[30]

The many obvious differences between the feudal and modern eras make it easy to overlook the similarities in the socioeconomic roles of knights and trustees. Although wealth management is now a paid profession, the essential normative demands of honor, selfless service, prudence, and loyalty—however often they may be violated in practice—remain unchanged in many respects from their origins in the relations among feudal nobles. The knightly ethic is still very much alive in contemporary wealth managers' vision of themselves and their work. See Figure 2.2 for a recent illustration.

Moreover, pledges and elite solidarity remain critical to the functioning of the socioeconomic system.[31] Just as the structure of feudal society and the distribution of wealth were held together by a "web of oaths," observers of modern capitalism have noted that "wealth, in a commercial age, is made up largely of promises"—including promises made and kept by

Armour for your assets

Figure 2.2. Illustration from a November 2014 *STEP Journal* article on protecting clients' wealth.

the professional class of wealth managers.[32] Formerly the standards of conduct for these actors were enshrined in ceremonies or in texts such as *Le Chanson de Roland* and the *Canterbury Tales*; now they are written into case law and professional codes of ethics.[33]

Of particular significance in the development of professional standards of conduct has been the emergence of the laws governing fiduciary behavior. "Fiduciary" is a general term describing a relationship that exists not only between trustees and beneficiaries but also between attorneys and clients as well as between corporate officers and shareholders. Fiduciaries of all types are obligated to behave with loyalty, honesty, integrity, good faith, and transparency, and to put the interests of principals above their own, avoiding any self-dealing.[34] But beyond these descriptors (which are practically knightly in their idealism) there is no uniform set of rules governing fiduciary duties: instead, norms arise within fields of practice and are enforced legally on a case-by-case basis rather than a statutory one. In the language of principal-agent theory, such relationships are "characterized by unusually high costs of specification and monitoring. The duty of loyalty replaces detailed contractual terms."[35]

For wealth managers, fiduciary duties counterbalance the powers they wield over clients and their wealth—ensuring, for example, that legal ownership of the assets a client has put in trust won't be abused to enrich the professional at the expense of the client's intended beneficiaries.[36] The fiduciary designation was originally so strict that it prohibited trustees from accepting any compensation for their role, except in the instances where consideration was stipulated by the settlor and written into the trust instrument. As a late eighteenth-century legal treatise explained, "The courts of equity look upon trusts as *honorary*, and as a burden upon the *honor* and *conscience* of the person intrusted [the trustee], and not [to be] undertaken upon mercenary motives."[37] This created a formidable, and intentional, barrier to professionalization.

The fiduciary duty of care, formalized in statutes such as the Uniform Prudent Investor Act in the United States, requires trustees to act with "reasonable care, skill and caution" and to "manage trust assets as a prudent investor would."[38] The standards are intentionally broad and open to interpretation, precisely because of the risk and uncertainty involved in trust administration. Included here are not only the risks of losses from investments but also the unknowns that arise over the long time frames attendant upon multigenerational property transfers. These are certainly not equivalent to the risks and uncertainties that medieval knights faced in defending the property of their feudal lords, but the analogies between the two conditions mean that in both cases, terms of service cannot be specified or standardized.[39]

Perhaps the most famous statement of this code was provided in 1928 by Justice Benjamin Cardozo, then serving on the highest court of the state of New York. Cardozo, who was later elevated to the Supreme Court of the United States, wrote for the majority in *Meinhard v. Salmon*: "A trustee is held to something stricter than the morals of the market place. Not honesty alone, but the punctilio of an honor the most sensitive, is then the standard of behavior. . . . [T]he level of conduct for fiduciaries [has] been kept at a level higher than that trodden by the crowd."[40] These are precisely the characteristics attributed to medieval knights: punctilio (a regard for formalities and etiquette), honor, honesty, and a sense of being above the crowd, bound to a duty "stricter than the morals of the market place." In fact, it reads like an updated portrait of the pilgrim knight in Chaucer's *Canterbury Tales*, who "loved chivalry, truth, honor . . . and all courtesy."[41]

The medieval becomes modern

But these historical continuities also raise the question: Why did an adaptation to feudal conditions survive the Middle Ages? That is, once feudal taxes and inheritance restrictions were lifted, what need did landed elites have for trusts and trustees? By the end of the seventeenth century land could be "devised by will," meaning that it was legally valid to transfer real property (not just money or goods) to one's heirs through a written document to be executed upon one's death.[42] Later the development of offshore financial centers made it possible for corporations based in places such as the Caribbean to offer many of the tax shelter functions once provided by trusts. These two factors would seem to make the practice of putting assets into trust as obsolete as the broadsword in an age of automatic weapons.

Yet trusts remain a popular—even indispensable—tool for wealth management, both for wealthy individuals and for corporations. And trusts require trustees. In other words, the continuing relevance of the trust for elites has perpetuated the need for trusteeship. But because of changes in the kinds of assets that trusts contain (a topic that will be addressed in greater detail in Chapter 4), there has been a parallel transformation in the roles and duties of trustees, leading to the emergence of the wealth management profession.

For centuries, trustees' responsibilities were quite simple: to hold (and possibly transfer) legal title to a piece of property. But as the impact of industrial capitalism changed the composition of wealth in the nineteenth century, a passive role was no longer tenable; when it came to managing financial wealth, trustees were obligated to take an active role. When trusts "ceased to be a conveyancing device for land and became instead a device for holding a portfolio of financial assets . . . [t]he transformation in the nature of wealth that led to the management trust brought about a parallel transformation in trusteeship."[43] As wealth became more fungible, with property increasingly superseded by financial assets, trusts provided elites with a means of control that was not easily duplicated through contracting or incorporation. How this altered the demands on volunteer trustees and led to the development of professional wealth management will be the subject of the next sections.

Stage one: From voluntarism to professionalization

During the nineteenth century, processes that had been under way in economic history since the Age of Exploration produced great merchant fortunes in Europe and North America. The basis of wealth shifted decisively from land to capital—a more fungible source of wealth requiring a different kind of attention and maintenance than landed estates. In England, the nineteenth century saw the repeal of the Bubble Act, allowing corporations—and corporate investment—to flourish as never before.[44] Suddenly trustees had tremendous amounts of cash to manage, and hundreds of joint stock companies in which to invest. Yet they did not have the right to invest in those securities unless specifically authorized to do so by the trust instrument. Most trust instruments, in the interests of protecting beneficiaries from "faithless feoffees," gave no such powers, leaving the trustee to act simply as a passive title holder for real estate.

A major step forward in the professionalization process occurred when the courts stepped in to expand trustees' powers of investment. In the United Kingdom, where trust law originated, this did not occur until the Trustee Investment Act of 1889, which allowed trustees to invest in U.K. government bonds or English land, even if the trust instrument did not confer powers of investment. As investment opportunities expanded, trustees were offered options sanctioned by the courts and the legislature for putting the trust capital to work. These so-called legal lists were usually limited to local real estate or government bonds. The limitations did not cause as much consternation as might be supposed, since the failure of the South Sea Company in 1720 continued to cast a long pall over trust finances, such that "trust practitioners argued that it was imprudent for a trustee to invest trust funds in equities on the stock market, even if he had power to do so."[45] So when they were granted the express power to invest in stocks later in the nineteenth century, trustees frequently played it safe by eschewing stocks on the legal lists in favor of the old standbys: land and bonds. It took more than a century—until the Trustee Act of 2000—before the U.K. courts awarded trustees full discretion to invest in equities as if they were the beneficial owners of the assets.[46]

These limitations on the autonomy of trustees were matched by the requirement of full personal liability for any losses incurred to the trust. That is, a trustee was required by law to repay from his own personal assets any loss in the value of the trust caused by his actions and decisions—even if the loss was incurred by accident and in good faith.[47] The risk of personal bankruptcy kept many trustees from investing in stocks, particularly since the courts maintained that trustees should neither be paid nor delegate any decision making to specialists, such as accountants.

In sociological terms, the role of the trustee was governed by the logic of the gift rather than the logic of compensation.[48]

Indeed, because trusts originate legally in the concept of the gift, the ordinary requirements of "consideration" (i.e., payment) to establish a contract did not apply.[49] Trustees were thus "economically celibate," barred from earning a fee for their efforts on behalf of settlors and beneficiaries.[50] This, combined with the burdens of full liability and limited investment discretion, helped maintain the "the whole tradition of the trust as a personal relationship," grounded in moral obligation and voluntarism, as opposed to professional service.[51]

The processes that would ultimately lead to acknowledgment of trustees as a professional class, and later to the emergence of wealth management as a distinct profession, began in the United States in 1830. The decision of the Massachusetts Supreme Court in the *Harvard College v. Amory* case established the "prudent man" rule, which gave legal recognition to the expertise of these actors and accorded them a measure of autonomy in investment decisions.[52] On the one hand, the rule simply codified the heretofore informal practices of elite solidarity, since "prudence" was defined by the courts in terms of the behavior of "businessmen from the upper circles of Boston society."[53] But the decision also represented a substantive and historical advance in offering recognition of trustees by the state—an essential element in the constitution of all professions.[54]

The timing and location of this first public acknowledgment of trustees as an emergent professional group was not coincidental: the American Northeast, unlike Great Britain and continental Europe, had no history of large tracts of land being tied up for generations in the hands of hereditary nobility or by plantation farming. Instead, the region grew wealthy through whaling and through the global trade in textiles, rum, and slaves. These businesses generated a huge profit, and with it the need for advice on the disposition of cash reserves greater than most families could spend in a generation.

In other words, the profession of trust and estate planning emerged concurrently with the transformation of capitalism itself. In some respects, the trustees employed by nineteenth-century Brahmin families had the same goals and motives as their medieval counterparts: the maintenance of class solidarity. Not only were trustees generally men of the same rank as the families they served, but they were instrumental in effecting the "institutional integration of a stable capitalist class."[55]

Despite this continuity of aims, however, trustees faced significant new demands under industrial capitalism. As wealth took on new forms, moving from material property to merchant capital, the need for expert assistance in managing wealth increased as well. The job required time and expertise far beyond what was demanded of the traditional, unpaid trustee of real property. In response to this need, *Trusts & Estates* magazine began publishing in 1904, creating the first public forum for professional discourse on wealth management. This was a critical step in marking the contours of a distinctive field of practice.[56]

So as the remnants of the old feudal economic system gave way to a new mode of creating wealth, trusteeship became a very different kind of job. After centuries of stability, major transformations occurred within a few decades. "The typical trustee at the end of the Victorian period was quite different from that at the beginning of the reign. He had become the manager of a fund, of a portfolio of investments, rather than

Which will you choose to manage the money you leave by will?

The Northern Trust Company		The Average Individual
Never dies	1	Life is uncertain
Is never absent or disabled	2	May travel or become ill
Is abundantly responsible	3	Is often financially irresponsible
Is free from prejudice	4	Is often prejudiced
Has a background of experience	5	Is rarely familiar with trusteeship
Has the facilities and organization	6	Must do everything himself
Makes regular and exact reports	7	Is inclined to shirk reporting
Makes a business of trusteeship	8	May be absorbed in his own affairs
Collective experience and judgment	9	One man's judgment

Figure 2.3. Northern Trust advertisement from 1917 on the advantages of using professional wealth management services. *Source:* Northern Trust Company Annual Report, 1917.

the guardian of a family's landed estate. . . . It was a skilled occupation undertaken for profit."[57] This point of inflection in the development of the profession is captured in a 1917 advertisement from Northern Trust, a Chicago-based organization specializing in trust administration (see Figure 2.3). The thrust of the advertisement is to persuade well-to-do individuals to turn to professionals rather than friends or family members for wealth management.

In the century that has elapsed since that advertisement was created, wealth management has been transformed by the increasing complexity of elites' investments, tax sheltering strategies, and organizational structures for holding assets.[58] Particularly in the past twenty to twenty-five years—coincident with the creation of STEP—protection of wealth from tax and other regulatory authorities has become "multifaceted and global in its operation."[59] Over the same period, there has been a dramatic increase in coordination among disparate industries offering products and services designed to help the wealthy stay that way, including banks, law firms, accounting agencies, and insurance providers as well as numerous boutique wealth management firms and individual practitioners.[60]

This global expansion and coordination demands a new kind of professional expertise, as "transnational" and "hypermobile" in its orientation as the capital and clientele it serves.[61] If trustees were, as one study put it, "the concrete human incarnation of this abstract functioning of law and money," it was perhaps inevitable that the internationalization of capital would drive professional transformation.[62] As trusteeship emerged in response to the feudal state, wealth management is an outgrowth of the supranational space created and inhabited by the world's wealthiest families.

Stage two: The rise of STEP

Despite the increasing recognition that early wealth management professionals enjoyed in the nineteenth and twentieth centuries, most practitioners remained isolated from one another, and their work was seen as one of the "havens for age and obscurity" in the financial sector.[63] A Liverpool accountant named George Tasker decried this state of affairs in a November 1990 letter to the editor of *Trusts & Estates* magazine—which, after eighty-six years in print, was still the only publication linking the diverse group of professionals engaged in wealth structuring and management. His letter drew hundreds of responses, with many suggesting that readers meet to share experiences and best practices. In early 1991, eighty-two practitioners attended the inaugural meeting of the Society for Trust and Estate Professionals in central London. One year later, STEP enrolled its one-thousandth member.

From these initial steps sprang a host of other institution-building activities and political activism, both on behalf of the profession and for its wealthy clients. One of the society's first members—Nick Jacob, who joined in October 1991 and is now a member of the board of directors—said it was originally intended to be purely a U.K. organization. But within a couple of months, it became clear that STEP was going to have an international membership, as branches formed in other jurisdictions at the initiative of practitioners. Worldwide, STEP members organize 572 events annually on a voluntary basis, amounting to more than two events for each working day of the year.[64]

STEP has also become very active in lobbying and legislation. Within the United Kingdom, it has lobbied Parliament to shut down amateur—or "cowboy"—will writers by restricting the trade to professionals such as STEP members.[65] The society is also active in offshore jurisdictions, where members regularly cooperate with elected officials to draft financial laws.[66] On the global front, STEP has been a key player in the struggle tax havens have waged against blacklisting by the OECD; the society's members crafted some of the rhetoric that won the battle of words, forcing a retreat on the part of the OECD, which had proposed sanctions against some jurisdictions.[67]

As STEP's membership has grown, the organization has also been increasingly active in establishing the formal boundaries of its expertise. Because most of those who practice trust and estate planning are also members of other professions, STEP has developed the Trust and Estate Practitioner certification to designate those specializing in services to wealthy clients. The TEP has become the de facto standard credential in the profession, recognized worldwide, much like the CPA for accountants.

Classified advertisements typically specify that the TEP credential is required or desirable for those applying for positions in the field (see the appendix to this chapter). And employers usually pay for their staff to take the certification classes, as it serves to enhance firms' status and professional credibility. This effect seems to be greater for the TEP than for other credentials. As Sherman, a BVI practitioner, put it, "I had to get a certification, and it was either a CTA [Chartered Tax Adviser] or a STEP qualification, and the STEP qualification was much more expected. So I did my STEP qualification over a couple of years. My firm supported it and recognized it as a very important professional qualification for me."

The TEP credential also serves symbolically to unite a global profession—a necessity given the wide range of backgrounds among STEP's global membership. The five weeklong

seminars through which the credential is earned are as much
a socialization process as a knowledge-delivery system.

The ties between the profession and higher education are
still developing. While professional knowledge is distinctively
"centered in and allied with the modern university," formal
degree programs in wealth management have only been established recently.[68] Law schools have offered specialized
courses in trust law for decades. But it was not until the au-
tumn of 2011 that a university offered a degree devoted to
wealth management. The University of Manchester, in cooperation with STEP, conferred the first B.Sc. degrees in management of trusts and estates in the spring of 2013, representing
another milestone in the professionalization process.

The rapid global spread of STEP, along with its growing
public role, suggests why some scholars have characterized
professional associations as among the most important but
least studied sources of institutional change in the world.[69]
Through its credentialing and degree programs as well as its
publications (such as the flagship *STEP Journal*), STEP has
created what scholars call an "epistemic community"—a
group of professionals who come from a variety of disciplinary
backgrounds but are united by their expertise and way of
looking at the world.[70] These communities are highly influential in the global political economy, effecting change in laws,
politics, and the boundaries of professional practice.

STEP has been particularly successful at establishing its
practices as global norms. Through lobbying and consulting
on laws (onshore and off) and by creating institutions—such
as the TEP training program—to diffuse professional expertise, STEP has been instrumental in the globalization of fi-

nancial and legal innovations. For example, STEP practitioners played a significant role in "translating" the trust concept so that it could be used in jurisdictions that did not previously recognize trusts. They also assisted in the creation of new variations on the trust—such as the VISTA trust-corporation combination in the British Virgin Islands (see Chapter 3)—that have become a major source of competitive advantage for the offshore world. This kind of "globalized localism," in which a practice emerging from a specific place and time becomes a worldwide standard, is a major source of institutional change transnationally.[71]

Another way that professional societies create global change is in defining their scope of practice. No matter how well established a profession, its terrain is always contested, dynamic, and subject to "ongoing claims and counterclaims."[72] Newly formed professions such as wealth management are continually under pressure to defend their current domain of expertise and to remain alert for opportunities to expand it. STEP has been very strategic in this regard. Not only has it fought to limit the practice of writing wills in the United Kingdom to STEP members and their professional peers, but it is taking the fight global. In a recent interview, Nick Jacob argued that "the most important area for our development in the future" lies in capturing the domains of will writing and estate planning in civil-law countries, such as those of continental Europe and South America. "'People die in civil-law countries just as much as they do in common-law countries and there are big divergences around the world in how estates are dealt with,' he says. 'That's masterminded in many of those jurisdictions by the notaries and they're fairly self-preserving, so it is quite difficult to get in on that act, but I still think we could have a big part to play.'"[73] Having taking the lead against "cowboy" will writers on its home turf in Britain, STEP is now poised to do battle with "mastermind" notaries abroad.

Such jurisdictional battles not only are consequential for the profession itself but also impact everyday life around the world, including for people who may have no contact with STEP or wealth managers. For example, Charles, a South African wealth manager, explained that the high level of trust failure in his country—85 percent of trusts are invalidated in court—is due largely to lack of professional standards and regulation. "Unqualified people," he said, "set up trusts with their brothers as trustees, and they get destroyed in court challenges." Trust failure of this kind is often very costly for the individuals involved, who must pay not only court costs but taxes and penalties on the assets that they thought were sequestered in the trust structure.[74] Charles continued, "This is why we're happy for STEP to come here and establish professional standards, so that trusts hold up in court. And so that people have to be registered and take regulatory exams in order to give advice [on trusts and estate planning]." This argument closely parallels the rationales given in the mid-nineteenth century for the rise of the American Medical Association and its attempts to set standards that would exclude "quacks" and other practitioners deemed illegitimate.[75] As the South African case indicates, there is a genuine public interest to defend; the solution offered by STEP just happens to coincide with the interests of the profession in restricting the right to practice.

Contemporary practice

Explaining how wealth management functions as a contemporary profession requires an account of its distinct body of expertise, its relationships to larger social structures, and its "symbolic terrain"—including positioning relative to other occupational groups. Status competition is a defining act of professionals, both within their larger social environments and within their own ranks. Defining and defending the boundaries of their expertise, as described above, is a matter not just of capturing fees but of positioning within a hierarchy.[76] This competition for rank is one way that professions establish themselves as a field of practice and contribute to "the institutional design of the social order."[77] To explore these dimensions of contemporary wealth management, this section will examine salaries, job satisfaction, and nonmonetary sources of compensation for practitioners.

Prestige, pay, and positioning

Among all the fields that have emerged in the modern division of labor, finance dominates in many ways, both through its transnational reach and through its command of payment and privilege.[78] While salaries are always an important component of professional status, they are accorded particular importance within finance.[79] By that measure, wealth management occupies an intermediate space in the field: not the lowest-paid, but nowhere near the high end. The average salaries in wealth management, which hover in the low to middle six figures, seem particularly modest in comparison to the human capital requirements of the positions.

For example, one recent advertisement offered $250,000 to $350,000 per annum for the director of wealth management for a client described as a "UUHNWI" (ultra-ultra-high-net-worth individual) based in Geneva. The candidate was expected to possess the following qualifications: at least twenty years' experience in the wealth management business, a TEP credential, the ability to serve as liaison between a multinational family and its team of advisers, and "exceptional diplomatic skills to ensure pristine coordination of very important people and their agendas." Concurrently, a private bank in Zurich offered $200,000 per annum for a multilingual trust manager with at least ten years' experience, to "administrate from A to Z a complex portfolio of structures such as trusts, companies and foundations, dealing directly with clients." (See the appendix to this chapter for the full text of these advertisements.)

These salaries are somewhat higher than the $175,000 average annual salary for financial managers, but considerably lower than the compensation packages in many investment firms.[80] For example, the base salary for a non-executive position such as managing director at Goldman Sachs is $500,000; at Morgan Stanley and Credit Suisse, the base salary is $400,000.[81] Annual bonuses average $500,000 in such firms.[82] Because finance is a global profession, these extremely high salaries are not just a U.S. phenomenon: in Europe and elsewhere, finance is one of the most highly compensated occupations, and its salaries are among the fastest-growing in any field of work.[83]

As these salary differentials suggest, wealth management suffers from a prestige problem within financial services. Many wealth managers who work for diversified multinational firms (i.e., firms that don't specialize in wealth management but offer multiple financial services) complain about being viewed as "cost centers"—doing high-cost, low-margin work for their firms, while the traders bring in the profits.[84] Highly personalized service, of the kind high-net-worth clients demand, is indeed costly to provide. As Erika, a wealth manager at a Swiss boutique firm, explained, "What we do is very, very expensive. . . . We're *supposed* to spend 60 to 70 cents for every franc we take in through fees. In practice, that often works out to about 72 or 73 cents of expense per franc we receive; but right now, we're spending way too much on clients. I can't tell you how much exactly, but it's unsustainable." This account is roughly consistent with data on wealth management worldwide, which show that the average pre-tax profit margin in the profession is 23 percent—or about 23 cents per dollar charged in fees.[85] This is more than 20 percent below the average 29 percent profit margin in financial asset management globally.[86]

In a sense, this level of intensity in client service advances the interests of wealth management by sharply delineating its boundaries vis-à-vis other occupational groups. Generally the status of professional work hinges on "the belief that it cannot be standardized, rationalized, or . . . 'commodified.'"[87] The service model enacted by wealth managers is opposed to standardization and commodification: rather than one-size-fits-all products, they create one-of-a-kind structures designed to fit the unique specifications of each client. Indeed, in this field, "personalization . . . increases proportionately as the size of the fortune to be managed increases."[88] Its commitment to individualized products and long-term relationships with clients distinguishes wealth management as a bit of an anachronism in an industry that is otherwise at the forefront of modernity.[89] Like haute couture, wealth management operates on a business model in which low profit margins are counterbalanced—at least in theory—by high social prestige for the profession.[90]

But while wealth management may enjoy prestige in the larger scheme of occupations, its position is less well regarded by peer professions within finance. In addition to bespoke service, rising compliance costs are driving lower profit margins in wealth management.[91] Compliance work—which ensures that an institution follows all the rules, laws, and regulations that govern its activities—is not only expensive but often resented and even stigmatized within finance.[92] As Bruce, a Geneva-based practitioner, observed of wealth management's image within financial services, "Bankers, including private bankers, understand their job as *growing clients' assets*, which also means growing profits for the bank; they regard compliance as a nuisance. A good wealth manager, on the other hand, has compliance in mind all the time, and is very conservative; he sees the job as *protecting clients' assets*. So private bankers often have real contempt for trust managers." One study of the private banking industry found that the wealth managers were mocked as the "Business Prevention Unit" because of the concerns they voiced about staying on the right side of the law.[93]

Bankers aren't fiduciaries in relation to their clients; wealth managers are. From that relational difference springs a host of consequences, including bankers' ability to behave in an economically rational way—opportunistic and exploitative of informational asymmetries—at the expense of their clients. The absence of fiduciary duty frees many (if not most) in the financial services industry to make huge profits and earn proportionally huge salaries and bonuses. An extreme example of this can be found in the case of investment bank Goldman Sachs, whose traders bragged in emails about ripping off clients in mortgage-backed securities deals.[94] When U.S. senator Susan Collins confronted Goldman executives in a subsequent congressional hearing with the question "Do you have a duty to act in the best interests of your clients?" the bankers could not answer in the affirmative.[95]

The fiduciary role that constrains wealth managers has its origins not only in voluntarism but also in the concept of the gift.[96] That puts fiduciaries, who are supposed to serve selflessly and without a motive for personal gain, in conflict with the norms of the finance industry. Philip, a Chicago-based wealth manager, made a direct link between the salary issue and the character traits necessary to do fiduciary work: "One of the things that characterize a first-rate trust administrator is humility. Because to do the job, you have to put the interests of another person [the client] first. You have to listen to your client tell you about themselves. This may be one reason why, in an institutional context, in a corporate context, we have a very different psychology and that may be tied to the compensation issue. We're in an industry where many people are very good at tooting their own horns, but trust administrators aren't like that. They really see themselves as in service."

This service orientation and humility are reflected not only in lower salaries but also in the hesitant way some wealth managers approach client billing. Robert, a Guernsey-based practitioner, said, "As a professional, you want a long-term relation with a client, not with their bank account. Instead of asking a client to *pay* the bill, you ask them to *approve* the bill; that tends to be easier, because it emphasizes that it's not their money being paid out—it belongs to the trust."

This ethic of "neutrality to the world of interests" may be connected to an increasingly gendered division of labor in wealth management.[97] Although men make up the majority of practitioners today, numerous interview participants suggested that women are increasingly occupying positions as fiduciaries—an observation supported by the credentialing courses I attended, which were all majority female in composition. To see how the gendering of the fiduciary role affects compensation, consider this example from Amelia, a wealth manager working in the Cayman Islands: "I've helped clients avoid disastrous investments—like the time I told a guy not to invest in a hedge fund that later tanked, and would have cost him about $500,000, or 70 percent [of his account]. But I didn't get paid anything more because I saved him from that disastrous investment. He probably never even knew that I'd done it." Several things are noteworthy about this story. First of all, there was no compensation or financial incentive for Amelia to save her client's fortune—it was not an act of economic rationality on her part. Had she simply let him make the bad investment, as a Goldman Sachs trader would have done, she might have lost a client and the fees he paid, but it would not have affected her salary.[98] Second, she received no recognition for this save; it was simply expected. The case exemplifies Philip's point about service and humility.

Making wealth serve human needs is less lucrative and prestigious than multiplying wealth for its own sake. If wealth management has an increasing number of female practitioners, this may be due in some degree to well-known processes in which professions shift from majority-male to majority-female as autonomy and earnings decrease.[99] This has happened in medicine and other fields, and may be occurring within this domain of finance: the combination of regulatory compliance costs and the high demands for client service may be making wealth management less attractive to men, creating more room for women to enter the profession. As Gabrielle, a fiduciary in the Seychelles, explained, "The women make things happen. . . . You'll find guys in portfolio management but not in the fiduciary department, where most of the work is carried on. And I think ladies have more of the criteria to deal with demanding clients—more patient, more diplomatic."

Wealth management, while it is a part of the financial services industry, is nevertheless very different from the rest of the field because of its path-dependent ties to the ethic of knightly service, loyalty, and self-effacement. But what was once a masculine ideal linked to the code of chivalry is— somewhat ironically—becoming associated with feminine behavior in contemporary practice.

Time and job satisfaction

Although wealth managers are paid less than many of their comparably skilled peers in finance, the participants in this study noted many nonmonetary forms of compensation that make the trade-off worthwhile to them. For one thing, most wealth managers work a forty-hour week, which is quite low compared to others in financial services.[100] This appeals to men and women alike. Alistair, a British practitioner who earlier had moved to the Cayman Islands to work as a futures trader, recalled, "I changed from trading because I realized it was an unsustainable lifestyle. Our open hours on the Cayman exchange were 3:00 a.m. to 7:00 p.m., because most of our clients were European [from Spain], and trading in S&Ps goes on twenty-four hours a day. It was intensely stressful. . . . As a career, it was brutal. It was not fun to drag myself out of bed at 2:00 a.m. every day to go to the office."

Drew, who left a lucrative partnership in a Canadian law practice to join a wealth management firm in London, expressed similar motivations for his career change. He added that wealth managers gain an acute sense of the personal costs of working hard to earn and grow a fortune through close proximity to the lives of their high-net-worth clients, many of whom become estranged from their families. Drew is a father of two children, and his decision to enter the relatively slower-paced, less demanding world of wealth management was motivated in part by the following story: "One client told me that he was home for a few days after a whirlwind of business trips and [was] sitting with his wife and daughter in the living room one morning. His wife said to his daughter, 'Go say hello to

Daddy.' And his daughter walked right by him, picked up the telephone, and said, 'Hello, Daddy.'" After relating this anecdote, Drew also observed with some amusement that most of the partners in his current firm would have gotten fired for working too few hours had they been working at the law practice he had left behind, where the norm was sixty-five to eighty hours of work per week.

Some wealth managers get the best of both worlds: a reduction in work hours without a financial penalty. This is possible for those who relocate to low- or no-tax jurisdictions, which means that their pay offshore ends up being equivalent (or nearly so) to the salary they took home after taxes while working in their home countries. For example, Luc, a Frenchman who moved to Saudi Arabia, where there is no income tax, said that when he worked in Paris, he was at the office from 8:00 a.m. to 8:00 p.m. most days, "but now in Riyadh, it's 9:00 to 5:00 for the same salary!"

There is also the opportunity to learn new wealth-generating techniques from clients who have made their own fortunes. Rafael, a Brazilian wealth manager based in Geneva, said, "I learn so much about business and how to make money from them—some of my clients are so smart. If they invest in something, I buy it, too." For professionals dedicated to preserving and protecting assets, this is a significant change of orientation and an opportunity from which they can benefit without breaching their fiduciary duty. Thus, between picking up moneymaking strategies from clients and basing themselves in a low- or nil-tax jurisdiction, wealth managers may actually do better financially than their salaries would suggest. "There is good business in being a fiduciary," said

Jason, an Australian wealth manager based in Guernsey. "You're not in the same league as your clients, but you can generate very substantial streams of income for yourself."

In addition, many participants in this study mentioned that they enjoyed much greater creativity, variety, and challenge in their day-to-day work compared to their peers in allied professions. As Sebastian, an English wealth manager based in Hong Kong, put it, "It's not like being an investment banker, where you're just filing papers for a company you care nothing about. . . . It's much more intellectually interesting and more satisfying. . . . Even if the clients are spoiled brats (and some of them really are), your work helps keep families together." This was a common refrain: almost every participant in the study mentioned "helping families" as a major source of satisfaction in everyday activities. This is also a major theme in STEP's presentation of the profession to the world. On the organization's website, under the heading "What Do STEP Members Do?" the answer is given as follows: "STEP members spend their professional lives working with families and tackling real problems."[101] For professionals whose counterparts in finance and law often spend more time engaging with papers than with people, being face-to-face and solving highly individualized problems (rather than routine or standardized ones) provide important sources of meaning and pleasure to daily work. Research on other occupational groups confirms that job satisfaction is linked to a strong sense of purpose, meaning, and engagement, net of salary levels.[102]

There are, of course, less noble motives for wealth managers' job satisfaction. Bruce, the American working in Geneva, said that *his* primary source of job satisfaction was the

"intellectual challenge of playing cat and mouse with tax authorities around the world." The appeal of this kind of multi-
dimensional international problem solving may be why the
profession lures people from academia: of the sixty-five participants in the sample, three were former professors, in the fields
of law, literature, and journalism. Others mentioned the at-
tractions of international travel, and what Stan—a Chicago-
based wealth manager—called the "tabloidesque aspect to this
area of practice." Eleanor, an American working in Switzerland, expanded on this theme: "It's like being a voyeur . . . the
client has to undress in front of you."

That is, in addition to satisfying curiosity of the intellectual
variety, wealth management feeds a more personal sort of interest in what was once called the "lifestyles of the rich and
famous." As Erika put it, "You get to meet unusual people, see
another level of society." In some cases that brings not only
proximity to great wealth and power but also the ability to influence people in those rarefied circles. Dieter, a German
wealth manager who spent many years working with high-
net-worth clients in Africa, said that that having the ear of the
world's most influential people was the most satisfying part of
his thirty-year career: "When you succeed and famous people
call you up for advice . . . that's a big deal. The [former] chair-
woman of the *Washington Post*, Katherine Graham, called me
to join her for lunch when she was coming to Nairobi to discuss Africa. The head of Africa for Boeing would come to me
and ask about people in Malawi or Zambia. I had ministers
from Zambia in my house as guests, stinking, smelling, but I
had them drunk at two o'clock in the morning, so I knew what
the budget for the country the next month would be. The

more success you have, the more you want. It's a drug . . .
you're carried forward."

Alternative business models

Although the majority of wealth managers are salaried, some
have taken the more lucrative route of striking out as sole practitioners. This alternative business model is riskier for the
practitioner but offers the potential to earn much more, since
income is based either on fees for specific à la carte services
or on a percentage of assets under management. The risk takes
the form of dependence on individual client relationships:
sole practitioners serve a much smaller group of clients than
those working under the umbrella of a larger firm. In addition, the sole practitioner takes on all the risks of liability and
regulatory compliance—costs that wealth managers working
in firms do not bear personally.

Though STEP does not keep track of how many of its
members work in firms and how many operate as sole practitioners, the interview data I collected gave a consistent picture
of the differences in the business models and the likely consequences for compensation. Luc, the Frenchman practicing in
Saudi Arabia, is typical of the salaried professionals I interviewed: he has twenty to thirty clients, whom he serves as part
of a team, and each client has between $30 million and $300
million in assets under management.

In contrast, Simon—an English sole practitioner working in
Singapore—has a client base of just fifteen families. His income derives from fees rather than a fixed salary: "My fee for
putting a structure in place—the value-added fee to me, if you

like—is $75,000, which represents about two solid months of work. You're not charging for your time, but for your expertise. You're selling your expertise. You're selling doing the job correctly and properly, and that the right advice is taken. It's another $100,000 just to gather advice from the relevant legal experts." Only someone well established as an expert can command compensation at this level; the reward is a much higher income than for salaried wealth managers, but the risks are commensurately higher.

In addition to the liability and compliance issues, the size of the client base itself presents a risk. Simon only works with ultra-ultra-high-net-worth clients, each of whom brings him "an absolute bare minimum" of $50 million in investable assets; "otherwise my fees are not economical for them," he said. Such clients are relatively rare, so if one of them takes his or her business elsewhere, the consequences could be devastating for Simon's income. In contrast, Luc's firm can take on more work from a broader client base (one that includes somewhat less wealthy people), so the loss of any individual account will not threaten the company's stability.

The sole practitioner model also has downsides for the client. The typical ultra-high-net-worth individual owns a complex multinational portfolio of assets requiring expertise in numerous domains of practice. Nancy, a sole practitioner based in Buenos Aires, describes her client base as follows: "I have about ten clients total. Each client can be quite complex. One client has eight trusts with a total of thirty underlying companies; another is the beneficiary of an old English trust containing land, boats all over the world, works of art, and houses all over the world." To serve these clients, Nancy—like

Simon—must draw on her personal network to gather advice from legal and tax experts globally; each of those consultations is charged on an hourly basis to the client, plus Nancy's fee to coordinate the advice into a coherent strategy. In this situation, clients not only bear heavy expenses but are extremely vulnerable: What happens when the sole practitioner dies or retires? What if his or her skills in seeking the best advice worldwide and integrating it for the client decline as a result of old age or illness? What if the sole practitioner takes on too large a client load, making him or her unable to respond to client inquiries in a timely fashion?

Such concerns, combined with a surge in the number of ultra-high-net-worth individuals in recent years, has led to the increasing popularity of "family offices," where a suite of professional wealth managers are employed full-time in the service of a single family or a small group of families.[103] The Rockefellers are thought to have innovated the structure for their own use in the late nineteenth century.[104] Family offices, which typically set fees as a percentage of assets under management—ranging from 0.25 percent to 1 percent—often cost $1 million or more annually, and are affordable only for those with $100 million or more in investable assets.[105] Bruce, the Geneva-based wealth manager, called such offices "one-stop-shopping for the super-rich."

Elsewhere, family offices have been described as a "vanity cost," and likened to owning a private jet in terms of offering privacy and control for an exorbitant price. But just as demand for large private jets continues to grow, so does that for the ultra-high level of customization offered by this service model:

assets under management in family offices are estimated to be $1.2 trillion and growing.[106] This rising demand has spawned a cottage industry: for a fee of up to $80,000, a "matchmaker" firm will recruit top wealth managers for ultra-high-net-worth individuals seeking to staff a family office.[107] In that rarefied labor market, wealth managers can command large incomes without exposing themselves to the risks of being a sole practitioner. However, some of those I interviewed opted to forgo this trade-off. Steve, the sole practitioner quoted above, decided that the risks were worth what he gained in job satisfaction: "I don't want to go in-house [as part of a family office] because you get caught up in the day-to-day politics of the family and lose the . . . variety and challenge of dealing with different people in different situations. That's the reward: variety."

Conclusion

Just as wealth management makes an unusual combination of demands on practitioners, it offers an unusual mix of rewards. Salaries are high compared to most kinds of work, but just middle-of-the-road with respect to other positions requiring comparable qualifications. While that may contribute to lower prestige for the profession, the nonmonetary compensations of the work are considerable. This includes the opportunity to do creative, intellectually challenging work, which is apparently rare in finance and law; there is also a genuine sense of meaning and the ability to make a difference for real people, both of which are missing in many occupations.[108] Finally, there is the appeal of gaining entry to, and potentially influencing, a realm of elites rarely glimpsed or accessed by outsiders.

This chapter has traced how the wealth management profession developed to this point from its temporally and culturally distant origins in the practice of trusteeship. It shows how this was driven by the changing nature of wealth, catalyzed by transformations in capitalism. What was once a tightly constrained role now requires global expertise. This evolution of wealth management from its medieval origins has been called a "revolution," since it paralleled upheavals in the scope and operation of the global economy.[109] The changes included not only the increasing fungibility of wealth but also a dramatic loosening of the legal restrictions on how that wealth could be deployed, whether by trustees or by corporations.

At the beginning of the nineteenth century, both trustees and corporations were held in close check by the courts and legislatures. Modern capitalism came into being only when lawmakers granted "corporations legal powers almost coextensive with those of natural persons . . . to engage in any lawful line or lines of business."[110] At the same time, trustees received professional recognition and greater decision-making autonomy, which they used to channel their clients' fortunes into the financing of the growing firms. By establishing a capital circuit between private and corporate wealth, trustees not only established themselves professionally but also were instrumental in creating capitalism in its modern form.[111]

This trajectory of professionalization calls to mind sociologist Lynne Zucker's analysis of economic development in the United States during the nineteenth and twentieth centuries.[112] What transformed a mostly isolated, agrarian economy into a global industrial and political power was the growth of trust in institutions—and most critically in professionals as the embodiment of those institutions. These professionals, including bankers and lawyers, bridged the immense geographical and social distances that characterized the United States when westward expansion and waves of immigration created a patchwork of widely divergent local cultures and norms. Financial professionals played a particularly important role: "The central fact of the transformation of the U.S. economic system is the proliferation of formal production of trust and creation of an active market for institutional-based trust. . . . Several trust-producing structures were critical in the production of trust during the early period of industrial formation in the United States: spread of rational bureaucratic organizations, professional credentialing, the service economy, including financial intermediaries and government, and regulation and legislation."[113]

In contemporary practice, interactions between clients and professionals often result in the transfer of vast flows of capital into trusts based offshore, out of reach of tax authorities and other forms of governance, but also out of the client's control. That this process often involves clients from developing countries underscores how closely connected the professionalization of wealth management is to the larger narrative of capitalism's development worldwide. Echoing their role in the United States in the nineteenth century, but on a much larger scale, wealth management professionals now play a critical role in bringing local wealth into global circulation. This makes them key actors in the global political economy.

At the same time, an essential part of the job remains keeping wealth outside the control of the state. Wealth management is still closely tied to its own history of resistance to governing authority, particularly where taxes are concerned. But along with the legacy of the "conveyancing dodge," the profession retains practices and norms—such as the code of fiduciary duty—that originate in medieval mores and culture. It is this combination of the material and ideal, instrumental and relational, that gives wealth management its unique character within the field of financial and legal services. The impact of this character on client relations will be the subject of Chapter 3.

APPENDIX

Sample job postings for wealth managers

Both of the following advertisements were placed on the STEP website by the recruitment firm AP Executive (www.ap -executive.com) in the summer of 2011.

Location: Switzerland: Geneva
Salary: US$250000–350000 per annum
STEP Experience: TEP Qualified
Key Skills/Keywords: Family office executive

Coordination of the senior advisers, liaison between the family organisation and family members, management of a team, spread in different jurisdictions, will form part of the agenda.

Our client, a UUHNWI, is looking for the head of his family office services. This executive senior level role requires a broad understanding of business and family issues and excellent leadership in providing administrative support to its family members. Coordination of the senior advisers, liaison between the family organisation and family members, management of a team, spread in different jurisdictions, will form part of the agenda. The successful applicant will have exceptional diplomatic skills to ensure pristine coordination of very important people and their agendas, and excellence in complex negotiations. With at least 20 years experience in successfully running a family office (single/multi) the ideal candidate could also be a senior private client practitioner (private bank, professional advisory firm) keen to move away from the commercial aspect of their job. This exciting opportunity will involve frequent travel across Europe.

Location: Switzerland: Zurich
Salary: CHF130000–160000 per annum
STEP Experience:
Key Skills/Keywords: Trust, STEP

Our client, a prestigious Private Bank, is now seeking a trust manager to join its team based in Zurich.

You will administrate from A to Z a complex portfolio of structures such as trust, companies and foundations, dealing directly with the clients.

This is an outstanding opportunity to join a dynamic institution offering first class solutions to its clients.

The successful candidate will hold the TEP designation, and have a proven track record of ten years experience in the industry. Fluency in English is required while German, Spanish or French would be valuable assets.

Please send your CV in English in order to apply to this exciting opportunity.

3

Client Relations

WEALTH MANAGERS HAVE EMPLOYMENT PATTERNS QUITE UNLIKE those of most of their professional peers in finance and law. While retaining legal counsel or consulting a financial adviser now commonly leads to short-term relationships, wealth managers maintain clients over the long term, sometimes amounting to lifetime employment.[1] One study characterized the profession in terms of "relationships of long and uncertain duration, usually measured in lives."[2] It is not uncommon to find wealth managers working with the children or grandchildren of their original clients.[3]

One reason for this is the extraordinary intimacy wealth management requires between client and professional. Like a family doctor or lawyer, a wealth manager is privy to highly sensitive information, but that information is not confined to just one domain. The doctor who knows everything about a patient's body rarely knows the contents of her bank account or estate plan. The wealth manager, in order to do his or her job properly, has to know everything. As Eleanor put it in the previous chapter, the client has to "undress" in front of the wealth manager. James, a London-based practitioner, described the level of familiarity required in even more vivid terms: "When people choose a TEP, first they sort based on competence, then they have to pick someone they want to know everything about them: about Mother's lesbian affairs, Brother's drug addiction, the spurned lovers bursting into the room."

Wealth managers need to know these intimate details of their clients' lives because so many of the factors that affect high-net-worth individuals also affect their fortunes. As a fiduciary, the wealth manager is bound to protect clients' wealth from risk: this includes not just financial risk but the threat of spendthrift heirs dissipating the family assets or of family members with embarrassing secrets who might be targeted for blackmail.

Another factor in the longevity of these relationships is that wealth managers, like the Persian court accountants described by Weber, end up holding their clients' purse strings.[4] Their detailed knowledge of the structures and laws governing their clients' fortunes gives the professionals enormous power, making them indispensable and difficult to replace. Mark, an English wealth manager based in Dubai, said of his own clients, "The relationships last for decades, and the structures we create last for longer than that. One of my clients said to me after years working with him, 'You know I can't sack you now. You know where everything is, you know everything about me. . . . It would take me an age to explain my business and assets to someone else.'" In other words, once past the trust barrier, wealth managers often maintain client relationships for life.

How wealth managers acquire these positions of trust and power in client relationships will be the focus of this chapter.

The professionals' task—signaling trustworthiness—is made particularly challenging because of the extreme wariness and skepticism of others' motives that characterizes many high-net-worth individuals.[5] Robert, a wealth manager working in Guernsey, observed that "a major downside of wealth that we see . . . is that people who have a lot of money can become very suspicious and isolated, because they become convinced that everyone who meets them is trying to take advantage of them." Often this suspicion is born of experience rather than paranoia. Many of the professionals interviewed for this study mentioned how wealth makes high-net-worth individuals the target of a variety of threats. As Mark put it, "People want to con them, scam them, rob them, kidnap them." These threats come not just from strangers but from their governments and even from their own families, further fueling suspicion on the part of clients that no one can be trusted. This suggests a fundamental puzzle in the relationships cultivated by wealth managers: how do they win the extraordinary depth of trust necessary to do their jobs from individuals who are so strongly inclined to be distrustful? And how do they manage this across the cultural and socioeconomic barriers that often separate them from their clients?

To some extent, wealth managers' clientele can fairly be described as "a politically and socially homogenous and autonomous group," united by a distinctive way of life and set of interests.[6] This is what is meant by terms such as "the jet set." Several participants in this study support this view of elite clients' essential sameness. Neal, an English-born wealth manager working in the Cayman Islands, said that "high-net-worth individuals are all pretty similar to one another—they're a pretty global bunch, with a lot more in common with each other than with the people in their own countries." Erika, the wealth manager based in Switzerland, echoed Neal's view, saying, "All wealthy families are basically the same." However, evidence from other participants in the study suggests that there remain important cultural variations in establishing trustworthiness—a conclusion that is supported by studies in other disciplines.[7] I'll explore this apparent paradox at the end of the chapter.

The first section examines the special role of trust in wealth management and how that distinguishes it from allied professions in finance and law. Then I review the challenges professionals face in working with the wealthy, to the extent that they represent a "geographically diverse but like-minded" group because of their shared experiences and interests at the top end of the global socioeconomic spectrum.[8] The third section delves into the cross-cultural differences that remain, and how wealth managers overcome those obstacles to establishing trusting relationships with clients.

The special role of trust in wealth management

As Chapter 2 showed, the practice of wealth management is distinguished by fiduciary obligations. This means that, unlike practitioners in finance and law, wealth managers are bound by special rules that foreground socioemotional aspects of client relations, such as trust. These rules are designed in part to protect potentially vulnerable clients from being exploited by people who know everything about them and who have de facto, and often de jure, control over their fortunes.[9] In consequence, the Cayman-based wealth manager Alistair said, "for this to work, they have to trust us."

Though some practical implications of the fiduciary ethic have changed over time—for example, wealth managers no longer have full personal responsibility for losses incurred by clients—there remains a strong sense of person-to-person obligation that has largely disappeared from other, more bureaucratized modern professions. As Elaine, an English wealth manager working in Dubai, noted, "They tell you lots of secrets, these clients, things they would never tell their bankers. You are their confidant. You are so trusted—you have to be totally confidential. A client will say to me, 'I want to leave money to my girlfriend, but I don't want my wife to know.'" Because of this special role, some wealth managers liken themselves to clerics or confidants.

In interviews, participants reached for these and other analogies in an effort to capture the special mix of socioemotional skills and character virtues needed for success in the profession. Trevor, a South African who owns a wealth management firm in Panama, defined his work as "stewardship," a term that evokes the role of clergy in its devotional connotations; appropriately enough, it derives from the medieval role of the steward, a highly trusted servant who managed a noble lord's household economy.[10] On a darker note, Sherman in the British Virgin Islands said, "We're a bit like the *consigliere* in *The Godfather*" in the sense of providing advice with absolute discretion and loyalty.

Marian, an American practitioner working in Los Angeles, quipped, "My ex-husband always used to say, 'She does social work for the rich.'" James, the London-based wealth manager quoted in Chapter 2, had a more serious take on this analogy: "Part of my job is social worker—I do deal with some tricky families. . . . It's about being there for the person and being someone they can rely on, often beyond the way that the person can rely on their own flesh and blood, because we don't stand to get an inheritance from them." James specializes in protecting elderly clients from exploitation by relatives who want to cut corners on hospital or nursing home care in order to preserve the family fortune for themselves to inherit.

As this suggests, the fiduciary role shades into social work through its connection to intrafamily conflict. For high-net-worth clients, many of whom are surrounded by impatient heirs and yes-men, the opportunity to talk through intensely personal problems with someone knowledgeable, discreet, and honest is a valuable service in and of itself.[11] Echoing James' remarks, Jason—an Australian wealth manager based in Guernsey—said of client relations in wealth management, "You're privy to a lot of very personal information, and you end up having conversations that you know and they know can't be had with anyone else, including the rest of their family." For high-net-worth clients, it seems, the family is not the high-trust environment envisioned by some social theories—particularly in economics, which "proposes that a continuum exists which places the family (high trust) at one pole and the impersonal market (low trust) at the other pole."[12]

It may also be that wealth lends a special dynamic to families: even documents from the mid-thirteenth century in England record court battles among nobles in which the proceedings are marked by "a widespread distrust of family wolves hungering after an inheritance."[13] Many of the professionals interviewed for this study mentioned that this remained a very real concern for clients. For example, Nadia, a wealth manager who sets up trust structures in Panama City, said that "we hear from settlors all the time, 'No one in my family knows that this structure exists; only you, me and my lawyer know about it.'" This often puts the wealth manager in the position of having to sort out familial conflicts after the client's death. Sometimes, as in Nadia's case, the professional's job includes breaking the news of the client's wealth and inheritance plan to the potential heirs and coping with any negative responses. In other cases, the professional may end up in the role of detective, trying to piece together clues about aspects of the client's fortune that were kept secret from everyone. Alistair, the Cayman-based wealth manager, recalled working with a "wealthy family in Jamaica" in which "the father died, not having told any single person all of his financial affairs; there was no one person who knew everything he had and where it was. He told each family member and a few trusted friends just little bits, but not the whole picture. And now, three years after his death, we're still locating his assets."

This degree of distrustfulness among the wealthy comes at a significant cost, often measured in fees to professionals charged with sorting out mysteries such as this, as well as familial conflicts.

Like family, but better

Through involvement in such struggles, wealth managers themselves often end up taking on a quasi-familial role vis-à-vis their clients and clients' relatives. Perhaps in recognition of the special intimacy and trust conferred on these professionals, the 1989 Guernsey Trusts Law states that a fiduciary must "observe the utmost good faith and act *en bon père de famille*"—a French phrase that translates literally as "good father of a family."[14] In practice, wealth managers are "usually recruited in a very personal way" by the actual fathers (rarely mothers) of high-net-worth families, with the relationship cultivated carefully to ensure that the professional represents the wishes and interests of the father after his death.[15] Some scholars have interpreted this in purely rational-bureaucratic terms: "The work of the fiduciary . . . occupies, after the death of the family founder, the place of abstract patriarchal authority in a family, but *what family beneficiaries literally trust is not an object or person imbued with positive family values such as love, amity and warm feelings, but a cold, rational construct of wealth—the trust and its trustee*."[16] However, this instrumental view is belied by the statements of participants in this study, who repeatedly emphasized that trusting client relationships hinged on mutually experienced bonds of emotion.

For example, Elaine in Dubai described her client relationships in terms that emphasized the emotional labor and caring involved: "They're asking you to take care of their family. You can't just think of it as another piece of business. . . . It's not just a matter of signing documents; it's the whole concept of doing the right thing for that family. You have to be able to say, 'Mr. A., don't worry—your kids are all going to be put through university. It's all going to be okay.' You have to be very businesslike. But also family-like."[17] Comments such as this point to a socioemotional aspect of the duties of loyalty and care stipulated in fiduciary law.[18] Beyond their rational-bureaucratic sense, in which "care" is intended to mean "prudence in business dealings," an additional layer of genuine interpersonal attachment may arise between professionals and clients.

Sometimes clients themselves underscore the familial quality of the relationship with their wealth managers. As Grace, a Los Angeles–based practitioner, recalled: "I worked with some clients in San Diego who said, 'Oh, we wished you were our daughter instead of the daughter we had.' When the father died, the daughter pestered her mother constantly for money, and we finally had to resign as trustee, because we couldn't work with the daughter."

Many participants in this study report that clients invite them to attend family weddings, to go on vacation with them, and even to sit by their deathbed. A few practitioners talked of crying at their desks after learning a client had died. As Sherman, the English wealth manager working in the BVI, put it, this intimacy with clients' lives gives a depth to his practice that is unlike his previous experience in banking: "It's very emotional. It's very real." The genuineness of the socio-emotional bond is connected to the sense of meaning and purpose that, as Chapter 2 showed, makes wealth management a particularly satisfying line of work for many practitioners.

The quasi-familial role does have some downsides. Their position of trust and intimacy with clients often makes wealth managers witnesses to some of the worst parts of family life. Many mentioned their distress at having to help clients disinherit their children and spouses. Nadia, a practitioner in Panama City, said with tears in her eyes that over the past

thirty years of her career, "I have watched families tear themselves apart over money. Tear themselves apart." Several mentioned their discomfort in abetting deceptions and betrayals
of clients' family members. Alistair, in the Cayman Islands,
said, "We may have a client with a mistress and children
[born out of wedlock] he wants to provide for, and it all has to
be kept totally private from the wife. We have to just put up
and shut up."

In countries where privacy, family harmony, and respect for
authority are particularly valued—notably China and the nations of the Arabian Peninsula—professionals often get drawn
into family battles as participants.[19] As Mark in Dubai explained, "Clients use us as swords and shields—to impart bad
news, and to carry out instructions without them being accountable. So a mother with sons at war comes to me and says
that she wants me to do something that would favor one son
at the expense of the other, and that I should never tell them.
Then she goes and tells them herself and they scream at me."

It is a testament to the depth of trust that such clients have
in their wealth managers that they invite the professional
to see and participate in the "backstage" activities of a family
life whose public image is otherwise carefully managed and
protected.[20]

Impact on client service

Determining whether a professional is worthy of such trust
and intimacy is understandably a major concern of elite clients. Several participants in this study told of clients who
purposely demanded extraordinary acts of service in order to

assess their trustworthiness in the early stages of their relationship. For example, Eleanor told of a new client who called
Eleanor's office in Geneva to say, "I'm outside a restaurant in
London and I just lost a bracelet—I need you to find it." In
other words, the client was asking her to locate a bracelet outside an unnamed restaurant in another country. Eleanor
somehow did this, billed for her time, and earned a loyal client
for decades to come. Mark, the English wealth manager based
in Dubai, explained that such outlandish requests are surprisingly common in the profession, in part as a way of testing
whether the practitioner is "worthy" of the client making a
long-term investment in the relationship: "The very rich are
willing to pay for that extra-special bespoke service, just
like suits. And they don't like change: they want to go to the
same doctor all their lives, the same dentist, and the same
lawyer or fiduciary."

With this in mind, elite clients may ask wealth management professionals to undergo a contemporary version of the
trials of Hercules. David, another English practitioner who is
nearing the end of a forty-year career in Hong Kong, had a
particularly impressive story of an impossible task set him by a
client bent on testing his trustworthiness:

> I was phoned up from Osaka once, by a client who said, "I'm
> sitting across from Owagi-san, who speaks no English, but we
> are bowing to each other. He has just said to me through a
> translator that he needs a thousand sides of smoked salmon
> by Tuesday, and I'm relying on you to get them." I said, "I'm
> your wealth manager, not your fishmonger." And the client
> said, "Well, today you're a fishmonger." So I had to ring up a

friend who knew the guy from Unilever who runs the smoked salmon plant in Scotland. And the plant manager made it happen. So I found out later that my client was testing me by setting me an impossible task—he told me that he was trying to see if I was really up to the kind of job he wanted me to do.

The story is reminiscent in some ways of the tales of knightly quests, complete with seemingly insurmountable obstacles and abject humiliations ("today you're a fishmonger")—with a shipment of smoked salmon in place of the Holy Grail. The question behind the impossible task remains consistent: *Are you truly devoted?*

Clients may also have a pragmatic reason for posing these tests: they allow the client to discover whether the wealth manager possesses the kind of social networks and influence necessary to provide extraordinary personal service. In David's case, being "up to the kind of job" the client wanted depended not just on personal resolve but also on knowing the right people, in this case a friend with connections at Unilever. This is consistent with previous research showing that elite professionals serve their clients in part by acting as commercial "matchmakers," facilitating opportunities that are not available publicly. For example, a study of nineteenth-century British lawyers showed how their familiarity with clients' business dealings allowed them to create whole new industries, such as the country's railroad system; the professionals established a kind of private market, accessible only to the upper crust of British society. Access to such opportunities hinged entirely on trust between clients and professionals, and the related perception of exclusivity. As the study concluded, "To avail one-self of opportunities, one has to be 'one of us.'"[21]

Such examples of social closure linked to markets abound in the remarks of wealth managers. Michael, a Guernsey-based wealth manager, says that he personally runs a multibillion-pound market in real estate and art, just by arranging trans-actions among his own clients. In fact, he employs a man in London exclusively to keep track of the private investment and sale opportunities that clients bring to his attention, "whether it's a Rembrandt, a department store, or a mansion." These private sales keep clients' names out of the newspapers and help protect their wealth from public scrutiny.

Michael volunteered another way that he was able to de-velop new investment opportunities for his clients as a result of social exclusivity: by participating in elite recreational ac-tivities. For example, he was able to alert clients to food as a promising investment sector because "when we tried to go shooting with clients, we were told that the cost is going to go up 30 percent next year, because wheat is getting so expen-sive, and it costs so much to feed the birds at the shooting range." Three participants in the study singled out shooting parties—along with other expensive elite activities, such as sailing and polo—as fruitful settings for creating business op-portunities with high-net-worth clients. Dieter, the German wealth manager quoted in Chapter 2, said this was a product of the traditional links between sport shooting and the landed gentry, as well as the necessarily small size of such groups: "Shooting has the greatest concentration of wealth. . . . Plus, you can only invite ten or so people, so you end up talking."

But in keeping with the quasi-familial role wealth managers often acquire in relation to their clients, the trust accorded to the professionals can lead to opportunities beyond the realm of business. Nigel, an English practitioner based in Singapore, has become a literal matchmaker for his clients, many of whom are too busy to date. Other participants in the study mentioned providing services of a highly personal, non-financial nature. Several specifically mentioned helping clients get treatment for their drug-addicted children—a particularly common problem in wealthy families.[22] Sherman, the practitioner in the British Virgin Islands, said, "I'm not qualified to counsel anyone on the use of drugs, but I can say, 'There's a facility that other clients have used for rehabilitation.'" The same social networks that allow many elite professionals to create special business opportunities for their clients give wealth managers—with their unusually intimate access to their clients' lives—the ability to offer an additional level of personalized service that distinguishes them from allied fields of work in finance and law.

Gaining the trust of high-net-worth individuals

Having established the extent and consequences of the trust and intimacy that characterize wealth managers' relationships with their clients, we return to the question of how the professionals earn that position. How do strangers acquire the status and access privileges of quasi–family members? Indeed, how do they manage in many cases to become *more* trusted than flesh-and-blood relations? Previous research suggests that part of the answer lies in the profession's distinctive set of demands.

Like all professions, wealth management requires simultaneous mastery of both a body of expert knowledge and a set of context-specific "mannerisms, attitudes and society rituals."[23] The French sociologist Pierre Bourdieu thus defined professionalism as "a technical competence which is inevitably social."[24] As the previous section illustrates, the highly personalized service afforded by wealth managers to their clients requires intense interaction, often in face-to-face settings; under those conditions, the minutiae of mannerisms and self-presentation become observable and significant. This is why, as Bourdieu explained, many professions "set such store on the seemingly most insignificant details of *dress, bearing*, physical and verbal *manners*."[25]

However, mere good manners in the ordinary sense of the term are not sufficient for success in wealth management; nor is a clean and neat appearance or a friendly demeanor. The social conventions of high-net-worth individuals represent a distinct and difficult-to-master set of norms and interaction rituals. As one recent study of elite London legal practices noted, "A common story told by junior lawyers is that wearing the right color socks and shoes is vital for success."[26] To an even greater and more detailed extent, wealth managers and their firms take care to present themselves in a way that signals trustworthiness, discretion, and reliability in the distinctive idiom of wealth.

For example, one firm where I conducted interviews maintains headquarters adjacent to Westminster Abbey. The office space, covered with neo-Gothic stonework on the outside, could double as a nineteenth-century gentlemen's club on the inside, with its lustrous wood paneling and sturdy leather sofas that may date to the firm's founding in the late 1800s. In this firm and others, I consistently saw practitioners present themselves in a style that could only be described as "neo-Tulkinghorn," featuring three-piece suits (a few with gold watch chains at the waist) and an array of discreet but costly jewelry, such as signet rings displaying a family coat of arms.

There is more to this than the "presentation of an 'up-market' image."[27] The signaling takes place at a frequency all but inaudible to everyone except members of the very upper reaches of the socioeconomic spectrum—people who not only would notice but could assign meaning and value to the wearing of braces instead of a belt, or a pocket watch instead of a wristwatch. These distinctions can be literally inaudible in that they extend to special ways of using language that would pass unnoticed by all but a select few. As James, a London wealth manager, said, "You [as an American] probably don't hear it, but anyone in this country would be able to tell that from the way I speak that I went to an independent school because I have the characteristic accent. Clients notice." In Bourdieu's terms, this is a form of "cultural capital," embodied in the speech of the wealth manager. As part of a larger constellation of dispositions, mannerisms, and modes of self-presentation, it constitutes part of an individual's habitus.

Professions, particularly those that require interaction with elites, all demand mastery of a particular habitus for successful job performance. As previous research has noted, "the physical body is an important facet of professionalism because it is symbolic of aspects of identity and the self, the embodied representation of a perceived identity."[28] What makes wealth management distinctive is the depth and complexity of this embodied performance of professionalism. Furthermore, the habitus of elites is by definition a "class-specific" phenomenon, grounded in cultural practices and norms transmitted through families, exclusive schools, and other institutions.[29] This means that many technically qualified professionals may lack the cultural capital necessary to gain the trust and respect of high-net-worth clients.

To the manor (and manner) born

As social psychologists have shown, similarity is a common basis for trustworthiness: that is, we trust people who seem like ourselves.[30] Thus, elites prefer wealth managers who are themselves from the upper reaches of the stratification spectrum — or who can convincingly play the part of someone from that background. As one study put it, "In short, gentlemen wish to have their money . . . dealt with by gentlemen."[31] This point was illustrated vividly in an anecdote James related concerning an aristocratic client:

> I have one client who's a know-it-all, and he's got management of his mother's estate and five or six trusts. He's always boasting, telling the same stories five or six times. He was talking about Portugal, and I was able to say, "Oh, fantastic, I was just out there playing golf." Or he shoots, and talked about signing papers while out shooting, and since I shoot, I was able to ask, "Oh, whereabouts?" and then keep up with him in conversation. The thing that finally shut him up was that

he came in one day to tell me that he'd just been at lunch with the prime minister's father-in-law, and I said, "Oh, Willie Astor! How's he doing?" It just happened by coincidence that I knew the fellow, and the client began to accept that I was his peer, and therefore trusted me with more information and authority.

This, ultimately, is the purpose of displaying the proper habitus in client interactions: the client invests the professional with trust, information, and authority. As this case illustrates, the time and effort required to enact or signal appropriate habitus can be quite considerable, even for those endowed with the right cultural capital during their upbringing.

As detailed in Chapter 2, wealth management until recently was an activity performed for elites by elites. This may be a result not just of convenience—elites cross paths in many walks of life, including as neighbors and family members—but of the social psychology of trust: the easiest way to signal similarity and trustworthiness to high-net-worth individuals is to be one of them.[32] One study described this historical pattern as follows: "Offspring who eventually specialized as trustees had themselves been socialized into dynastic families, and as a result were prepared culturally and ideologically to assume the management of other dynastic families' money."[33] More recent research suggests that this remains a common mode of entry into the profession.[34] By virtue of their need to earn a living, these professionals are what Bourdieu called "the dominated fraction of the dominant class."[35]

Several participants in this study were very forthcoming about the impact on their career of their own family origins—

particularly in terms of the repertoire of experiences, dispositions, and mannerisms conferred by their upbringing. Dieter,
quoted in Chapter 2, was born into a family of European
nobles who lost their fortune in World War II. Nevertheless, he
bore the title of count, and had it printed on his engraved business cards. He claimed that the title, along with the deport-
ment that was part of his upbringing, allowed him to rise to
the top of the profession despite having gone to a public high
school and not continued on to university. James, quoted
above, made a similar observation about his family background becoming the basis for his career: "That's the reason I
got into this: I have some trusts that I'm the beneficiary of, we
have some land, and I understand what it's like to have to
manage a family fortune and succession process. A lot of my
clients are not dissimilar to me—just a few years older."

While this traditional point of entry into wealth management continues to provide the profession with new practitioners, the supply of down-at-heel nobles and the heirs of
smaller family fortunes is inadequate to meet the growing demand. Many firms report that "it has become exceedingly
difficult to find suitably skilled fiduciary staff"; almost half the
firms responding to a recent STEP survey said that they have
"more difficulty finding fiduciary skills than any other."[36]

Alternative routes to gaining the trust of elites

With the explosion in demand for wealth managers worldwide,
the profession might have been expected to follow the lead of
top law firms in creating habitus "training" programs: pre-
paring individuals from middle- or working-class backgrounds

to work with elite clients by educating them in the finer points of upper-class self-presentation and interaction norms.[37] But this seems to be a rarity. STEP, the professional society, offers no training in social skills for wealth managers, and barely mentions the subject in its educational materials. In any case, the success of such programs in transmitting habitus is unknown. This may be because, as Bourdieu suggested, it is difficult to teach "what comes without saying."[38]

The task of learning the correct habitus for wealth management is made even more complex by the significance accorded to behavioral taboos—things that must not be done, many of which would be considered normal business practice in other settings. For example, most of the professionals interviewed for this study claimed that to gain new clients, it was imperative to approach high-net-worth individuals indirectly, without alluding to money, business, or selling in a forthright manner. As a rule, their firms don't market themselves publicly, and individual professionals do not prospect for new business, at least in any of the conventional ways. Alex, a British-born wealth manager based in Singapore, said of his firm: "We don't advertise, we'll never advertise—all our business comes through referrals."

To the extent that wealth managers recruit new clients, they do so through encounters organized around clients' hobbies and leisure pursuits. Erika, the wealth manager in Geneva, described one of her most successful colleagues as a master of acquiring clients through informal encounters: "He never comes back from vacation without new clients. Of course, he stays at the right hotels. Once I went to the opera with him, and we were standing in the lobby during an intermission, having a drink, and I watched him talk to some strangers. Before long, they were telling him their life stories, and by the time the intermission was over, they had exchanged cards and he had a new client. He did *nothing*—I watched him! Actually, what he did was listen with great interest and attention. He made them the center."

Along the lines of making the client the center of attention, Amelia, an English practitioner working in the Cayman Islands, related the story of a colleague in London who achieved this aim in a more planned and strategic fashion. Like a hunter stalking skittish prey, this wealth manager plotted for months to get close to the client; after arranging a face-to-face meeting in the client's office, he then devised a "lure" to draw the client's interest without arousing suspicion:

> The best prospecting story I ever heard was from a quiet, understated guy who really knows his stuff and is incredibly successful. He identified this very rich Asian guy after reading about him in *The Economist*, saying that the guy was really interested in certain types of tubes that go into certain types of bridge. So David goes and finds out about this building material that the Asian is obsessed with; he even gets hold of the trade magazine for whatever, cement construction, and finds out all about the precise thing that the client is interested in. Then he rips out the article in the magazine, sent it with a personal note to the Asian client, and that's how he gets through the gatekeepers and gets the first meeting. The client decides to give David five minutes. David goes in thinking, "I'm just going to get the guy to open a checking account." The client asks, "What do you want from this meeting?" So

> David says, "I know you come to London a lot and probably
> need a credit card or checkbook facility." Instead of selling big
> fancy investments, he chose the simplest, least threatening
> thing in the world, and the guy went for it. And now he's one
> of David's biggest clients.

This strategy of doing business through indirection and side-long approaches to clients is an essential component of the habitus of wealth management, and makes it particularly difficult to teach. This is evident from STEP's few attempts to provide guidance on the subject. In meeting a new client, the STEP course texts advise, "do not immediately proceed to the business at hand"; "be interested, leaning slightly toward the client, head nodding but *not too much*," and, most surprising, "do not make a preliminary analysis of the client's needs."[39] Having explained what should *not* be done, however, the STEP texts are less explicit about what wealth managers *are* supposed to say and do in client interactions.

Dieter, the formerly down-at-heel count, attempted to address such issues with a habitus "training" program he created for the private bank he headed. This was the only case I encountered in the study of an employer-sponsored training program that addressed issues of professional demeanor and the dos and don'ts of client relations. Each year Dieter would bring a small group of junior people in the firm to an "academy . . . [to] focus entirely on nonbanking issues, like etiquette and demeanor." With actors trained to play the roles of potential customers, the count delivered the course content himself:

I tell people, "You are thirty to thirty-five years old, and our preferred client is fifty-five, is a company owner, has 1,000 employees and sales of $50 million, head of the Rotary Club in his city, president of his golf club, he deals on the highest levels with politicians and other business people; and now you come to him and ask for his money." . . . If you are young and don't have the status the client has, you must be attractive. . . . You have to have essence, which is attractive to other people and bridges the status and age gaps with the clients. You must have an image of trustworthiness, all qualitative, subjective things, which are difficult to find. You need to be service oriented, which means not only technical skills, but to be modest and devoted . . . because you're dealing with people who command a thousand people a day, and they're used to deference and speedy execution.

Dieter's description of the modesty, devotion, and service orientation of a successful wealth manager is reminiscent of the knightly ethic, and of Philip's reflections on humility in Chapter 2. As for being attractive and cultivating "essence," the count did not claim to create those qualities in his employees. Rather, he said, he first hired people with the potential to interest wealthy clients, then taught them how to make the most of what they already had. The success of that effort—that is, whether a professional acquired the correct habitus for working with high-net-worth clients—is ultimately determined by the clients themselves. Indeed, Dieter was always soliciting feedback, asking clients and their friends, "Which asset managers do you find attractive and trustworthy?"

Perhaps surprisingly, Dieter did not suggest that his trainees try to make themselves seem more "attractive and trustworthy" by changing their skill sets—for example, by learning to shoot or play golf if they did not already do so. Instead, he hired people who came endowed with high levels of cultural capital and showed them how to display those assets to best advantage vis-à-vis high-net-worth individuals. As an example, Dieter explained that he hired a former opera singer, since many wealthy clients enjoy the opera. According to Dieter, this former singer made himself attractive to clients through his connections to the opera world: "When we go to the Salzburg music festival, he ensures that we have lunch with Ricardo Muti, the conductor, or Cecilia Bartoli, the singer. So everyone wants to have him around." In other words, high-net-worth clients seem to be looking for wealth managers whose social networks can give them access to extraordinary experiences and service.

Dieter's approach to recruiting is similar in spirit to the strategies of many professional service firms that cater to elites: they hire people who have been presocialized and endowed with cultural capital through prior life experiences. If this does not include coming from a well-to-do family, attendance at elite educational institutions is often accepted as a substitute. James mentioned his "independent school" accent as a competitive advantage in his career—something valued not only by his employers but also by his clients. Similarly, Neal noted that "for someone coming into the profession, it's very important to have the right names on your CV in terms of education qualifications—to have gone to the right schools. Clients really look for that; it's important to them. It's like

brand identity." Thus, law firms and other providers of elite
professional services will hire almost exclusively the graduates
of elite universities, in order to get employees who are presocialized in the habitus of the high-net-worth clientele.[40]

Where wealth management seems to depart from the pattern of other professional services is in the breadth and intensity of the habitus professionals are expected to master in order
to do their jobs. This may account for the lack of formal
training programs in the profession: the outlay of time and
money required to teach behaviors and dispositions that have
traditionally been transferred over decades within families
may simply be too great for any business venture to bear. Individual firms are likely ill-equipped to make such heavy investments in transmitting this curriculum, particularly when the
results are uncertain: as Bourdieu suggests, it is questionable
whether habitus can ever be taught, since it is learned through
unconscious mimesis rather than conscious imitation or effort.[41] This may be why, when I asked wealth managers from
elite family backgrounds how they acquire the social skills to
succeed in their jobs, some gave a perplexed look, as if they
had never considered behaving any other way. As Sebastian
put it, "You just do it, don't you?"

For those professionals not "to the manor born," one of the
most common means of acquiring professional habitus among
the wealth managers in this study was what might be called
the method of "accidental apprenticeship." This is another way
to "just do it," consisting of an unplanned, unintentional and
mostly cost-free training in how to interact successfully with
the very rich. Dieter essentially specialized in finding and recruiting people who had undergone this sort of apprenticeship.

His own habitus enabled him to recognize in others the qualities that might appeal to elites; he then helped recruits cultivate and expand the assets they already possessed. In essence, he acted as a Pygmalion for the wealth management profession.

Participants who described their entry into wealth management as "accidental" were not university educated and described their family backgrounds as working-class. Among those who came to the profession in this way was Nick, an Englishman who began work as a boat builder, and then—upon the collapse of that industry in the early 1990s—found new employment as a crew member on yachts competing in the America's Cup races, one of the favorite sporting events of the ultra-rich. As he explained, "I came from a very poor background myself, [but] . . . by doing lots of yachting around the world, I've dealt with a lot of high-net-worth individuals. Someone walks into my business and says they have $40 million, it doesn't really faze me." Similarly, Javier said that he used his sailing skills to rise above the career limitations he experienced as a son of a low-ranking member of the Argentinian navy. In general, he said, "it's very unusual for Argentinians to get work abroad; even within [multinational firms], people from the Argentinian offices don't really get to work in other cities." That, combined with his class origins, frustrated his aspirations to an international business career. As someone who has "sailed from very, very young," Javier occasionally competed in races for fun; then, "by participating in a regatta in Curaçao, I met the two most important guys at a [wealth management] firm in Miami, and that led to a job offer."

Another "accidental" path into the profession came through clerical work in wealth management firms. Elaine, a native of Guernsey, happened to get her first job after high school as a temporary secretary at Rothschild Bank; some twenty years into her career, she had just been promoted to director of the wealth management practice for one of the largest banks in the world. Likewise, Sherman—the Englishman I interviewed in the British Virgin Islands—told me that he started work as a clerical apprentice in a London retail bank shortly after finishing secondary school. Because of his skill at accounting, he was assigned to a difficult task in the trusts department, setting his career in motion. Thirty-five years later, he observed, "I help clients buy yachts and luxury properties, and I stay at their homes, I know their children. With a couple dozen of them, I go on short vacations." In all three cases, the path to mastering the professional habitus of wealth management was idiosyncratic, unplanned, and time-consuming, unfolding over decades. These individuals didn't just stumble into a job; they also found themselves in a new domain of dispositions, tastes, and habits.

This route provides the profession with a larger labor market than it previously had, but supply still remains inadequate to demand. Despite this, and the profession's extensive demands for mastery of elite social skills as well as technical skills, labor scarcity has not resulted in an increase in salaries. One reason may be downward price pressures from the industry's main source of new clients: the developing world, which is generating new millionaires at a rapid pace.

Crossing cultures

The center of gravity in the wealth management profession is shifting eastward and southward, from its traditional centers in North America and Europe to Africa and Asia.[42] A recent report suggests that Singapore is poised to usurp Switzerland's place as the global center of offshore finance.[43] This shift carries a number of implications. As suggested earlier, it may change the industry's pricing structure: all of the professionals interviewed for this study mentioned that their clients from Asia and the Middle East were extremely price-sensitive, forcing across-the-board reductions in the professionals' fees when they worked with these clients. Mark, the English wealth manager in Dubai, conceived of the struggle over pricing as a cultural issue: "This is a haggling country. It's even worse if you go farther east, to India and Pakistan. In the West, we're used to paying sticker prices. But when I meet with clients and they ask me what things cost, and I tell them, they say, 'Yes, but what is the price for *me*?' And then I tell them again the sticker price and they say, 'Oh, you must be giving me your famous English humor.'" This clash of expectations echoes what the anthropologist Clifford Geertz observed in "the bazaar economy," where pricing stemmed not from shared norms about value but rather from particularistic relations.[44]

Compensation for wealth managers has long been a fraught topic. In the West, the old English tradition of friends and kin serving as unpaid trustees of land yielded only grudgingly to the American-led practice of treating wealth managers as professionals and paying them for their skills.[45] It took more than a century of court cases and statutes to make payment the standard. In the rest of the world, these issues are just coming to the fore, and practitioners end up addressing them one client at a time. Lian, a native of China who spent most of her adult life in England, became accustomed in her U.K. wealth management practice to what she termed "European complacency" about paying professional fees. When she returned to China in 2007, she had to revise her business model, because her European pricing structure caused her to "lose a lot of clients" and she had to "cut, cut, cut to stay competitive" in that market. Lian said she had forgotten "how Chinese people were—obsessed with hard bargaining and getting the lowest possible price, being distrustful of service providers."

As Lian's remarks suggest, one driver of these pricing demands seems to be trust—or rather, lack of trust. Numerous participants described how clients from the BRICS countries in particular were characterized not only by the distrustfulness common to high-net-worth individuals but also by an additional layer of suspicion born of experience with corrupt governments and shady business dealings. Because of these experiences, such clients typically have little trust in professionals, organizations, or the rule of law. Sebastian, the English wealth manager based in Hong Kong, works mainly with older Chinese clients who lived through the Cultural Revolution and vividly recall the seizure of their family's wealth by the government. Such an experience of losing control makes the value propositions of wealth management a "hard sell": "When you propose to elderly Chinese gentlemen, 'Look, I'll tell you what, how about you give me control of your assets and I'll hold on to them for you and your kids until you need them, at which point I may or may not give them [the assets] to you? And by the way, you'll be paying me a hefty fee all the while,' the elderly Chinese gentlemen laugh very hard for a long time." These observations are supported by scholarly research indicating a "psychological impediment in Chinese culture against relinquishing ownership over one's property to another person."[46] More generally, research in social psychology suggests that trust in professionals and organizations is more likely to arise among individuals in countries where income inequality and corruption are low, and where the rule of law provides strong protections for property rights and contracts.[47] This is not the case for many wealthy people from developing countries, creating a significant additional challenge for wealth managers.

Translating trust

Culture affects the kinds of signals that indicate trustworthiness, as well as how those signals are interpreted.[48] As a result, trust is more likely to develop among those who share the same norms and assumptions about "the types of actions that indicate whether trust is warranted."[49] This is a particularly important challenge for wealth managers, because the clients' lack of trust in institutions places the whole weight of the professional relationship on individual practitioners. As Luc, the Frenchman working in Riyadh, put it, his business hinges on establishing "personal trust, because Saudi Arabian clients don't trust firms or legal systems per se, but rather individuals." For the majority of wealth managers who were born and raised in Europe and North America, these differing signal systems for expressing trustworthiness pose a formidable obstacle to gaining the trust of clients from other cultures.

This may be related to wealth managers' observations about the differences they experience in their relationships with cli-

ents from "old money"—that is, from families that have been
wealthy for generations—and those from "new money." Most
of the "old money" clients are from developed countries with
a stable rule of law, giving them some basis for trust in professionals in organizations. These effects are intensified for
people in countries where Protestantism is the dominant form
of religious practice.[50] This includes the United Kingdom, the
United States, and Canada, as well as many other former
British colonies. So the widespread acceptance of key elements of wealth management—such as the trust—in such jurisdictions may be due not just to the shared common-law
system in those countries but also to a set of cultural dispositions stemming in part from religious practice. Louis, an elderly and aristocratic wealth manager in London, expressed
one consequence of this connection between national culture
and trust: "As Brits, we're all hardwired for trusteeship. Everything is in trust here. Little tiny trusts from people's wills to
keep the organ going at the village church . . . there are thousands of these. The whole of English life is permeated, effectively, with assuring continuity, of protecting the bell tower of
their Norman church. We're hardwired to think of trusts and
how they operate, and making decisions as trustees." This
smooths the path of gaining clients' trust in countries such as
Great Britain and its former colonies.

But practitioners working in countries where "new money"
is the norm, often in a context of religious and cultural traditions alien to the Anglo-Saxon world, face a formidable set of
challenges. It takes time, patience, and skill to translate the
culturally specific signals through which trusting relationships
are formed. In the meantime, many wealth managers based

in developing countries find that they are working blind: clients often withhold crucial information from them. Several of those interviewed for the study mentioned clients, particularly in Asia and the Arabian Peninsula, who did not disclose the full extent and location of their assets or their possession of a secondary nationality. This creates significant legal and professional liability for wealth managers.

Those who succeed in overcoming this distrust must find a way to "indigenize" the trust and other wealth management tools, making them "legitimate, recognizable and appealing" in terms of the client's native culture.[51] This demands an act of translation from the wealth manager, not just through language but also by aligning the beliefs and values of different meaning systems. Bruce, the American wealth manager based in Geneva, speaks Arabic fluently and works frequently with clients from the Arabian Peninsula. When he tries to explain why they should use a trust structure, he says, Arab clients are particularly distrustful:

> They want to *own* things . . . so they can't understand why they should agree to give up that ownership and keep control. . . . Culturally, it's an alien concept. They say, "Why should I trust you?" That's a tough one, so I have to explain in terms of concepts that are already in their culture, like *amana*—this basic idea of trust, so that you can go off with the caravan to Syria, for example, and say to someone trustworthy, "I'm leaving for a few months, please take care of my stuff, and if I don't come back, please make sure my stuff goes to my son/wife/et cetera." The Prophet Muhammed was one of those people that other people found really trustworthy,

and he was often asked to take care of their stuff for them, knowing he'd take better care of it than his own stuff.

For Bruce, as for many wealth managers working in countries whose histories and cultures militate against trust in professionals, the main challenge of client relations consists in articulating the local with the global. He solves the problem of client skepticism—"Why should I trust you?"—by drawing on the history of Islam, which permeates both the environment and the worldview of his clients. Not only does *amana* (in Arabic, أمانة) mean "trustworthiness," but it is also the second key attribute of the Prophet Muhammed, giving it a powerful positive significance for Arab Muslim clients. The success of Bruce's strategy—fluency not only in the local language but in key cultural and religious concepts as well—is consistent with research suggesting that in the absence of ethnic similarities between interaction partners, adaptation to local norms helps outsiders appear more trustworthy.[52]

Luc, who like Bruce works primarily with Saudis, described taking a similar approach in client relations. Although he does not speak Arabic, he goes out of his way to demonstrate his knowledge of and respect for the local culture and to frame his work in locally meaningful terms. For example, he explains to Saudi clients the similarities between trusts and the traditional Islamic *vaqf* (وقف), an ancient form of charitable foundation that has several important features in common with trusts, including the function of passing wealth from one generation of a family to the next and the separation of ownership from control through the management of assets by a third party (called a *mutawallī* or المتولي), whose role is similar to that of a common-law trustee.[53] According to Weber, the *vaqf* was originally developed so that private wealth could accumulate free of feudal taxation—an important historical commonality with the common-law trust.[54]

In fact, wealth managers working in the Arab world might have an advantage in terms of indigenizing the trust concept for Muslim clients: the *vaqf* predates the trust by several centuries, and may be one of the many practices imported to Europe in the Middle Ages by pilgrims and Crusaders returning from the Holy Land. In support of this, there is evidence of its traditional structure and terms being used as a template for some of the earliest trusts created in England.[55] In this sense, wealth managers are *re*indigenizing the trust for modern Islamic societies.

But what of wealth managers working with clients from other religious and cultural groups? How do they translate the concepts and tools of wealth management into terms that inspire trust in clients? The pattern of putting new wine in old bottles, as Bruce and Luc did with Saudi clients, seems to hold across cultures. Sebastian, who described the challenges of selling his services to clients who lived through China's political upheavals, says that those who ultimately accept the Western wealth management paradigm are "sold by the dynasty concept." That is, Sebastian's Chinese clients appreciate the way that the structures he creates dovetail with traditional patriarchal authority and allow them to extend that authority beyond their natural life spans: "They really love the idea of being able to control their families from beyond the grave. These are people who have everything they want—the only thing they don't have is immortality, and they really want it.

They love the idea of a perpetual trust, and so what you usually end up doing with these clients is creating a perpetual trust with an intricately detailed letter of wishes, specifying that 'my grandson's second son gets X, but only if he does Y.' Very specific conditions, tight control." Sebastian succeeds in gaining the trust of his Chinese clients to the extent that his work coheres with local culture. In Weberian terms, he wraps a traditional form of authority in a Western rational-legal structure, protecting and expanding the power of the patriarch.[56]

In this sense, Sebastian and others like him play an important role in globalization. They belong to a larger class of "globalizing agents," mainly in finance: these are actors who bridge the local and global levels, armed with "enough local knowledge to mobilize judiciously the cultural elements needed to orchestrate the new economic practice."[57]

In trusts we trust?

But there are limits to this ability to bridge the local and global. While contemporary wealth management sits well in certain respects with the values of societies organized around traditional forms of authority, some issues remain problematic. The difficulties seem to arise particularly frequently in connection with trusts. Although wealth managers have other tools at their disposal (see Chapter 4), trusts have become an indispensable feature of financial planning both for high-net-worth individuals and for corporations.[58] This global norm—which involves a rational-legal form of authority and invests considerable control in professionals—runs into resistance with clients from cultures characterized by strong patriarchal authority. Elias, a Panamanian wealth manager, observes, "One of the main characteristics of Latin American clients, which are 98 percent of the people I work with, they feel that trusts don't give them enough control. . . . They are desperate for control, and they don't like trusts very much. They don't trust trusts!"

In response to this common obstacle to the formation of trusting client relationships, wealth managers—along with professionals in allied realms—have sought to institutionalize solutions. There has been particular interest in accommodating the cultural preferences of high-net-worth individuals in the Asia-Pacific region, who share norms of patriarchal authority with Latin Americans but represent a much bigger client base: Asians are the fastest-growing population of high-net-worth individuals in the world, and already possess more than twice the wealth of the high-net-worth population of Latin America.[59] In response to this growing market power, some jurisdictions have purposely created laws to address the conflicts over control that have been so problematic with Asian clients. Frank, an English practitioner who draws on thirty years of international experience in teaching the STEP training courses, observed that "the British Virgin Islands developed the VISTA [Virgin Islands Special Trusts Act] corporation expressly to attract Asian high-net-worth clients, because the rules created firms held by a trustee, but in which a trustee was not allowed to make any inquiries into the underlying firm—the nature of its business, how it operates, who operates it, et cetera." The BVI, in its determination to create a financial environment with maximum appeal to wealthy Asians, created a new form of trust designed to provide extraordinary privacy and control for clients.[60] Under the VISTA law, a trust holds shares of a client's ongoing business operation, but whereas a traditional trust would require the trustee to be fully informed of, and possibly involved in, the day-to-day operations of that business, VISTA eliminates those obligations. This turns the underlying business into what Frank called a "black box," allowing the client to maintain control over the source of his wealth and shroud in secrecy many of the activities that otherwise would have to be disclosed to the wealth manager.

Although VISTA has been a resounding success (see Chapter 4 for details), some sources of cultural conflict can't be legislated away. They have to be worked out one client, or even one interaction, at a time. A recurring theme in the interviews for this study was the frustration many practitioners experienced at having to educate clients about ownership and control of their assets. This was a particular problem for clients with assets held in trust, since those are legally owned by the wealth manager. Neville, a practitioner based in Guernsey, said that the issue broke down across both the lines of culture and those of "old money" versus "new money":

> The "old money" clients are typically landed U.K. clients, and they are very comfortable with the idea of the trust—that the money is not theirs, they just have the enjoyment of it, and don't have much influence over the way those assets are managed. With the more entrepreneurial "new money," the settlor usually sees the assets as his own and wants to direct how they're invested. It takes a while for them to grasp the idea that it's not their money once they put it in trust. This is all the

more so for clients from emerging markets because they're less interested in setting up generational transfer than protecting their assets from the regimes in their home countries, and making a safe pile of assets they can use if they have to flee the country.

There are limits, in other words, to how much a practitioner can indigenize the tools and rules of contemporary wealth management to fit the local norms and expectations of clients.

Testing the boundaries

Sometimes global norms must prevail because they carry the force of law and its associated sanctions. Often this entails wealth managers having to say no to their clients in order to keep them within the bounds of the law. Bruce, the American wealth manager, recounted one such case: "I had one Arab client who asked me to send him $100,000 from company funds so that he could buy a Ferrari. I had to say no, and he said, 'What do you mean, no?' I said, 'This is a company and you're a shareholder, so perhaps you're requesting a distribution?' I had to coach him on the right words to use, and said, 'Would you please delete those emails you sent me requesting the cash for the Ferrari?'" By treating the company as what Bruce called "a personal bank account," the client put both himself and Bruce in danger of breaking the law. By saying no, Bruce protected them both, but he also risked losing the client's trust and his business.

In this case, the practitioner kept his client. But in many instances, wealth managers find themselves confronted with an insurmountable cultural barrier. Such cases arise particularly around taboos—the "ultimate values" of a culture.[61] Sometimes this is a matter of religion: in majority-Islamic countries, for example, the belief that "God will provide" poses a major obstacle to the basic purposes of wealth management. Elaine, an English practitioner in Dubai, says this belief even extends to a resistance on the part of her clients to buying insurance, as they consider it *haram*—forbidden by Islamic law—to protect themselves against misfortune. Mark elaborated, saying of his clients in Dubai and elsewhere on the Arabian Peninsula, "When it comes to planning, there's a feeling of '*Inshallah*—if God wants things to happen in a certain way, it will.' It's actually an insult to God to try to plan. They only reconsider and work with us when they see other families going wrong because of lack of plans. It's a whole modernizing thing." For some clients, it seems, the practical problems they face can provide the impetus necessary to make a leap of faith, overcoming cultural barriers to trust in professional advice based in a different view of the world.[62]

Wealth managers must also help clients make this leap of faith in the face of secular taboos. Discussion of death, for example, represents a major hurdle for individuals of many cultural and religious backgrounds. Arjun, a Mauritian practitioner of Indian origin, says that he faces this problem with both Hindu and Christian clients: "When it comes to Indians, and I see this also in Africa, you cannot really discuss succession planning with them, because they believe that talking about death is bad luck." Similar nonreligious ideas about death, fate, and planning have played a significant role in shaping client preferences in China, necessitating a number of cultural adaptations to bridge the practices of global finance with local beliefs.[63] Sebastian, like many others I interviewed, relies on euphemism: "There is a suspicion among elderly Chinese gentlemen that to contemplate death is to invite it, so we avoid very assiduously the use of the *d*-word. Instead, we talk about 'when the children are on their own,' or 'when you're no longer able to control your assets.'" For some practitioners, however, such circumlocutions impinge on their ability to deliver client service. They feel that the inability to be honest and direct hinders the formation of a genuinely trusting relationship.

As a result, a subset of individuals I interviewed simply decline to work with clients of certain cultures, in the belief that the barriers to trust are insurmountable. Morris, a practitioner in New York with forty years' experience, exclusively works with Americans, but will only take on members of certain ethnic and religious groups as clients: "I don't even want to see Chinese people, because it's almost insulting to talk about death. I specialize in Jews and Italians, because they're very family oriented. I can't work with WASPs, because I ask questions from my New York Jewish background, which may be offensive to someone from other backgrounds. So if a WASP comes to me for estate planning, I will usually refer them to someone else." Morris also limits his clientele to those within ten years of his own age, because "when I talk to young people, I can take them down the path and the patterns I've seen . . .

but I can't really relate to them, even though I've been through their stage of life. There's an age-sensitivity to this work."

Morris is an extreme example of a larger phenomenon: the link between social identity and trust, and the implications of that connection for relations between professionals and clients. In some client interactions, only certain aspects of social identity contribute to trust, while others militate against it. For example, Shivani, an English wealth manager of Indian descent, described how her youth and gender initially worked against her with an elderly male Indian client. At first the client made it clear that, as a traditional Indian patriarch, he was uncomfortable being advised by a young woman. But over time, Shivani said, he became impressed by her technical competence and ability to solve any problem he brought to her. Yet he expressed his trust not in rationalized terms—*I have confidence in my wealth manager because she is technically competent*—but rather in a new emphasis on Shivani's ethnicity. This did not erase her age and gender, but rather reframed them in terms consistent with the traditional authority structure of the Indian family: "He eventually decided he was glad I was Indian and in meetings with the money management team [who were all white and European] he would sometimes turn to me and say, 'You're Indian, you'll understand my point.' Now he acts like my father, and he knows that I advise him like a father. He advises me like a daughter, and recommends restaurants to me."

Shivani's case illustrates a way that the physical body can influence the interactions between professionals and clients, in addition to the dispositions and demeanors of habitus.[64] In this instance, the relevant characteristics Shivani embodied were demographic—age, gender, and ethnicity. What began as a relationship that challenged the client's beliefs about the proper exercise of authority (an older man being advised by a younger woman) shifted to one that mirrored traditional Indian family relations, cemented by a shared ethnicity. This social identity version of putting new wine in old bottles is a common strategy of coping with the entry of a stranger into a position of trust, although it is often deployed unconsciously.[65]

Conclusion

The levels of disclosure, intimacy, and frankness necessary to protect clients' wealth (and assess the true threats to their fortunes) are well above and beyond the norm in professional interactions. According to the participants in this study, clients' reluctance to bestow this kind of trust is pervasive, even among the "old money" clients whose families have relied on professional wealth management services for generations. The problem is even more acute among clients from the developing world, whose experiences with corrupt governments and weak rule of law makes them particularly loath to relinquish information or control over their assets. In addition, clients from many cultural backgrounds harbor taboos and family grudges that make it difficult to talk honestly and openly about issues that affect their wealth.

This puts an unusual burden on individual practitioners: they are charged with embodying trust in a highly personal way for each client. In some families, the wealth manager acts almost as a member of the family, privy to its most compromising secrets, enlisted in its battles, and occasionally serving as the surrogate for the authority of a deceased patriarch. In this sense, the professional's position of trust is based an unusual combination of rational-bureaucratic expertise and socioemotional bonds.

In consequence of this quasi-familial intimacy, the professionals' physical presence—including their demographic characteristics as well as their dispositions and demeanors—take on an importance equal to that of their technical competencies. From the point of view of the client, the physical appearance of the practitioner may be one of the few signals of service quality and trustworthiness available: "As there are no goods for inspection, the customer has to trust the practitioner himself . . . and trust is bestowed on those who appear to be respectable."[66] Of course, what is trustworthy or respectable may vary across settings, particularly cross-nationally, posing an additional challenge to the professionals to "indigenize" their expertise and manner of self-presentation.

Unlike many contemporary professional activities, which can take place through the intermediation of the Internet or the telephone, the provision of client service in wealth management remains very much an embodied activity that takes place in face-to-face interactions.[67] This is characteristic of certain luxury services where professionals are called upon not only to display technical competence but also to manage their cultural capital and social identity in ways that win the trust of high-net-worth clients.[68] As the evidence in this chapter demonstrates, the skillful presentation of self in client interactions— what Bourdieu called the "labor of representation"—is as real a form of work as the preparation of an asset management plan.[69] This is "a fundamental, and often overlooked, aspect of the professionalization process."[70]

Having focused in this chapter on the socioemotional and cultural aspects of client relations, I will look next at how wealth managers solve the distinctive problems that high-net-worth individuals bring to them. These problems, and the development of appropriate solutions, often vary by culture and national context. This drives the creation of new forms of asset protection, putting wealth management—despite its fundamentally conservative orientation—at the forefront of financial and legal innovation globally.

4

Tactics and Techniques
of Wealth Management

WEALTH MANAGERS' IMMERSION IN THE LIFE-WORLDS OF THEIR clientele, as described in Chapter 3, is essential to the development of the distinctive strategic orientation necessary to protect large private fortunes.[1] I began to get a sense of how distinctive this perspective really was while interviewing Alan, an English banker and trustee who had worked for decades in the British Virgin Islands. While discussing the benefits of international wealth planning using offshore financial centers such as the BVI, he observed that "if Bill Gates had set up Microsoft offshore, he'd be a rich man by now." Taking this for a bit of English humor, I laughed. But then Alan added, "I mean, *seriously* rich." I looked up from my notes to find him gazing back at me in complete earnest.

Bill Gates' $79 billion personal fortune has put him at the head of the *Forbes* list of the world's wealthiest people for sixteen out of the past twenty-one years; in light of this record, most people would never imagine criticizing Gates' wealth management strategy. But from the perspective of professionals who work regularly with ultra-high-net-worth clients,

Gates' failure to make use of offshore financial centers—at least in the protection of his private fortune—constitutes a significant and deeply troubling omission. In his frustration, Alan sounded much like lawyers and financial advisers for the middle class when they describe clients who fail to write a will or purchase life insurance.[2] To him it seemed that an obvious, easy, and highly beneficial strategy was being overlooked.

To understand how someone could look at Bill Gates' massive fortune and conclude that he had missed a few tricks or been poorly advised, one has to appreciate what constitutes the norm in the wealth management industry. As Chapter 3 showed, it is common for practitioners to work with clients who have tens of millions of dollars, if not hundreds of millions, in assets under professional management. While there are still "landed gentry," whose wealth is confined to real property within the boundaries of a single country, this has become the exceptional case. The new norm is to hold a wide variety of assets—many of them globally mobile and fungible—in multiple jurisdictions in a complex of financial-legal structures. In this milieu, the use of offshore financial centers is a given.

Multiple residences, frequent travel, and intensive capital mobility requirements are defining characteristics of this group. For example, Mark, the English lawyer now based in Dubai, described his practice as follows: "A typical client . . . has assets in a dozen different jurisdictions and family members in another half a dozen jurisdictions, and they need a bunch of wonks to make sure that they're holding their wealth in the most efficient way possible and don't lose their wealth to unnecessary taxes or get caught up in probate. We also want to make sure the owners of the wealth avoid the family disputes that destroy the wealth."

Similarly, Alistair, an English wealth manager based in the Cayman Islands, said that among the thirty-five clients he advises, the international complexity of their wealth was a common denominator: "Each client will have at least one trust—maybe four—with at least one underlying company— maybe three—and they're all designed to do different things. Right down to a wife's structure and a girlfriend's structure." Such situations, involving provisions for mistresses as well as long-term relationships and children kept secret from the client's legally recognized family, are apparently so common as to have become something of a cliché in the offshore world. More than twenty-five years ago, Lloyd's Bank International profiled a typical client for offshore wealth managers as a male business owner in his forties who uses an offshore trust to leave his fortune to his mistress, avoiding not only the tax laws of his home country but the inheritance laws as well.[3]

As this example suggests, wealth management has traversed a vast distance from its origins in the passive holding of title to landed property. Chapter 2 showed how this transformation was driven in large part by changes in capitalism and the nature of wealth itself. In the defense of this wealth, knightly service through the skillful deployment of arms gave way to legal maneuvering, which became increasingly complex and innovative as industrial capital supplanted land as the primary form taken by family fortunes.

By the end of the nineteenth century, the economist Thorstein Veblen was moved to observe the swift transition that had taken place during his lifetime, not only in the foundations of wealth but also in the means of keeping and growing it: "The economic basis of the leisure class, then as later, was the possession of wealth; but the methods of accumulating wealth, and the gifts required for holding it, have changed. . . . Simple aggression and unrestrained violence in great measure gave place to shrewd practice and chicanery, as the best approved method of accumulating wealth."[4] These changes were driven in part by the growing significance of wealth managers during the Gilded Age, and undoubtedly contributed to their advancement as a profession. This chapter explores how those practices have evolved and manifested a century later, driven by the internationalization of wealth and the emergence of "hypermobile" capital.[5]

Just as the profession was transformed in the nineteenth century by the increasing fungibility of wealth, so, too, did wealth management metamorphose under the influence of globalization. As Mark explained: "In the late 1990s, a new breed of super-rich, the *Forbes* billionaire class, exploded in numbers and haven't stopped growing. Who would have guessed in the 1980s that you could have an industry charging individuals for trust and estate services? And the reason is, those individuals have the wealth equivalent to small countries." The timeline described by Mark and by several other participants in this study coincides roughly with the phenomenon that social scientists now term "financialization."[6] In particular, the combination of loosened currency controls and decreasing regulation of financial markets in the 1970s and 1980s led to an explosion of international commerce and of profits derived from investment.[7]

One result was the emergence of a new group of elites in need of wealth management services—people who, along with their fortunes, have become so mobile that they seem to exist between nation-states, rather than within the ordinary territorial boundaries that the law assumes.[8] This new, "multi-territorial" client required a different kind of service, one focused not on making the most of legal and financial opportunities within a given state but on exploiting the conflicts and gaps *between* the laws of individual countries.[9] This technique, known as "regulatory arbitrage," is now part of a basic wealth management strategy for many clients.[10]

In keeping with these changes, wealth management firms have altered the way they present themselves to clients, shifting from a message of institutional stability—as shown in the Northern Trust advertisement in Chapter 2—to one of institutional nimbleness in the international arena. For example, one firm that advertised at STEP's 2012 inaugural meeting in South Africa distributed handouts that read: "We specialize in complex cross-border solutions." Their offerings ranged from "bespoke international tax structures" and "property, yacht and aircraft acquisitions, onshore and offshore," to "emigration and immigration" and "tax-efficient divorce settlements." These diverse activities all hinge on managing and maximizing client benefit from the legal gaps and conflicts involved in cross-border transactions.

The essence of this "regulatory arbitrage" has been to foreground a contemporary version of that "shrewd practice and chicanery" Veblen identified more than a century ago. This modern practice involves innovative financial-legal activity that "operates within the letter but against the spirit of the law."[11] What seems most troubling to observers is that while such tactics are perfectly legal, they represent a "heads I win, tails you lose" approach to rules and regulations. As one U.S. congressional committee put it, clients of wealth management services treat "regulations as a one-way street, to be relied upon when supportive of the desired return position [e.g., profit opportunity] and to be disregarded when contrary to such a position."[12]

The indispensable offshore financial centers

As the congressional rebuke suggests, another common feature of the clients of wealth managers is an unwillingness to submit to constraints imposed by law and government. A desire to reduce their tax bill is only the beginning—and for some individuals (such as those from nil-tax jurisdictions like the United Arab Emirates) it is entirely beside the point. It would be more accurate to say that many high-net-worth individuals desire to "escape what they regard as onerous, unreasonable or capricious restrictions imposed by governments."[13] These maneuvers range from the relatively benign, such as evading the "prohibition against interest payments in some Moslem countries," to the more sinister, like "arms dealing and the evasion of international sanctions and embargoes."[14] What all those restrictions have in common is that they limit participation in global financial markets, which are the primary site of wealth generation in the contemporary political economy.[15]

Wealth managers "liberate" capital from these limitations on growth and mobility, freeing clients to accumulate wealth unfettered. Ironically enough, shifting wealth away from one set of sovereign constraints requires recourse to another set of states: ones that use their sovereignty in a different way, to compete for and shelter assets that have been "liberated" from other places. As a result of this competition for the finances of the world's elites, the use of offshore financial institutions has become an essential component of wealth management plans for corporations and individuals alike.

The significance of these zones to the practice of wealth management is suggested by the treatment they receive in the STEP training program. In the introductory course for the TEP diploma, the textbook opens with a discussion of off-shore and devotes the first twenty-eight pages (11 percent of the book) to the subject. That is, the very first thing that wealth managers in training read about are the uses of offshore finan-cial centers in defending private fortunes. This comes before any discussion of the tools of the trade or the kinds of prob-lems that high-net-worth clients typically face.

Characteristic features of the offshore financial centers

While not all offshore financial centers (OFCs) are actually offshore—landlocked Switzerland is a particularly notable case—many are islands or have some other type of geograph-ical or political separateness that they can exploit to their ad-vantage in a "bitterly competitive market" to attract the wealth of elites.[16] OFCs can be found in every corner of the globe, from the English Channel to the South Pacific, and from the

Caribbean to the Indian Ocean. In total, OFCs contain an estimated $8.9 billion in private wealth, along with trillions more in corporate wealth.[17] Of the seventy to eighty OFCs worldwide, Switzerland dominates the field with 26 percent of private offshore wealth, originating mostly from Europe, the Middle East, and Africa. Hong Kong and Singapore hold 16 percent of offshore wealth, coming mostly from elsewhere in Asia. Finally, Panama and the Caribbean islands hold about 13 percent of offshore wealth, mostly originating elsewhere in the Americas.[18] In addition to these leading centers, there are dozens of others competing for the same business, from the well-known Channel Islands of Jersey and Guernsey—centrally positioned between the United Kingdom and continental Europe—to the more remote and obscure, such as Labuan, in the Malaysian archipelago, and the Cook Islands, situated in the South Pacific about halfway between Tahiti and Fiji.

As diverse as these OFCs are, what they all have in common is a few key features that make them not just tax havens but zones of freedom from regulation and accountability. STEP's introductory course book for the TEP credential defines OFCs as locations with the following characteristics:

> - politically stable government
> - stable economy
> - geographical and convenient accessibility so far as time zones are concerned (as this promotes administrative efficiency and also facilitates a closer customer working relationship)
> - a wide choice of reputable banks and other institutions
> - modern, reliable communications

> ➤ a low-tax or tax-free environment
> ➤ an appropriate official language (English?)
> ➤ excellent support services, including a choice of quality legal and accounting firms
> ➤ sensible and effective regulation and supervision
> ➤ high ethical standards in government, the professions, and commerce
> ➤ laws that are clear and fair, applied by a competent judiciary[19]

This description emphasizes stability and convenience, making the use of OFCs seem as benign as buying life insurance or making a will. Indeed, the text repeatedly justifies recourse to offshore finance as a matter of simple prudence and good sense, with observations such as "It is only natural for an individual, particularly one who has worked hard all his life in order to accumulate real wealth, to seek some form of insurance against the vicissitudes of life."[20] However, what the text defines as "vicissitudes of life" are not natural disasters or sudden death but things that many legal systems regard as obligations that are taken on voluntarily and must be fulfilled, such as payment of creditors.

This is where the disagreement about the true nature and purpose of OFCs comes to a head. While STEP and many wealth management practitioners see the use of offshore finance as legitimate and necessary, most outside the industry see it as a transparent scam. As one observer put it recently, "Offshore is a project of wealth and powerful elites to help them take the benefits from society without paying for them. . . . [T]he whole point is to offer escape routes from the duties that come with living in and obtaining benefits from society."[21] Specifically, there is widespread agreement that the financial activity that takes place offshore is, at best, "fictional."[22] That is, assets are never really deposited there, but instead are treated "as if" they passed through offshore institutions, though in reality these banks and firms are nothing more than "closets with computers."[23] The result is a system that provides secrecy and legal cover for a variety of activities that benefit a few at the expense of most. These range from criminal acts (such as laundering the proceeds of drug deals or corruption) to strategies that are legal but socially destructive. While the vast majority of wealth management practitioners avoid the former at all costs, they are implicated in the latter with most of their clients.[24] In other words, offshore finance is widely viewed as being "on a collision course with civil society."[25]

In historical perspective, this is par for the course: a complete definition of OFCs must take account of their position at the tail end of a long succession of liminal spaces where the "dirty work" of finance occurs. This is rooted in cultural practices going back centuries, in which unsavory but necessary financial activities were quarantined in specially designated zones. In medieval Europe, money changers were segregated from the rest of society: for example, in 1141, King Louis VII of France restricted the practice to a single bridge over the Seine, right next to a prison.[26] Lending money at interest, an even more transgressive activity in light of the Catholic prohibition against usury, was famously the province of ghettoized Jews; although many European kings availed themselves of this service, the practitioners were relegated to the margins of civilization, like butchers and executioners.[27] One of the major advances pioneered by OFCs was to turn this isolation— usually a source of shame—into an advantage. As they discovered, "a sovereign right to write the law . . . can be used as a competitive asset."[28]

The "fiction of fragmentation"

With the loosening of currency controls and the increasing ease of international travel and communication, wealth management strategies now hinge on scattering assets as far and wide as possible. The number and variety of offshore jurisdictions provides the essential structural support for this approach, as does the geographical remoteness of many OFCs. Specifically, the use of offshore jurisdictions to protect assets from tax and regulation exploits a vulnerability of the nation-state system that has governed the global political economy since the Treaty of Westphalia in 1684.

In that system, each nation is treated as a separate juridical entity, free to make its own laws and to disregard those of other nations. The result is a patchwork system, loosely held together in places by the coordination mechanisms of international law and by treaties among individual countries. But these mechanisms are relatively few and weak compared to the power of sovereign laws. As one study concluded, "The distinctive feature about the rules that govern the behavior of parties to cross border financial transactions is the absence of a single, unitary legal system."[29] For centuries after Westphalia, as long as mobility of people and capital remained low, this lack of a unitary legal system meant little. But as global transit has grown increasingly easy and rapid, the existence of large gaps in the legal system—"regulatory voids"—has become increasingly problematic.[30] OFCs, aided by wealth managers, exploit these voids and conflicts to their advantage in attracting business from high-net-worth individuals.

For example, an OFC can pass legislation that specifically and intentionally contravenes the laws of onshore jurisdictions. This commonly includes laws pertaining to taxation, as well as to the rights of creditors and heirs, so that judgments onshore against individuals whose assets are held offshore—for legal purposes, if not in reality—cannot be enforced. Since a fundamental principal of law holds that no sovereign state is obliged to enforce the laws or judgements of a foreign country, there is little the onshore state can do to enforce its claims.[31] International legal institutions have thus far remained relatively weak in terms of their ability to resolve such disputes or force convergence in legal regimes.[32]

OFCs, along with the wealth management profession, thrive economically and politically on this lack of coordination and on the failure of the international legal system to catch up to the realities of globally mobile people and capital. Each OFC designs its legal regime in ways that not only separate it from onshore but also distinguish it from competing offshore jurisdictions, each catering to different segments of the high-net-worth market. In such environments, "at the edge of the law," innovation thrives as professionals and lawmakers "compete by creating unique innovative structures, contracts and country combinations" to address the kind of culturally specific concerns and problems described in Chapter 3.[33] The rapid pace of financial-legal innovation creates a double fragmentation—within the offshore world as well as between onshore and offshore.

This provides wealth managers with the means to execute a "divide-and-conquer" strategy to protect clients' assets. That is, the wealth gets divided among a variety of OFCs so as to conquer the legal authority of onshore states seeking to tax or regulate it. The general approach is to apply legal regimes selectively to individual components of a client's wealth—a stock portfolio, a house, a business, or a yacht—with two objectives in mind. First, each asset should be placed in the jurisdiction most favorable to the client's interests, whether that be minimizing taxes or defeating the claims of creditors and heirs; whatever the goal, there is a jurisdiction competing to distinguish itself in providing the best possible protections from onshore authorities. Second, the assets must be dispersed as widely as possible, in as complex a structure as possible; this makes the full extent of a client's wealth, as well its true ownership, very difficult to assess.[34] The intended effect is to erase clients and their assets from public view. One offshore wealth management has even made this its motto: the legend on its website reads, "I want to be invisible."[35]

The hazards of fortune

The complexity characteristic of the finances of many high-net-worth individuals is both a source of employment for wealth managers and a product of their work. But it is not just that elites have more problems; rather, their problems are often of a different nature than people of ordinary means experience. As Mark in Dubai explained: "If you are a leader of small country, one of your family members might want to rise up and kill you and take your wealth." This and other political risks come in addition to the threats posed by lawsuits, regulators, and tax authorities. Great fortunes are targets of attack by a great variety of actors.

This seems to affect the perceptions of wealth managers and their clients in such a way that *most* obligations come to be seen as onerous and unjust. For example, one wealth management training textbook describes the claims of creditors as "risks," like the threat of a natural disaster, rather than as obligations that borrowers take on voluntarily.[36] Others threats include the legal system itself, in the form of an "aggressively litigious society," "onerous regulation," and of course "confiscatory" taxation.[37]

For ultra-high-net-worth clients, it seems, being obliged to honor their debts, pay the costs of government, and otherwise obey the laws of the land are offenses to liberty. The desire to escape these obligations fuels the popularity of offshore strategies in wealth management, in the name of self-defense (or wealth defense). As one recent study of OFCs put it, only partly in jest, "a peculiar mixture of characters populates this world: castle-owning members of ancient continental European aristocracies, fanatical supporters of American libertarian writer Ayn Rand, members of the world's intelligence services, global criminals, British public schoolboys, assorted lords and ladies and bankers galore. *Its bugbears are government, laws and taxes, and its slogan is freedom.*"[38]

These observations are corroborated by the remarks of participants in this study. Drew, the Canadian wealth manager who moved to London to reduce his work hours, said that many of his clients "go to extreme lengths to protect their assets, like moving away from friends and family to remote tax haven islands, just to avoid taxes—it's insane." Nick, the Englishman working in Panama, added that above all, his clients "want privacy . . . they think if they give their names [on financial documents], the IRS will come and seize all their assets, make them hand over gold to the Fed. I've had clients who are so paranoid that they said they've had teeth removed so that the feds couldn't monitor them."

In light of this, the objectives of most wealth management clients—according to the participants in this study—are protective and conservative rather than aggressive and acquisitive. The wealth manager is employed not to grow the fortune but to preserve it against the many hazards facing it. Michael, the Guernsey-based wealth manager, observed this among his ultra-wealthy clients: "The minimum client is about GBP 50 million; there are some multibillionaires. They are diverse in nationality and interests: some own teams, some fund villages in Africa or handicapped people in Romania. But what they all want to do is keep what they've got—not make the extra 2 or 3 percent." One might think this safety-first orientation was characteristic only of the ultra-high-net-worth clients, but it seems to be shared across the spectrum of people who employ wealth managers. George and Mary, a team working in New Jersey with clients on the low end of the high-net-worth band ($1 million or more in investable assets), made similar comments about these clients' desire to "minimize risk" and preserve capital above all.

Thus what Erika said of her boutique firm in Zurich also seems to be true of other wealth management enterprises: "We're trying to provide security and preserve assets; we're like a protection firm." She added that this orientation extended far beyond the way the firm managed clients' assets. Rather, it included the minute details of client interactions, all carefully choreographed to protect clients and their fortunes. For example, Erika said that the partners in her firm never go out to lunch with clients and are never seen in public with them, so that the clients can avoid being identified as the sort of people who employ wealth managers. Similarly, Paul in Dubai has developed a kind of mail routing service to preserve the confidentiality of his European clients: "I have a German client and a relationship with a Swiss *banque privé*. The banker, when he crosses the border to visit his client in Germany, doesn't wear a suit or tie, doesn't carry papers, because the moment the German border authorities see a banker, they ask, 'Who are you going to see?' So in order to get the paperwork to the meeting, my banker friend sends it to me here in Dubai, and I send it on to Germany!"

As these examples suggest, part of what wealth managers must do to protect clients and their fortunes is to break or obscure any link between the two. The goal of all the tactics and techniques is to separate individuals from their wealth, in the eyes of the law and of any outside observers, while still allowing clients the use and benefit of that wealth.

The way it used to be done was very simple and "analog": with suitcases full of cash transported by hand to offshore banks. Several participants in this study mentioned that until recently this was standard operating procedure, at least for the fungible portion of clients' fortunes. Drew, the Canadian wealth manager working in London, observed that "the offshore centers were very much like Grisham's *The Firm*—

people showed up with suitcases of cash to the Cayman Islands, and nobody asked any questions." Similarly, Paul in Dubai mentioned a Kuwaiti client who smuggled the equivalent of about $9 million out of the country in suitcases during the first Gulf War, moving the "luggage" across Iraq and into the safety of a Jordanian bank account. Steve, one of the English wealth managers based in Hong Kong, said that when he worked in the British Virgin Islands in the early 1990s, "there was a lot of cash being flown in on private planes, and the biggest complaint of the [BVI] banks was that they had too few cash-counting machines and they broke down from overuse."

But efforts to make international transmission of wealth more transparent and accountable—while failing in many respects—have certainly been successful in shutting down this method of capital mobility.[39] Between tightened coordination in the global banking system (with accompanying threats to blacklist jurisdictions in which financial institutions accept suspect funds) and legal strictures imposed on wealth managers to conduct thorough "know-your-client" reviews (including determining the source of clients' funds), contemporary wealth managers must turn to other methods to achieve the same ends. For some clients, the change comes as an unwelcome surprise. Hassan, a practitioner based in Mauritius, said that the biggest challenge in his day-to-day work was "to make the client understand that the way we do business now is different than it was ten years ago. Twenty-five years ago you could walk into a bank in Jersey with a suitcase full of money and say you wanted to deposit it, and it would be no problem. You can't do that anymore. Even to create transfers from bank to bank, you have to document the source of the funds. Clients who are 'old school' aren't used to being asked for proof of residence, the origins of their funds, and their passports. They ask, 'Why are you asking me this? You never used to ask me this stuff.' We have to educate them about how finance works in this day and age."

The following sections examine in greater detail "how finance works in this day and age" by looking at how wealth managers deploy three key financial-legal tools—trusts, corporations, and foundations—to solve the problems high-net-worth clients bring them. (A detailed review of the three structures, along with a comparison of their relative advantages as wealth management tools, can be found in the appendix to this chapter.) These problems usually fall into one of three categories. The first stems from living in a politically unstable or corrupt country. The second arises for people living in countries with stable and functional governments that work too well for the liking of high-net-worth individuals in terms of enforcing taxation, court judgments, and other legal matters inimical to wealth preservation. Finally, a set of problems that seems to be common around the world concerns family: wealth can be dissipated quickly by spendthrift heirs and intrafamilial conflicts.[40] Each of these threats to wealth can be mitigated, if not eliminated, by skillful financial-legal management.

Problems connected to political instability and corruption

Some of the world's most corrupt and unstable countries are also major sources of new demand for financial services. The very factors that allow individuals to "get rich quick," such as weak rule of law, also make it difficult to hold on to that wealth. For elites in those countries, taxation is of little to no concern.[41] Instead, they are seeking safe havens for their fortunes as well as for themselves. This usually means putting their assets in an offshore structure, with the help of a wealth manager.[42] Alistair, the English practitioner working in the Cayman Islands, outlined the general problem facing high-net-worth individuals in developing economies: "As you go down from first world from to second world to third world, you slide down a scale of due process . . . you get into a world in which theft of your assets without due process is common. There are bad countries out there that do not follow due process, and that's another reason why OFCs thrive: if you're in an unstable country, with a regime that does not have your interests at heart, would you keep your money there? Probably not. If you're born there, grew up there, you don't just leave easily. So leaving the country isn't an option; but your money can leave."

Beyond these general risks associated with political instability, each country or region in the developing world seems to have a distinctive "risk profile" in terms of the threats posed to private wealth.

For example, South Africa's history of apartheid government gives a racial dimension to the concerns of high-net-worth individuals. Charles, the South African wealth manager, observed that "the older white families who have generated a lot of wealth over a long period of time, they have a lot of reservations about the intentions of the current government and the possibility of the Communist Party coming to power. They're looking at getting their assets offshore and keeping secrecy." In other words, these are families who grew rich under the

apartheid system and who are now fearful of race-based retribution, expressed through confiscation of their wealth.
These concerns are not totally unfounded, as there have
been calls by members of the ruling African National Congress to seize white-owned farms for redistribution to black
citizens.[43]

For African clients, Mauritius is favored as a "new and fast-
growing conduit haven" close to home.[44] Located in the
Indian Ocean between Africa and the Indian subcontinent,
Mauritius has become a key player in the economies of both
regions. In addition to its convenient location, it offers a stable
and relatively "clean" governance environment. Data from
Transparency International indicate that Mauritius has one of
the most trustworthy public sectors in the region: of the forty-
seven countries in sub-Saharan Africa, it ranks near the top of
the list for freedom from government corruption.[45] This has
led to comparisons between Mauritius and the historical financial centers of Europe. Hassan, a Mauritian native who
runs a wealth management firm on the island, described its
appeal to clients from Africa: "Mauritius is safe and well-
regulated. If you're from Kenya, instead of bringing your
profits into Africa, well, Africa is Africa. These foreign na-
tionals prefer to park their money here for future use. Kind of
like people used to use Switzerland in the Second World War
to park money because of political uncertainty in their home
countries." As Switzerland loses its ability to protect parked
assets from investigation and seizure by other nations, Mauritius gains business.[46] Gayatri, another native Mauritian practitioner, observed this among her own clients, who were giving
up their numbered Swiss accounts: "Because of the attacks on

client confidentiality in Switzerland, many of the bank accounts are being moved to Mauritius."

While high-net-worth individuals in Africa and India seem to be primarily concerned with avoiding corruption, those from China and Russia—where private wealth is growing faster than almost anywhere else in the world—face a somewhat different set of concerns. In addition to corruption, those countries' political history is littered with purges, show trials, and disappearances.[47] This makes avoidance of political reprisals a major consideration. Drew, the Canadian practitioner based in London, observed of the Chinese case: "It's a lawless society. Most Chinese people are terrified by what the government is going to do to them and their wealth in the future, and they want an escape plan. Every once in a while the government will turn on you and say, 'It's your turn—you're now a pauper.' So they want an escape plan . . . so that if the government turns on them, they can walk into the nearest British, Canadian, or U.S. embassy, get out of China, and have a pile of cash waiting for them offshore." As for what kind of offshore structure contains that "pile of cash," the answer is: usually not a trust.

In theory, trusts could be a good solution to protecting assets. But in practice, they are not the preferred tool for high-net-worth individuals who originate in politically unstable nations. Chapter 3 described how many wealthy people who have lived under Communist regimes are disinclined to the kind of faith in fiduciaries necessary to establish a trust. Furthermore, there have been several high-profile failures in the use of trusts to protect assets from government seizure. For example, Yukos Oil chairman Mikhail Khodorkovsky, a political enemy of Vladimir Putin, attempted to save his company from seizure by the Putin government by putting the majority of his shares in a Guernsey trust, but since Russia's legal system is based on civil law and the country was not a signatory to the Hague Convention on Trusts, Khodorkovsky's move was unsuccessful.[48]

In light of this, individuals from Russia and China generally seem to prefer protecting their assets through means that increase their control over their fortunes as well as over their own fates and those of their loved ones. Some simply "invest" in a U.K., U.S., or Canadian residence permit through those countries' "investor visa" programs. The U.K. program is particularly popular among Russian and Chinese elites: for an investment of at least £2 million (most of which must be placed in U.K. stocks and bonds) applicants not only acquire the right to live and work in the United Kingdom for themselves but can also bring their spouses and dependents along without any of the usual red tape, such as English-language proficiency requirements. In 2014 Chinese received 43 percent of such visas; Russians, 22 percent.[49]

High-end real estate—particularly in London and New York City—is also a popular choice for wealthy Chinese and Russians. In many cases, such properties are never occupied by the owners or anyone else; they are purchased simply to "park their wealth, a safe haven in an uncertain world."[50] As a result of this practice, an estimated 30 percent of luxury properties in Manhattan are unoccupied for at least ten months of the year; furthermore, most of these properties are sold for cash, meaning that there are no mortgage documents to provide clues to the owner's identity.[51] For additional privacy protection, many such properties (in London as well as in

New York) are purchased through offshore entities, rather than in the name of an individual.[52]

When clients from developing countries use offshore structures, they often prefer the control afforded by corporations. For Chinese high-net-worth individuals, the Cayman Islands are second only to Hong Kong as the favored locale for basing offshore firms.[53] While Cayman Islands corporations ease legal entry for investments in the North and South American markets, the primary appeal of creating such a corporation seems to be tax avoidance. Firms incorporated there can be used as a temporary holding area for profits made in China through investments or other activities; in a practice known as "round-tripping," the profits are then brought back into China disguised as "foreign investment," which is generally untaxed.[54]

Wealthy Indians use the island nation of Mauritius for similar purposes. An estimated 40 percent of foreign investment coming into India originates in Mauritius, largely because of the special tax treaty between the two countries.[55] Treaties such as this—known collectively as double taxation avoidance agreements, or DTAAs—govern how nations divide up the "spoils" of tax revenues among themselves. The agreement between Mauritius and India provides the island with a major competitive advantage compared to other offshore centers. As Arjun, a native Mauritian practitioner, put it, "You can do quite a lot of planning in Mauritius that isn't possible in other jurisdictions because of the DTAA. If you have a client who wants a structure to hold shares in an Indian company, he could do that with a Jersey trust, but it [Jersey] doesn't have a DTAA with India. . . . By going through an offshore vehicle incorporated in Mauritius, you get huge tax-favored status.

The normal tax rate would be 18 percent, but by going through Mauritius, you only pay 3 percent on profits." In addition to reduced corporate income tax, Mauritius has zero capital gains tax, compared to the 20 percent rate in India. All told, "round-tripping" through Mauritius costs India an estimated $7 billion in annual tax revenues, but India has thus far been reluctant to crack down on the practice for fear of losing foreign investment.[56]

As for the BVI, the favored offshore locale for Russian corporations and one of the top ten for Chinese firms, its primary appeal seems to be the streamlined access it provides to London's real estate and financial markets because it is a U.K. territory.[57] Russians channeled $31.7 billion to the BVI in the first quarter of 2013 alone.[58] Chinese clients' use of BVI corporations accounts for approximately 30 percent of the island's annual revenues.[59] For those concerned about asset seizures by their governments, "the additional layers of confidentiality in place for BVI companies" provide peace of mind.[60] But there is also a social element. As one British lawyer claimed, "Our [Chinese] clients say that you haven't really arrived if you don't have at least one BVI company to your name."[61]

Ned, a New Zealander practicing in the Cook Islands, said that the hold of BVI corporations on the Asian market is so strong that many Asian clients refer to offshore corporations in general as "BVIs," as in "I want to put my fortune into BVIs." As a result, Ned says, he finds it very difficult to persuade them to consider incorporating in other jurisdictions, even if it would plainly be more advantageous for them to do so. Similarly, Bruce—the American wealth manager working in Switzerland—said that "Russian clients just want the same asset structures as their friends have, regardless of whether their friends' solution really fits for the client's situation. So, for example, they'll say, 'I want a Cayman or BVI company.' We explain why that's not a good idea, and they often say, 'I don't care. I want one. My friends have them.' Having the same thing their friends do makes them feel safe." Thus, in addressing fears about government seizure of their wealth, high-net-worth individuals gain a sense of safety from the familiar: not only do they prefer the well-known corporate structure, but they prefer to locate it in places that are familiar to their social peers, net of economic considerations.

Like Russians and Chinese, wealthy individuals from Latin America are uncertain about the rule of law in their countries and concerned about corruption. Kidnapping is a major issue for high-net-worth families in this region, since low-paid (or sometimes unpaid) government employees can be bribed to reveal the names of taxpayers and depositors reporting high levels of wealth. Sherman, the Englishman practicing in the BVI, said that he had been told by clients from Brazil and Mexico that "you can go down to a bank and for U.S. $100 get the names and addresses of all depositors with accounts over $100 million." Along the same lines, Frank—the Englishman based in Cyprus—said that several of his Latin American clients required him to use code names for the client's family members in all conversations and documents, to reduce the chance of them being linked to information about the family fortune and thus becoming targets of kidnapping attempts.

These concerns about safety and privacy motivate clients to work with wealth managers to get their assets offshore—out of local banks and off the radar of local authorities. In addition, Latin Americans have long-standing concerns about their countries' economic policies and the due process that applies to government seizure of assets. As Carlos, a practitioner in Buenos Aires, explained, "My clients want to get their money out of their countries because they want to get money away from being robbed by the governments. Brutal confiscation! Their very first concern is not taxation but being robbed by the government. In Argentina you have 30 percent inflation a year, so banks, authorized by the government, will take your dollars and give you pesos—so they're giving you pennies on the dollar and seizing your hard currency." The solution, Carlos said, was for clients to hold their wealth in U.S. dollars.

The easiest way to do that is to keep wealth in Panama, which uses the U.S. dollar as its official currency. It also offers the convenience of Spanish as the official language, as well as geographical proximity to rest of Latin America. Most important, Panama is among the most politically stable countries in the region, enjoying historically low inflation rates.[62] This is one reason for the significance of the Panama Papers, in which decades' worth of documents from a single Panama City–based wealth management firm were disclosed to journalists. Panama has created an important niche for itself in the global wealth management industry, making it popular among international elites from all walks of life. It attracted everyone from Chinese actor Jackie Chan and Argentinian soccer star Lionel Messi, to heads of state in Europe, Africa, and Asia. A leak from a less significant offshore jurisdiction than Panama would have been unlikely to be so revealing.

Since Panama has made the foundation form one of its specialties within the offshore industry, much of the wealth flowing into the country goes into foundations rather than trusts. This may be why, as mentioned in Bruce's comments above, Latin American clients prefer to place their wealth in foundations.

They could, in theory, use offshore corporations for the same purpose, but the preference for foundations may be an artifact of using Panama as the OFC of choice. Forced heirship may be the deciding factor: in civil-law Latin America, individuals' freedom to determine how their wealth gets distributed after death is highly restricted. As Carlos said of Argentina, "We have the highest forced-heirship rate outside of Muslim countries—80 percent of assets should go to your kids." Corporate structures leave assets subject to those inheritance laws, but Panama's laws specifically forbid the application of any foreign heirship rules to assets held in Panamanian foundations.[63]

First-world problems: Functional government and rule of law

For high-net-worth individuals in countries with well-developed political institutions and economies, sometimes government works a little too effectively and reliably for their liking. Unlike their counterparts from Latin America, Russia, or China, wealthy people from Europe and North America are generally not worried about political retribution, kidnapping, or rampant inflation. But they share a desire to overcome restrictions on their ability to keep and distribute their wealth. In the developed countries, that resistance generally takes the form of efforts to avoid taxation as well as payment to creditors, divorcing spouses, and disgruntled heirs.

For such clients, wealth managers develop strategies designed to make themselves and their assets impervious to applications of onshore law. The strategies for achieving this vary depending on the kind of laws the client wishes to avoid. In general, this falls into three categories: the laws related to taxation, those that govern obligations to creditors, and restrictions on lucrative trading opportunities. Each of these issues will be addressed in detail below.

Tax avoidance

When it comes to taxation, the law distinguishes clearly between avoidance and evasion: the former is lawful, while the latter is not. Tax avoidance involves using every legally permitted means to reduce the client's tax bill. The target is a substantial reduction not only in taxes on income but also in taxes on capital gains, inheritance, and real property. STEP's position—based on public statements from its leadership as well as the organization's training manuals—is that *some* taxation is legitimate but that the policies of many onshore governments are excessive and unjust. One prominent wealth manager, speaking at a STEP conference that drew thousands of practitioners from all over the world, spoke of the U.K. tax authorities as "the robber barons of the Inland Revenue"—a statement greeted with nods and knowing chuckles from the audience. Through remarks such as these, which recur frequently in STEP events and publications, the organization frames tax avoidance as a form of self-defense against illegitimate exercise of government authority—which also seems to be how clients see their position in hiring wealth managers. They might be called "right-wing anarchists," except that they seem to support eliminating state power only as it applies to themselves.[64]

In terms of protecting private fortunes from the state's power to tax, trusts and foundations continue to fulfill their historical roles. Corporations are rarely used for this purpose by wealthy individuals from developed nations, since their governments long ago passed legislation to circumvent corporate tax shelter strategies.[65] For clients with fairly simple arrays of assets—that is, involving just one or two countries and sources of wealth—there may be no need to go offshore; foundations and trusts in their home countries afford all the protection they need. This is particularly the case for clients whose primary concerns revolve around inheritance tax. Morris—the New York practitioner—described one client, a Goldman Sachs partner, who challenged him to develop a more effective tax avoidance strategy than the client's law firm had created. This was an opportunity for the wealth manager to show off the special skills his profession could offer: "So I say to him, 'How would you like to give your kids $50 million, and keep control of the $100 million you now have, and give zero to the IRS, instead of the plan your lawyers gave you, where you give $50 million to your kids and $50 million to the IRS?' So the next question is of course, 'How do you do that?' So I explain that he can set up a charitable foundation, with his children on the board to dispense as they see fit. As I always tell people, the estate tax in our country is a voluntary tax—you only pay if you don't plan." As this example indicates, foundations are used even in common-law jurisdictions such as the United States, where trusts are readily available. For example, there are now an estimated 40,000 family foundations in the United States, with total assets estimated to be in the hundreds of billions of dollars.[66]

As Morris indicated, control is the main appeal for clients who choose foundations to reduce their tax bills. While founders and their family members do not own the foundation's assets, they control how those assets are managed, and they can pay themselves a substantial salary as foundation officers. These salaries serve as a way to transfer wealth within families without the assets being subject to inheritance tax. And because foundations are allowed to exist in perpetuity, due to their (ostensibly) charitable purposes, this tax-free wealth transfer can go on indefinitely across generations. This is crucial to preserving the family fortune, which might otherwise dissipate within two or three generations because of the tax on intergenerational transfers, along with other forces.[67] The foundation can thus be used to achieve some of the same goals as a trust, but without the necessity of employing a trustee or requesting distributions. This control comes at a price, however: in many jurisdictions, a foundation's capital gains are subject to taxation. In the United States, this amounts to just 1 to 2 percent, versus the statutory rate of 20 percent on capital gains, so the trade-off may be worthwhile for some clients. However, they must also be willing to give up a large measure of privacy (foundation records are public in many jurisdictions) and to give away a certain amount of their wealth each year for charitable purposes.[68]

Ingvar Kamprad, Swedish founder of the multinational furniture retailer IKEA, has used foundation structures to become a multibillionaire. By putting his firm's assets and his personal wealth into "loosely regulated" Netherlands and Liechtenstein foundations in the 1980s, Kamprad was able to build his fortune in part through tax avoidance on a heroic scale.[69] On annual revenues of $28 billion, his foundations pay tax at a rate of about 3.5 percent—saving billions in corporate, capital gains, and personal income taxes for Kamprad, his

firm, and his family.[70] However, the lack of privacy surrounding foundations has also exposed Kamprad to several
embarrassing public inquiries, including an investigative report by *The Economist*, which concluded that while the structure "handsomely rewards the founding Kamprad family and
makes IKEA immune to a takeover," it was also one of the
world's "least generous" charities.[71] These and other revelations
led Kamprad to double the foundations' charitable giving.[72]

With tax avoidance becoming an increasingly contentious
public issue—particularly following the global economic crisis
of 2008—many high-net-worth individuals desire more privacy than a foundation can provide. For them, trusts may
offer a better solution. And now that so many jurisdictions
have abolished the rule against perpetuities (discussed at
greater length in the appendix to this chapter), trusts can compete with foundations in terms of longevity.[73] In addition to
their traditional uses to preserve property within individual
countries, trusts are increasingly being deployed in transnational tax avoidance plans. A recent article in the *STEP
Journal* detailed a strategy for "stacking" trusts in multiple
countries to help international couples avoid inheritance
taxes. The plan illustrates the "divide-and-conquer" strategy
characteristic of so many wealth management plans, in that it
hinges on spreading assets between trusts in different countries so as to defeat policy goals, including redistribution and
the prevention of multigenerational concentrations of wealth.

In the example, a couple with one member from the United
States and the other from the United Kingdom face a problem:
when they die, their fortune will be subject to a 40 percent tax
in *both* countries, which would drastically reduce the amount
that could be passed to their children. To prevent this, their

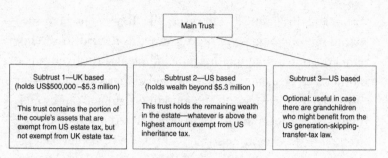

Figure 4.1. Stacked trusts for avoiding inheritance tax.

wealth manager suggests creating a structure that "takes advantage of benefits available under both systems."[74] In this case, the benefits are exclusions of certain amounts of wealth from inheritance tax: in the United Kingdom, up to £325,000 (approximately $500,000) can be transferred tax-free; in the United States, the threshold is $5.3 million. With the stacked trusts illustrated in Figure 4.1, the couple's fortune can pass to their heirs completely tax free in both countries.

Instead of having the worst of both worlds, with their wealth subject to a huge tax in two countries, the couple using this structure achieves the best of both worlds, deferring all taxes until the second spouse's death, and thereafter allowing "the maximum amount possible to pass free of death taxes."[75] (Understanding of this structure and its benefits may be enhanced by reviewing the appendix to this chapter.)

Debt avoidance

Among high-net-worth individuals, perhaps the only figure as reviled as the tax collector is the debt collector. Historically, trusts have been the favored instrument for avoiding both. But while other structures have arisen to rival the trust for tax avoidance, nothing has challenged the trust's primacy in frustrating creditors. For five centuries, trusts have been used to make "wealthy individuals effectively debt-proof"— impervious to creditors and to any judgments in creditors' favor.[76] By transferring all their assets to an associate to hold on trust, elites could run up huge debts based on their family name and then claim—lawfully—that they owned no assets that could be used to pay the debts.

This ruse was so commonly used, to such prejudicial effect on creditors, that the Statute of Elizabeth was created in 1571 to stop the practice. The statute allowed creditors to appeal to the courts for legal nullification of trusts created to avoid debt repayment. By declaring the trusts void, the courts granted creditors the right to seize the assets they contained. This rule marked a crucial development in modern capitalism, establishing protections for creditors that were essential in the expansion of commerce and faith in the rule of law.

But this didn't stop wealthy families from using trusts to avoid their debts: wealth managers simply modified the trust structure so as to limit beneficiaries' rights and access to trust assets. Entities such as the "spendthrift trust" and the "express trust" were created for this purpose. They gave trustees absolute discretion to make distributions only as they saw fit, and to cut off beneficiaries who got into financial trouble. Such "discretionary trusts," as they were known collectively, increased the legal distance between beneficiaries and trust assets.

In a traditional trust arrangement, beneficiaries could claim that they did not *own* any of the wealth held in the structure, but creditors might argue that those beneficiaries had the *expectation* of distributions from the trust. Based on those expectations, trust assets were sometimes attached to pay debts. With a discretionary trust, however, even the expectation of distributions was eliminated: beneficiaries would have no fixed entitlement to anything, at any time. This arrangement served to protect the family fortune from wayward heirs, "effectively frustrat[ing] the claims upon the trust assets by A's creditors or trustee in bankruptcy as, in each case, there are no assets belonging to A that may be attached."[77]

To the extent that these maneuvers went unchallenged, they gave special legal protection to the wealthy, relieving them of the obligation to pay their debts.[78] But when creditors pursued their claims through the courts, judges were repeatedly obliged to reiterate the principles behind the Statute of Elizabeth. In a particularly well-known case, *Re Butterworth* (1882), the decision read: "A man is not entitled to go into a hazardous business and immediately before doing so settle all his property voluntarily upon trust, the object being this: 'If I succeed in business, I make a fortune for myself. If I fail, I leave my creditors unpaid. They will bear the loss.' This is the very thing which the Statute of Elizabeth was meant to prevent."[79] Onshore, this principle has remained largely intact. However, in recent decades there has been an increasingly aggressive movement on the part of offshore jurisdictions to thwart the Statute of Elizabeth and thereby to render wealthy individuals "debt-proof" once again.

As bankruptcy laws tightened to be tougher on debtors of ordinary means, the options expanded for elites seeking to avoid their obligations.[80] Many of these options involved permutations of the trust structure that collectively came to be known as "asset protection trusts." While any trust can be used to shield assets from creditors—as the case of "spendthrift trusts" exemplifies—a new breed of structures has arisen in offshore jurisdictions that have sought competitive advantage specifically through repeal of the Statute of Elizabeth. These asset protection vehicles are discretionary trusts with the added wealth defense measure of being based in countries with laws specifying that trust assets shall be inaccessible to creditors.[81]

This strategy was pioneered by the Cook Islands. Their 1989 International Trusts Act states that assets held in the country's trusts will not be subject to the judgment of any foreign court or accessible to any foreign creditors. The act was originally created by a lawyer based in Denver, Colorado, seeking a way to help his well-to-do clients, who were mainly physicians and other professionals vulnerable to tort lawsuits.[82] But this new legal "product" became popular among all manner of wealthy individuals—so popular that twenty-five other jurisdictions have enacted similar asset protection legislation, including the Bahamas, Belize, and fourteen U.S. states.[83]

Despite the proliferation of this model, the Cook Islands retain ongoing dominance in asset protection due to the country's unbroken track record of stonewalling the legal authority of other nations. Cook Islands law has prevented the U.S. government from collecting the $37.6 million judgment it won in 2007 against author Kevin Trudeau for fraudulent business practices, as well as the $8 million judgment it won the same year against an Oklahoma property developer who defaulted on his loans from Fannie Mae; both Trudeau and the property developer put their assets in Cook Islands trusts.[84] To date, no effort to break a Cook Islands asset protection trust has been successful. Many creditors don't even try, since pursuing a claim against a trust based there requires litigating in the Cook Islands; this means sending a legal team on a long and costly journey—fifteen hours of flight time from New York, plus billable hours.[85] As a result, "many creditors will settle for cents on the dollar, rather than face the expense of a long and difficult lawsuit halfway across the Pacific."[86]

The Cook Islands have been blacklisted twice—first in 2000 by the intergovernmental Financial Action Task Force, and then again in 2015 by the European Union's Executive Commission—for being an "uncooperative jurisdiction" within the world financial system.[87] In spite of this, the asset protection trust business continues to thrive. According to the most recent information available from the Cook Islands government, obtained via a phone call made by one of the research participants during our interview, the wealth management industry contributes 10 to 15 percent of the country's GDP; this was "similar to what the pearl industry used to be," according to Roger, the native New Zealander who made the phone call. Since the pearl industry was "virtually decimated" by disease in 2000, the Cook Islands needs the wealth management industry more than ever and is unlikely to curtail asset protection services, even in the face of international sanctions.[88] As a result, said Ned, one of the New Zealanders practicing in the islands, "Cook Islands trusts . . . are set up to say, 'Here we are: come get us, and good luck.'"

Avoiding trade restrictions

While asset protection trusts were originally designed to avoid debt obligations, they have proved useful at circumventing all manner of legislation, since they effectively put wealth "outside the rule of law."[89] For example, part of the fortune that financier Marc Rich made from trading oil with Iran, in violation of the U.S. embargo, ended up in a $100 million Cook Islands trust whose beneficiary was his ex-wife Denise.[90] So while Marc Rich fled to Switzerland to escape criminal prosecution, part of his fortune escaped capture by fleeing to the Cook Islands. Similarly, R. Allen Stanford put some of the proceeds from his $7 billion illegal investment scheme into a Cook Islands structure he dubbed the "Baby Mama Trust," benefiting his mistress, with whom he had two children. While Stanford is serving a 110-year prison sentence, the trust and its assets appear to be untouched by ongoing litigation.[91] As one recent study of international financial crime concluded, "Trusts . . . prove such a hurdle to investigation, prosecution (or civil judgment) and asset recovery that they are seldom prioritized in investigations."[92]

On the other side of the world, trusts in the Isle of Man and the Cayman Islands helped catapult the American Wyly brothers onto the *Forbes* billionaires list by enabling them to avoid insider trading laws for thirteen years. By placing $1 billion of their companies' shares in a "maze" of dozens of trusts, they netted more than $550 million in capital gains, tax free.[93] Although the U.S. Securities and Exchange Commission argued successfully in a recent lawsuit that the brothers "knowingly sought to bypass securities disclosure laws" with their offshore trust strategy, no real sanctions may result. The $400 million judgment against the Wylys might never be paid, because their lawyers are arguing—with centuries of legal precedent in their favor—that the brothers neither owned nor controlled the $380 million remaining in the trusts they created.[94] To bolster this claim, one of the brothers recently filed for bankruptcy protection.[95]

Another interesting case of using trusts to avoid laws limiting profit opportunities is provided by Baroness Carmen Thyssen-Bornemisza of Spain, whose private art collection—valued at billions of dollars—is owned through trusts in the Cook Islands and other jurisdictions.[96] This mode of ownership is designed not so much to avoid creditors or taxes but to get around limitations on the sale and movement of fine art. Ordinarily, the works she owns—including paintings by Van Gogh and Manet—would be subject to tight legal controls. Art of that caliber is often considered not just private property but part of a nation's patrimony, subject to the UNESCO Convention of 1970 on the Means of Prohibiting and Preventing the Illegal Import, Export and Transfer of Ownership of Cultural Property.[97] Putting the art collection in trust avoids what Thyssen-Bornemisza's lawyer calls the "nightmare" of these national legal restrictions. "It's convenient," he said. "You have more freedom to move the assets, not just buying or selling, but also circulation."[98] By increasing the mobility of her art collection, the trust structure also maximizes Thyssen-Bornemisza's opportunities to make a profit, allowing her to sell the works to the highest bidder, anywhere in the world.

Vexed relations: Divorce, inheritance, and family businesses

Just as wealth management has grown by providing elites with freedom from legal restrictions on how they grow and trade their fortunes, the profession has expanded its influence by developing creative ways to work around the laws governing financial obligations to family members. As Chapter 3's section on wealth management in the BRICS showed, concerns about who will inherit a family fortune are not restricted to elites in the developed countries. In fact, high-net-worth individuals around the world face a trio of family-related concerns in common: not just inheritance but also divorce and the management of a family business can dissipate wealth if it is not structured properly.

The need for professional intervention to protect family fortunes illustrates the special importance of wealth managers as "inside outsiders" in the lives of high-net-worth individuals.[99] As powerful as such individuals are, their wealth seems to impart a certain fragility to their families. This necessitates "the work of professional administrators, who as guardians of fortunes, also become instrumental in holding together family organizations, almost in spite of family members themselves."[100] The structural reinforcements to the family consist primarily of trusts, with the addition of corporations in some cases. The following sections will illustrate how such structures can be used to address the threats that arise around divorce, inheritance, and family businesses.

Divorce

The dissolution of marriages constitutes such a threat to wealth that it has spawned a subspecialty of financial advisory services—distinct from wealth management—known as "divorce financial analysis."[101] STEP itself has hosted a number of dedicated seminars on the subject, with titles such as "The Business of Divorce," suggesting how significant an area of practice this represents. The topic came up frequently in the interviews for this study, and the solutions to divorce-related crises always took the form of trusts. Such divorce-protection trusts were almost always discretionary—providing beneficiaries with funds not as an entitlement but only at the discretion of the trustee—and often located offshore, just for extra protection against onshore court judgments.

To illustrate how important such a trust could be in protecting clients' wealth against the threat of divorce, Alistair—the English practitioner working in the Cayman Islands—related the story of a local client whose ex-wife had just won a huge marital settlement in the Cayman courts. The client, who was the beneficiary of a discretionary trust Alistair managed, asked for a huge distribution to pay the settlement, an amount that for all intents and purposes would have emptied the trust. Alistair refused. The client was stunned. "Then it began to dawn on him, apparently for the first time," Alistair said, "what it really meant to separate [beneficial] ownership from control. He saw the light, and realized I could protect him from being cleaned out by the divorce." The client went back to the judge with a letter from Alistair stating that the distribution request had been denied by the owner of the assets (the trustee); therefore, the client's main source of income (the trust) remained secure and untouchable by the court. But sometimes even discretionary structures are not sufficient to protect trust assets. In an increasing number of high-profile cases, divorce courts of several countries have treated trusts of which one spouse is a discretionary beneficiary as marital assets, to be divided when the couple splits. One of the best-known such cases was the Poon divorce in Hong Kong, in which the ex-wife persuaded the court that the couple's marital assets should be defined to include the $1.5 billion discretionary trust of which her ex-husband was a beneficiary.[102] In 2014 the Court of Final Appeal awarded the ex-wife 50 percent of the marital wealth, including assets from the trust.[103] The same year, in "the most expensive divorce in history," a Swiss court awarded half of Russian billionaire Dmitry Rybolovlev's $9.5 billion fortune to his ex-wife, Elena Rybolovleva. The fortune included assets held in discretionary trusts, which had apparently been established specifically to avoid any claims his wife might make in divorce proceedings: "In the [divorce] suit, Rybolovleva said the billionaire moved many of his assets, including jewels, furniture and the yacht, under the control of two trusts, Aries and Virgo, that he established in Cyprus in 2005, a few weeks after she refused to sign a postnuptial agreement he offered her."[104] Rybolovlev's strategy backfired, although it took his ex-wife nearly six years of court proceedings to uncover and break the trusts.

In light of such developments, some wealthy families are taking preemptive measures to protect their fortunes from being dissipated through divorce. In a speech at STEP's 2012

South Africa conference, Nick Jacob—a founding member of the organization and a current member of its board of directors—described a clever strategy used by one of his clients when their adult children began to marry. To protect the trusts the clients had set up for each of their children, the clients set up smaller trusts specifically to benefit the children's new spouses in case of divorce. That is, if the clients' children and their spouses ever split, the ex-spouses would still benefit from trusts set up by their in-laws. The idea, Jacob said, was to "throw a bone to the divorcing sons- and daughters-in-law, heading off challenges to the *real* family wealth, which was contained in the larger trusts to which the clients' children were beneficiaries." The hope was that the courts would see these smaller trusts for the divorcing spouses as offsetting or negating any claims the exes might make to the larger trusts. The stroke of genius in this plan, Jacob added, was the incentive the clients added: if the couples stayed together, the assets in the trusts for the sons- and daughters-in-law would pass directly to any children they had.

Inheritance

Historically, trusts have been used by wealthy people to ensure that they maintain some control over who gets their wealth when they die. "The origin of the Trust," wrote the late Frederic Maitland, one of the great legal authorities on the subject, is that "the Englishman . . . would like to provide for his daughters and younger sons. That is the root of the matter."[105] As discussed in Chapter 2, practices such as primogeniture—in which the eldest male inherited the entire family estate—meant dispossession and penury for many women when their fathers or husbands died, and for many younger sons as well. Trusts for these economically vulnerable family members offered a safety net.[106] Trusts were also useful in protecting the wealth inherited by daughters, in case they happened to marry spendthrift husbands. During the centuries when the doctrine of couverture was in force, husbands automatically assumed ownership of any assets women brought into marriage. Trusts, administered on the women's behalf by a male trustee, were the only way married women could maintain separate property.[107]

Although primogeniture and couverture are long gone, there are still many situations in which wealthy individuals fear that the "wrong" people will inherit their fortune or that the "right" people will be excluded. The increasing prevalence of multiple marriages, with children and/or stepchildren from each one, creates considerable complexity and uncertainty with regard to inheritance rights.[108] The inheritance rights of children born out of wedlock, or of unmarried partners, are also murky and potentially the source of conflicts that can dissipate wealth.[109] And then there is the offshore-world stereotype of the wealthy individual with a secret girlfriend (or boyfriend): what Nadia—the Panamanian practitioner—called "the typical high-net-worth person . . . [who] is married but has a special friend he wants to take care of."[110] Such cases illustrate how "legal and tax systems struggle to keep up with the pace of social change, or choose to ignore it altogether."[111] This puts wealth managers, a generally conservative lot in their approach to asset preservation, in an unexpected position at the forefront of transformations in family and gender roles.

The rapid pace of change is suggested by current practice on the Arabian Peninsula, where wealth managers are now routinely asked to mitigate the disadvantages that Islamic law imposes on daughters' inheritance rights. Since shari'a also tightly limits testamentary freedom—the degree to which individuals can choose how their assets are distributed after their death—those who wish their daughters to have an equal share of the family fortune must find offshore alternatives. Elaine, the English practitioner working in Dubai, explained that her clients are increasingly turning to her for workarounds to restore distributional equity:

> Arabs are getting their daughters educated, and they're trying to protect them, since they're taking over family businesses, sitting on boards of directors; in Kuwait they're sitting in Parliament. Typically, you'll see sheikhas not walking behind their husbands, like before, but walking with their husbands, holding hands. That's a big change since I first arrived here in 1994. We're hearing a lot of women who say, "My dad didn't want me to stay home and have babies, but participate in the family business." So fathers are changing their estate planning: they're creating trusts and taking out life insurance, which is kind of *haram* in Islam, but they do it because their sons are going to get the family business under shari'a law, and they want their daughters to have an equal share.

In the Muslim world, as in Europe and North America, change in family relationships and gender roles shapes the uses of wealth management techniques. The significance of these factors is often overlooked in discussions that focus on taxation and public policy.

Indeed, getting around restrictions on inheritance ranks alongside tax and debt avoidance on the list of classic motivations for establishing trusts. Increasingly, all three objectives lead to offshore solutions. Creating trusts onshore, even in jurisdictions that recognize the trust structure legally, can be risky when the objective is to override rules concerning inheritance (or divorce). In case of disputes, courts may "pierce" onshore trusts to seize assets for distribution to heirs who have been excluded from benefits on the basis of "spiteful and egregious" provisions.[112]

To prevent trust assets from being dissipated in such disputes, or "clawed back" by excluded heirs, contemporary wealth management practice suggests moving as much of an individual's fortune as possible into an offshore trust. Assets that cannot be moved, such as land, should be owned by an offshore corporation whose shares are held in an offshore trust, "in order to preserve at least the impression that the trust assets are located in the offshore jurisdiction."[113] This distances the assets not only from the heirs but also from the jurisdiction of onshore courts. Just for a final measure of security, in the event an onshore court *does* claim authority over assets held offshore in an inheritance dispute, a number of offshore financial centers have created legislation to block enforcement: the Cayman Islands, the Bahamas, Bermuda, the Cook Islands, and the Turks and Caicos all have enacted laws that specifically deny recognition to foreign court rulings on heirship rights.[114] That this has become a point of jurisdictional competition in the offshore world suggests how much high-net-worth individuals value the ability to circumvent inheritance laws.

Family business

Control of family businesses has been another catalyst for jurisdictional competition and innovation offshore. Entirely new regimes of trust law such as STAR (described in greater detail below) and VISTA (described in Chapter 3), along with entirely new institutional roles, such as that of trust "protector," have arisen expressly to address the concerns of family business founders about what happens to their enterprises, both during their lifetimes and after their deaths. It has long been common for individuals who made their wealth through the operations of a family business to put shares of the business in trust for tax purposes. As described above, offshore ownership of a business can dramatically reduce taxes on corporate profits and capital gains. In addition, the trust structure allows the shares to be transferred free of inheritance tax when the company founder dies. But this still leaves many uncertainties surrounding business control and succession. As Nadia, the Panamanian practitioner, explained:

> If you have someone who has inherited a business from his father, he wants to control what happens to that patrimony—he doesn't want the business to be split up through forced heirship rules, spreading the shares in the business among people the settlor knows won't get along or don't have the skills or interest to be involved in the business. Maybe they

have a bohemian in the family—one child is a musician, one is a dancer—they live in Paris or London, and they know that if those kids inherit the shares in that business, the kids will just sell their shares right away. The kids may not want to *asuciar los manos* [dirty their hands] with the family business, especially if it's grown up around something like agriculture. And the settlors don't want someone who doesn't know the business to be involved in the family business without qualifications.

The solution for many contemporary high-net-worth individuals in this position is an offshore trust such as a VISTA or STAR structure, with a "protector" appointed for good measure.

As described in Chapter 3, the VISTA trust allows family business founders to put their firms in trust—thereby reaping many tax advantages—without losing management control of the underlying business. Traditionally, trustees are held responsible for the management of all the assets held in trust, and can be held liable to repay any losses if they mismanage an underlying business.[115] However, the trustees may lack the skills to do this well. Furthermore, they are obliged to act in the best financial interests of beneficiaries, which may lie in selling the business outright. In both cases, the settlor cannot intervene, either to manage the business or to prevent its sale, because attempting to exert any management control would risk the trust structure being declared a sham, and having to repay any tax benefits.

VISTA legislation resolves this problem in two ways. First, it creates a new kind of trust law by explicitly removing trustees' obligations and liabilities with regard to any business owned by the trust.[116] Second, it allows the trust settlor—usually the same person who founded the family business—to appoint a "protector," an individual or firm vested with the power to direct and, if necessary, remove trustees. The protector takes orders from the trust's settlor, providing a way for the settlor to continue in the management and control of his or her underlying business without putting the trust structure at risk of being invalidated as a sham. The protector can prevent a business from being sold by the trustee, and can also preserve the business against liquidation in case of bankruptcy proceedings against the settlor.[117]

Yet another alternative for family business owners, in the form of the Special Trusts Alternative Regime (STAR) structure, was created by the Cayman Islands in 1997. It offers two distinctive qualities compared to trusts in other jurisdictions. First, STAR structures are "purpose trusts": unlike traditional trusts, which by law must benefit persons, Cayman trusts need not benefit anyone; instead, they can be created solely to advance a purpose, such as holding shares in a corporation. Onshore, the only "purpose trusts" permitted in law must have charitable objectives. The Caymans' legislation extended the idea to include commercial and political ends as well. Second, STAR trusts can last forever; for this reason, they are often known as "dynastic trusts." These two characteristics combine to ensure that a family business can remain intact in perpetuity, no matter what the founders' heirs might wish. While individuals may receive distributions from a STAR trust, they have none of the beneficiary rights associated with a traditional trust; most important, they cannot override the settlor's wishes. A STAR trust can therefore "resist any attempt by the beneficiaries to break the trust, or, alternatively, . . . resist any attempt by the beneficiaries to persuade the trustees to sell the shares (or the underlying assets) and for the proceeds to be invested elsewhere, perhaps in more profitable ventures. The settlor's primary wish, to provide for the continuation of the family business for generations to come, will, therefore, be guaranteed."[118] Settlors who put their business into a STAR trust not only reap the usual tax benefits of the offshore structure but also exert a measure of control over the disposition of their firms that is otherwise unobtainable.

Conclusion

Wealth managers use trusts, corporations, and foundations as tools to liberate clients from the rule of law, and to release clients' wealth from constraints on growth and mobility. Tax avoidance—which gets the lion's share of headlines whenever wealth management makes the news—is only the tip of the iceberg. The larger objective is defending wealth from the many risks it faces, both from without (in the form of political retribution or creditors) and from within (in the form of divorcing spouses or spendthrift heirs). There are many more possibilities for achieving these aims than can be explored within this chapter. There is also continual innovation taking place, driven by legislative action onshore to make certain practices illegal, as well as by counterlegislation offshore designed to create new alternatives and opportunities.[119] A key element of the professional's job is to keep abreast of these changes and to innovate on the basis of the new possibilities they present.

Through skillful regulatory arbitrage, use of offshore financial centers, and insertion of legal distance between clients and their assets, wealth managers can neutralize many political risks and make many forms of legislation and regulation optional, if not irrelevant. With good professional advice, clients can pick and choose the laws to which they wish to be subject—and they usually choose the ones that maximize their ability to control their wealth. This has significant implications for states and the development of economic inequality, which will be explored in subsequent chapters.

APPENDIX

Trusts, firms, and foundations as the building blocks of wealth management

The key tools of contemporary wealth management are three legal structures that can be used alone or in combination, depending upon the client's needs: trusts, corporations, and foundations. While these tools are rather restricted onshore in terms of how they can be used to protect wealth, they have been varied and improved upon with great ingenuity over the past decades in offshore jurisdictions, creating numerous variations that can be deployed to solve the problems elites face in retaining their wealth. The offshore setting plays a key role

in these strategies because it provides a permissive environment for financial-legal creativity—specifically, "innovation
that allows actors to greatly minimize, if not fully escape cen-
tralized country laws, in favor of alternative legal systems."[120]

The analysis here is limited to legal uses of those structures;
this excludes a vast realm of illegal activity. Further, this discussion can only provide a sketch of the wide variety of strategic
structural combinations used in wealth management. The
purpose is simply to illustrate the basic patterns and workings
of wealth defense systems.

Trusts. Trusts, which have been described briefly in the previous chapters, are devices for protecting wealth from taxes,
creditors, and regulators. This protection is achieved through
a legal fiction with financial consequences: dividing ownership into two components. In practice, this means that when
trusts are created, the benefits of ownership go to one set of
actors, while the obligations (such as the payment of taxes) go
to another set. The actors with the obligations are called fiduciaries, while the actors who enjoy the benefits are called
beneficiaries.[121]

From a strategic point of view, three key features have made
trusts a perennial favorite for wealth defense. The first is secrecy. The identities of trust beneficiaries, and the existence
of the structure itself, are not publicly registered. This creates
a useful obscurity and uncertainty with respect to ownership.
Trusts protect wealth from regulation, taxation, and seizure by
"shroud[ing] assets in cast-iron secrecy," making it very difficult to impose responsibility for any costs or legal restrictions
connected to the assets.[122] These include limitations on the

movement of the assets, as well as on the payment of creditors, taxes, or court-ordered fines and settlements. One legal scholar boiled down the trust concept to this simple idea: "A trust is a device for enabling one to enjoy . . . the benefits of ownership without subjection to all the duties and liabilities resulting from ownership."[123]

These liabilities may be cultural and political as well as financial. For example, Luc—the Frenchman who works in Saudi Arabia—said that his clients favor the use of trusts to keep them technically free of shari'a violations. To be seen to violate shari'a by borrowing or lending money at interest, both of which are almost unavoidable in the contemporary global economy, would disqualify clients from holding public office in the kingdom, or in any of the nearby United Arab Emirates. So for those with aspirations to political leadership, the preferred solution is to move their assets offshore into a trust structure. Legally and geographically, this maximizes the distance between them and ownership of those assets, along with anything done to maintain or grow them; this includes the use of conventional mortgages or insurance, both of which are *haram* (forbidden) under shari'a. While offshore corporations and "Islamic finance" can be alternative solutions to these problems of maintaining religious compliance, they do not provide the privacy that Luc's clients are seeking.

In addition to secrecy, a second key advantage of trusts in wealth management is the sparseness of regulation surrounding this type of structure, particularly compared to alternatives such as firms and foundations. Crucially, trusts are not taxed as entities, the way firms are; the assets held in trust are taxed and regulated based on the jurisdiction where the legal owner (the wealth manager) lives.[124] This is one way that offshore plays an important role in the profession's strategic tool kit: by offering a "home base," free of tax and regulation, for wealth managers and the assets they own on clients' behalf. The reduction or absence of such constraints helps wealth managers protect clients' fortunes from being "frittered away" in transaction and compliance costs.

Using offshore trusts in this way, a Russian national living in London could benefit from a multimillion-dollar portfolio of U.S. stocks held in a Cayman Islands trust without paying tax on the profits, because he is not the legal owner of the assets. The wealth manager is the only one liable for the any legal obligations associated with the portfolio, and since the Caymans impose no tax on capital gains or income, profits can accrue without impediment. For the same reason— divided ownership—the trust assets are untouchable by any creditors or disgruntled heirs of the Russian client.[125] Finally, should the Cayman trust be threatened by an unwanted obligation, or if a more attractive legal regime becomes available elsewhere, the trust can be equipped with a "flee clause," which automatically moves the structure to a new jurisdiction at minimal cost.[126]

Flee clauses are one of many innovations that exist only in offshore trusts legislation; they are not a part of traditional trust law or practice. Another key offshore innovation is to give trusts the ability to endure forever, known formally as the "abolition of the rule against perpetuities."[127] Traditional onshore trusts have a built-in life span of just over a century. This practice was called the "rule against perpetuities" because it prohibited assets from being tied up in perpetuity by a single entity;

the rule also ensured that assets held in trust could not escape taxation forever. From the point of view of wealthy individuals with dynastic ambitions, this constituted a significant disadvantage compared to alternative structures such as corporations and foundations, which are not subject to time limitations on their life spans. Starting in the 1980s, however, offshore jurisdictions (and even some onshore jurisdictions hoping to compete with the OFCs) began eliminating the rule against perpetuities, allowing wealth held in trust to remain forever sheltered from taxation, creditors, and other "threats."[128]

Both the elimination of the rule against perpetuities and the innovation of the flee clause are examples of a third way that trusts play a key strategic role in contemporary wealth management: their flexibility of design, which exceeds that of competing institutions.[129] One reason for this flexibility lies in the structural basis of the trust itself. Formally, the law defines trusts as "a fiduciary relationship with respect to property."[130] The key term here is *relationship*, which can be structured legally with as much freedom as relationships have in private life. Trusts offer even greater flexibility than contracts do, because contracts must account for contingencies; but over the multigenerational time frame envisioned in trust structures, there is no way to predict, let alone specify, all the contingencies that will arise. So the pragmatic solution has been to dispense with contracting altogether and instead to endow professionals with broad discretionary powers within the general remit of managing assets in the best interests of the trust's beneficiaries. In a fiduciary relationship, "the duty of loyalty replaces detailed contractual terms."[131]

The built-in flexibility of the trust receives maximum scope for expression in offshore jurisdictions. In OFCs, the financial laws are often written by wealth managers themselves, who seek to innovate and improve upon the traditional model.[132] This allows professionals not only to create innovative solutions to clients' problems—solutions that would not be possible onshore—but also to intensify the complexity that protects clients' fortunes. Besides flee clauses, other examples of offshore innovation include the Virgin Islands Special Trust Act (VISTA), first mentioned in Chapter 3, and the Cayman Islands' Special Trusts Alternative Regime (STAR) structure, described earlier in this chapter. STAR—by offering unprecedented levels of control and privacy to settlors, and allowing trusts to exist in perpetuity—not only makes the Cayman Islands one of the leading destinations for the fortunes of wealthy Asian families but also "creates a whole new legal framework" for trusts.[133]

Foundations. As described in Chapter 3, many high-net-worth individuals from civil-law countries have great difficulty accepting the loss of personal control over their wealth connected with putting assets into trust. As Elias, the Panamanian wealth manager, said of his predominantly Latin American clientele, "they don't trust trusts." This distrust, much to the frustration of the professionals, often trumps economic self-interest on the part of the client. Louis, a London practitioner, observed that in his experience, "many, many French people have missed out on very, very advantageous tax planning because they haven't been able to bring themselves to separate themselves from their assets and give them over to trustees. The civil-law mind-set just doesn't allow them to think that way."

This reluctance to put assets into trust is particularly marked among of clients from the BRICS countries, where wealth is growing fastest but generalized trust in others or in the rule of law is extremely low.[134]

With the strongest new sources of demand for wealth management services coming from countries where trusts range from what Bruce called a "hard sell" to an outright deal-breaker, practitioners must find alternatives. Or they must accede to the demands of clients against their better judgment as professionals. As Bruce put it, "The South American clients usually form foundations, because the founder maintains signature authority on the foundation's bank account. It doesn't matter there are tax risks with this structure, or that trusts are factually a better solution—the client wants what he wants, and it's his money."

Foundations, which originate in Roman law, are superficially similar to trusts in some ways. Like a trust, a foundation can hold all manner of assets, from corporations to stocks and real estate. A foundation's purposes may be philanthropic, but they are not restricted to that realm; many foundations offshore are created for commercial or private wealth management purposes.[135] The foundation's assets are protected from taxation, and distributions can be made to beneficiaries under terms similar to those offered by trusts. And like trusts, foundations are funded by an individual transferring assets into the structure. Nominally, "asset contributors cede rights of ownership, control and beneficial interest to the foundation."[136] But in practice, foundations allow high-net-worth individuals far more control over their wealth than trusts.

Specifically, the law of foundations allows several things that would put a trust structure at risk of being declared a sham—that is, legally invalidated. First, the person who establishes the foundation can be both a beneficiary and a member of the foundation's managing council (similar to a firm's board of directors). As a member of the managing council, the founder—instead of a trustee—directs how the foundation's assets are invested and managed. This is particularly appealing to individuals who put assets such as a family business into their foundations. And crucially, a founder can take assets from the foundation at his or her own discretion, instead of requesting distributions from a trustee, as would be necessary if the assets were held in trust.[137]

Like corporations, foundations have the status of persons in the eyes of the law, and must be publicly registered in consequence. In some respects, this is convenient: unlike a trust, which is a relationship rather than a legal person, a foundation or a firm can open a bank account and enter into contracts. And unlike a trust, foundations can exist in perpetuity. This structure is particularly useful for individuals in civil-law countries that do not recognize trusts, since the quasi-corporate "face" of the foundation gives it a ready-made place in legal and financial transactions in those jurisdictions. For many clients from civil-law jurisdictions, this combination of traits would seem to make the foundation a best-of-both-worlds proposition. As Parvita—a Mauritius practitioner—put it, "The foundation is dressed like a corporation yet has the soul of a trust."

However, foundations do have four significant downsides compared to trusts. For one thing, there is greater administrative complexity and thus higher transaction costs, which create a drain on the wealth held in the structure. Much like corporations, foundations are required to establish bylaws and articles, to create regular financial statements for the managing council to review, and to provide for audits.[138] Second, in many jurisdictions, foundations are subject to taxation, and transfers of assets into noncharitable foundations can be taxed.[139] Third, as a legal person that owns assets, foundations can be sued and go bankrupt.[140] This is in contrast to a trust arrangement, in which there is no legal personality, but only a "natural person" (the fiduciary) who holds only partial ownership rights; this makes it difficult to access the trust assets through lawsuits.

Finally, foundations have a drawback with respect to preserving the anonymity of the founders. The structures are established through means of a foundation deed—similar to a corporate charter—which must be filed with the government where the foundation is based.[141] In many jurisdictions, this means that the name of the founder becomes a matter of public record, undermining the privacy that so many high-net-worth individuals seek. However, legislation offshore has sought to address this problem and make foundation law in those jurisdictions more attractive. For example, both Panama and the Seychelles allow foundations to appoint "nominee founders": individuals or entities, usually law firms, who lend their names (for a fee) to substitute for those of the true founders in the public documents. This keeps the real names of the founders secret.[142] In addition, foundations are untaxed in both jurisdictions.[143] Such offshore modifications serve to narrow the gap between foundations and competing structures.

Corporations. Like trusts, corporations emerged from English law, albeit several centuries later. But while trusts have retained "nearly unlimited flexibility in design," the corporate form has been "encumbered with restrictions of a regulatory character, designed to protect creditors and shareholders."[144] This is partly because, almost immediately after their emergence in the seventeenth century, corporations became associated with fraud and the instigation of economic crises.[145] After one particularly serious crisis, the South Sea Bubble of 1720, the government drastically tightened restrictions on the establishment of new corporations—restrictions that endured for a century. During this time, many commercial enterprises were organized through trusts; these were known as "deed of settlement" firms.[146]

By the mid-nineteenth century, corporations were once again made widely available, and by the twentieth century they had become the dominant form of organization for manufacturing and trading. However, a succession of further corporate crises, particularly in the past thirty years, has attracted even more regulatory attention to firms, again restricting their management and activities.[147] This certainly has not eliminated the use of firms or the occurrence of fraud, but it has raised the transaction costs attached to corporate profits.

The form remains popular for three reasons. First, it is universally recognized: unlike the trust, which is a product of England's unique ecclesiastical equity courts and their rulings based on moral right, the corporation was created by statute law, which exists worldwide.[148] This has made corporations an excellent vehicle for global trading, as exemplified by the multinational corporation. Second, the corporate form offers limited liability, meaning that if a firm incurs debts or goes bankrupt, its officers and shareholders are not personally responsible for paying the creditors. Third, corporations are not time-limited: as long as they have operating capital, they can stay in business.

Given that corporations were designed for trading and profit-making, it is perhaps surprising that they should be used in wealth management, which focuses on capital preservation. But when corporate structures are deployed to protect private fortunes, they are almost always in the form of private limited firms incorporated offshore. These corporations are passive asset-holding vehicles; they don't trade, and thus they are subject to far fewer regulations than the corporations associated with onshore commercial activity. Offshore firms are typically quite easy to create—requiring little documentation and approximately $800 to $6,000 in upfront expenses—and they have few transaction costs related to upkeep and compliance.[149] But the biggest wealth protection benefits of offshore corporations derive from their use as tax shelters. By placing assets that would otherwise be subject to taxes on wealth, capital gains, or income under the nominal ownership of a company based in a country with no or low taxation, high-net-worth individuals can save a great deal of money.

In addition to saving on tax and administration costs, another key attraction of the offshore corporation is the level of control it provides to wealth managers' clients. They can be granted signature authority on the company bank account and be issued a company credit card, allowing them to draw cash from the firm at will.[150] Onshore corporations are subject to regulatory limits on the distribution of capital and are required to submit regular financial statements to the board of directors, as well as to auditors and tax authorities. Offshore legislation generally lightens or eliminates these requirements. In particular, most OFCs allow much more freedom in the distribution of capital than is permitted onshore, making the offshore firm like "a money box, or . . . a glorified bank account for the personal use of the client."[151]

However, some onshore jurisdictions have caught up with the use of offshore corporations for wealth defense. The United States, many of the EU member states, and most of the G20 nations have enacted laws that tax their citizens' offshore companies—and the assets they contain—as if they were held onshore.[152] This has given rise to further innovation in offshore legislation, much of it designed to promote anonymity and privacy by obscuring firms' true ownership. In onshore firms, the names of a corporation's directors and shareholders would ordinarily be part of the public record. This allows others to ascertain who owns and controls the firm and therefore who bears the legal responsibility for its actions.

Offshore, however, there are several ways of obscuring the identities of a firm's directors and shareholders. The most common is the use of "nominees": individuals and firms who substitute their names in the public record for those of the true shareholders and directors. These nominees do not act independently; rather, they act on behalf of those who really own and control the firm. The latter are known as the "beneficial owners"—the same terminology used to describe the beneficiaries of trusts. The nominees not only lend their names to protect the beneficial owners' identities in the public record but also vote in accordance with the beneficial owner's instructions, assign all dividends to the beneficial owner, and agree not to transfer the shares without express direction from the beneficial owner.[153] In return for these services, which constitute a major part of the business model for offshore financial centers, the nominees receive a fee—a "rent," so to speak, on the use of their names. The use of such "straw men" or "front men" makes it very difficult and costly to link the beneficial owner to the firm; as a result, the beneficial owner's wealth is protected from the claims of tax and regulatory authorities, as well as those of creditors and heirs.[154]

In addition, a few offshore jurisdictions allow the use of "bearer shares," which are a way of issuing corporate stock without specifying a particular owner. Rather, the owner of a bearer share is literally whoever happens to be holding the stock certificate at any moment in time. This provides strong privacy protections, because as long as one does not have the shares in hand, one can say truthfully under oath, "I do not own that firm." And if any officers of the firm are ever questioned about its ownership, they can also truthfully say, "I don't know who owns the company, because bearer shares were issued." In other words, bearer shares make it impossible to know who owns a company, and that makes it impossible to assign legal responsibility for any taxes, fines, or debts the company incurs.[155]

The three structures compared and combined. As the previous sections indicate, contemporary wealth management practice uses trusts, foundations, and firms to serve similar ends. While trusts are still the dominant tool for the profession—as indicated by the name of the Society of Trust and Estate Practitioners—innovations in offshore legislation are reducing the distinctions between the three asset-holding structures. As one legal scholar put it, we should "think of the trust as a competitor, locked in a sort of Darwinian struggle against other modes of business organization and finance, particularly the corporation."[156] Thus we see offshore legislation giving trusts more corporation-like features (particularly in terms of control, as in the STAR and VISTA structures), while offshore corporations are acquiring more trust-like features (particularly privacy, through the use of bearer shares and nominee shareholders and directors). Even foundations, which already unite some of the best features of firms and trusts, are being modified to increase their appeal—such as being made more trust-like in Panama and Seychelles, where founders' names are kept secret and foundations are not subject to tax. Table 4.1 compares the three modes of holding assets.

While offshore innovations have reduced many of the differences among trusts, foundations, and corporations, each form still offers distinctive advantages and disadvantages for wealth managers and their clients. Thus a typical wealth management strategy combines two structures and sometimes uses all three. A common solution is the "combined trust-company structure."[157] This involves moving an onshore business into an offshore corporation—run by nominee directors acting on the instructions of the client—and then creating an offshore trust to own all the shares issued by the firm.

This solves several problems at once. For example, many high-net-worth individuals wish to shelter the profits of their businesses from tax and regulation, or to protect the firm from

Table 4.1. Comparing corporations and trusts

	Trusts	Foundations	Corporations
Primary purpose	Holding and distributing wealth in the best interests of beneficiaries	Holding and distributing wealth for charitable purposes (offshore, may be used for private benefit)	Trading and commerce; maximization of shareholder value (offshore, may be asset-holding only)
Ownership	Divided between beneficiaries and trustees; trustees compensated	Foundations own the assets they contain	Shareholders, who pay for shares and may lose the capital they invest
Legal status	Not a legal entity, but a private agreement; recognized only in common-law countries	Separate legal entity recognized worldwide	Separate legal entity recognized worldwide
Management	Trustees	Councilors	Directors
Tax liability	Trustees liable for tax on income from trust assets; beneficiaries liable for tax on distributions (offshore, taxes may be reduced or eliminated)	Subject to income, excise, and gift taxes (offshore, taxes may be reduced or eliminated)	Income taxed twice: once at corporate level, and again when distributed to shareholders (offshore, taxes may be reduced or eliminated)

	Trust	Foundation	Corporation
Asset protection	Trust assets inaccessible to creditors and litigants; trusts cannot go bankrupt	Foundation assets may be attached by creditors and litigants; foundations can go bankrupt	Corporate assets can be attached by creditors and litigants; corporations can go bankrupt
Privacy	No registration; name of trustee may be public record in some jurisdictions, but identities of beneficiaries remain secret	Foundation deed must be publicly registered, disclosing name of founder and councilors (offshore, nominees may be used)	Corporations must be publicly registered, disclosing names of directors and shareholders (offshore, nominees may be used)
Compliance costs	Few to no reporting requirements or limits on liquidity and distributions	Required financial reporting, plus mandatory minimum distributions (offshore, these rules may be loosened)	Required financial reporting, plus limits on liquidity and distributions (offshore, these rules may be loosened)
Ease of migration	Relatively easy and low-cost to move a trust from one jurisdiction to another (offshore, automatic with "flee clauses")	More difficult and costly to move a foundation from one jurisdiction to another	More difficult and costly to move a corporation from one jurisdiction to another
Time limitations	Subject to rule against perpetuities (offshore, rule has been eliminated)	None	None

creditors and litigation, by moving it into an offshore trust, but that means losing control of the business to the new owner, the trustee. The trustee, for his or her part, generally does not have the expertise to run the business and does not want the associated liability for running it profitably.[158] However, if the business is simply moved to an offshore corporation, with the founder retaining control through stock ownership, another problem arises: what happens to the stock when the owner dies? The shares form part of the deceased person's estate and can be transferred only with the consent of a probate judge—which can involve a long and costly procedure and create a tax liability for the heirs.[159] This is obviously contrary to the intent of the client, who wishes to shelter as much of his or her fortune as possible from tax and any sort of legal proceedings. The trust-company combination maximizes both features clients value: protection and control.

This idea was illustrated in Figure 1.1, based on a typical client scenario from a STEP training manual. In that instance, a single Cayman Islands trust held shares in two underlying companies: one based in the BVI and engaged in active commercial activity, and another in Bermuda, which held a portfolio of financial securities. By structuring the assets in this way, maximum protection from tax and regulation can be achieved. As a STEP training manual explains: "In this manner, the trustee continues to hold legal title to the company's shares (and hence the underlying assets) notwithstanding the beneficial owner's death. There is a continuity of ownership of the shares of the underlying company by the trustee. In these circumstances it is not necessary to transfer the shares on the beneficial owner's death in accordance with the will of the deceased. Nor is it necessary to include the value of the shares in the application for probate."[160] The trust-company combination achieves best-of-both-worlds results for a client with a fairly simple array of assets.

But for those with larger and more complex fortunes, it is sometimes desirable to distribute assets among a greater number of structures, arranged in more organizational layers. While more costly to create and administer, these complex structures also provide enhanced privacy and access to resources. A World Bank study of these structures concluded that "the use of tiered entities affords a beneficial owner further opportunities to pocket integral pieces of relevant legal ownership, control, and assets across multiple jurisdictional boundaries. All this makes it easier for him or her (a) to access financial institutions in the names of different entities, which serve the same ultimate end, and (b) to maintain control over the primary corporate vehicle (that is, the vehicle holding, receiving, or transferring the asset). Tiered entities enable the beneficial owner to meet these goals while remaining wholly obscured by a convolutedly indirect hierarchy."[161]

As an example, consider Figure 4.2, which presents a structure suitable for clients with a net worth of at least $100 million.[162] Each layer is labeled for clarity. Layer 5 represents the underlying assets: a family business, two portfolios of financial securities, a yacht, and some real estate. These, in turn, are held in a classic trust-company combination structure, with the companies in layer 4 and the trusts in layer 3. Each asset is "ring-fenced" within a separate corporation in order to isolate the risks and duties associated with owning it. If tax or a legal judgment falls on one of the assets, having the assets

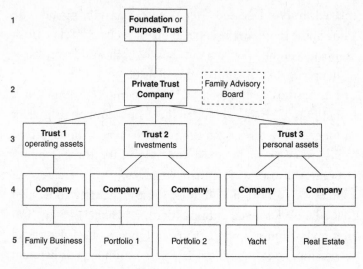

Figure 4.2. Private trust company structure.

separated into different holding companies means that a threat to one won't affect the rest. Each of the firms in layer 4 can also seek external financing—for example, the yacht or real estate could be used as collateral for a loan—which could in turn be borrowed by the companies holding the family business or portfolios. Paying back those loans at interest can generate tax savings.

Layer 3 consists of the trusts that own the shares of the underlying corporations. In this case, the trusts are organized thematically, segregating operating assets from investments and personal assets. As described above, this protects the wealth held in layer 4 from inheritance tax and probate proceedings. In addition, layer 3 ensures that any liabilities from the underlying companies do not flow upward: if the investments incur losses or the family business goes bankrupt, the layer of three separate trusts underscores the separation of the three classes of assets. This makes it difficult for creditors or tax authorities to argue that the structures are related and can be pooled to pay off any debts incurred by the others.

Layer 2, the private trust company (PTC), is a corporation wholly owned and directed by a single family. Its purpose in this structure is to own and manage the underlying trusts. As a corporation, the private trust company enjoys an unlimited life span—providing the continuity essential to long-term wealth preservation—but offers much more control than would be possible using a third-party trust company.[163] The private trust company also provides limited liability to the family advisory board at its helm, which is essential given the many risks to which the widely varied underlying assets are exposed.[164]

The private trust company is an explicitly dynastic tool, designed to institutionalize multigenerational concentration of wealth by ensuring continuity of its management, along with seamless intergenerational transfer of assets. Several leading firms in contemporary wealth management practice (including Northern Trust and Bessemer Trust) began as private trust companies in the nineteenth century, each serving a single family. In contemporary usage, the advantage of using private trust companies hinges on their family advisory boards, which "provide for future generations to take over and run the affairs of the family as a director of the PTC."[165]

Atop this elaborate "layer cake" of trusts and corporations sits an offshore foundation, or sometimes a purpose trust—a special type of offshore trust that need not have beneficiaries.[166] Layer 1 exists solely to own the shares of the private trust company, insulating it completely from regulation and public scrutiny. In this structure, the foundation or the purpose trust enjoys the legal status of an "'unowned' economic entity."[167] This means that no natural person can be identified as the owner of the underlying assets or be held accountable for any taxes or judgements attached to those assets. No wonder, then, that this arrangement, centered on the private trust company, has been described as "the masterstroke in a series of aggressive planning techniques (tax-driven and otherwise) that are used by the very wealthy to secure and grow a fortune for untold generations to come."[168]

Wealth Management and Inequality

MANY CULTURES HAVE SOME VARIATION OF THE CHINESE PROVERB "Sandals to sandals in three generations." In Italian, this gets a rather poetic phrasing—"From the stables to the stars and back in three generations"—but it conveys the same idea: private wealth dissipates quickly. In the usual course of events, the fortune earned by the first generation is spent by the children and gone by the grandchildren's time. As the Germans put it, "Erwerben, vererben, verderben": earn it, bequeath it, destroy it.[1]

The role of the wealth manager is to arrest this process. Through the techniques described in the previous chapter, they seek to slow or halt the dissipation of family fortunes. Ultimately, this means shoring up a larger system of inequality: by keeping private wealth intact within families and thwarting the usual processes through which assets get redistributed, wealth managers contribute to enduring patterns of stratification. Using legal and financial tools, they can turn one generation's surplus into dynastic privilege. As one study put it, "Only the fiduciary control of wealth under appropriate arrangements can slow the process of dissolution, and finally outlast it through institutions."[2]

The rise of wealth managers as a professional group coincides with a dramatic rise in wealth-based stratification since the 1980s.[3] Some have attributed these rising levels of inequality to directly to professional intervention. For example, one study of trusts concluded that "trusteeing of wealth . . . has led to increased concentration of wealth."[4] Others have made the link indirectly, pointing to wealth managers' role in helping their clients avoid billions in tax payments.[5] Of particular concern is the use of offshore finance, which has been characterized as "the biggest force for shifting wealth and power from poor to rich in history."[6]

I will not attempt to quantify the contribution of wealth managers in this growing global problem, because the data necessary to make such estimates are not available (more on this below). Instead, what this study can add to the growing body of research on inequality is a more precise understanding of the *mechanisms* underlying the phenomenon. I will expand on the review of wealth management techniques from Chapter 4 to show how their deployment not only makes it possible for clients to keep a larger proportion of their wealth than would otherwise be possible but also ensures that the surplus capital is allocated in ways that allow it to grow, protected from many risks and losses to which the wealth of others is vulnerable. The key processes are avoidance of taxes, debts, and penalties, along with access to exclusive investment opportunities not available on the open market, and finally the concentration of wealth over multiple generations through inheritance. So while this chapter cannot make claims such as "wealth managers are responsible for X percent of global economic inequality," it can offer insights on the broad consequences of wealth management techniques for the development and persistence of stratification regimes around the world.

Finally, I take a novel approach to inequality here by focusing on wealth rather than income. While the global financial crisis of 2008 renewed interest in the "1 percent" and concentrations of economic power more generally, the new stream of research that arose from the crisis centered almost exclusively on the analysis of income. Yet wealth captures far more of what matters conceptually about inequality, such as life chances, access to education, job market opportunities, and political power. While income often varies—due to bonuses, windfalls, unemployment, and taxation—wealth is more stable and can be passed down to future generations, creating enduring socioeconomic configurations. Empirically, what little we do know of wealth inequality suggests that it is a much larger problem, and growing much faster, than income inequality.[7]

However, wealth is difficult to study; data on income are far easier to obtain. Most governments track income as part of their taxation systems and make those records public. In contrast, the size and ownership of private fortunes are obscured, often through the intervention of wealth managers. The wealthy are almost totally excluded from any publicly available data on inequality.[8] Surveys "systematically underrepresent the rich and do not reflect the holdings of the super-rich."[9] Indeed, the members of the Forbes 400 are explicitly excluded even from data sets that oversample on wealth, such as the Survey of Consumer Finances.[10] Some individuals pay to be left off the Forbes 400 list, in order to protect their privacy even further.[11] Finally, the use of trusts and unregistered asset-holding structures offshore contributes significantly to the strategic obscurity surrounding the true extent of wealth inequality.[12]

In fact, increased interest in inequality has brought to light how carefully the "politically dangerous" information needed to estimate the extent of wealth disparities has been obscured.[13] In many jurisdictions wealth managers face civil or criminal penalties if they divulge any information about clients' capital flows. Should suspicions arise that their clients are engaging in illegal activities, the STEP training manuals caution practitioner about reporting those concerns to anyone, due to "strict confidentiality statutes, which not only ensure that the disclosure of client information to third parties is actionable in a civil court, but also render the offending professional liable to a fine and/or imprisonment for a criminal offense."[14]

The data that occasionally do come to light on the assets and wealth management strategies of elites generally emerge from two sources. The first is lawsuits, which often generate public trial records in which the magnitude and structure of individuals' wealth are exposed; examples include the Pritzker case mentioned in Chapter 1, and the Wyly case discussed in Chapter 4. These data, while highly suggestive, are unsystematic and likely to be biased, limiting their value for analysis and generalization.

The same can be said of the second major data source: theft. In recent years, there have been several high-profile cases of employees from offshore banks and other wealth management firms leaking client data to governments and journalists; this includes private account information taken from organizations in Liechtenstein, Luxembourg, and parts of the Caribbean. Most recently, an anonymous source leaked 11.5 million files encompassing nearly forty years' worth of client data from the Panama-based firm Mossack Fonseca. These files revealed billions held offshore by business leaders, celebrities, and politicians—a virtual "who's who" of the global elite. This included several billion held in offshore trusts for the benefit of Russian president Vladimir Putin. These likely represent only a small fraction of the trust assets beneficially owned by Putin, according to anti-corruption activist Alexei Navalny: "The reaction in Russia is: 'Ha, ha, they only found two billion?' It's petty cash for personal expenses."[15] However, it is unlikely that these claims will be substantiated with further evidence: barring another leak that happens to include data on Putin or his associates, the Russian president's offshore holdings will remain under strict privacy protections. These conditions point up the urgency of examining not just wealth inequality but the protections that have arisen around this quasi-taboo information.[16]

The problem with inequality

Not all forms of inequality constitute social problems, particularly in liberal capitalist democracies. On the contrary, some types of inequality are widely regarded as necessary and desirable in a system of short-term social and economic rewards and sanctions.[17] However, if "inequality" is understood as shorthand for "differential access to opportunities and advantages in multiple domains of social life," the issue becomes clearer. Inequality is problematic when it creates multigenerational barriers to the availability of capital, education, employment, and political representation.[18]

Wealth versus income

Wealth, also known as "net worth," is the surplus of assets one owns once all basic needs have been met and debts discharged. If wealth is our stock of accumulated resources, income is the *flow* of those resources into our individual and household economic systems.[19] Most people use income to pay for daily needs and debt service; what is not consumed in this way can be saved, becoming a stock of wealth. This provides stability, opportunity, and security.[20] In contrast, income can vary considerably in the short term, both because of windfalls (such as bonuses) and because of misfortunes (such as unemployment).

While income is measured in the short term—as an hourly or monthly rate, or as an annual salary—wealth permits us to think long-term, and potentially to change our position within the socioeconomic structure. As one study put it: "Wealth is a special form of money not used to purchase milk and shoes and other life necessities. More often it is used to create opportunities, secure a desired stature and standard of living, or pass class status along to one's children. In this sense the command over resources that wealth entails is more encompassing than is income or education, and closer in meaning and theoretical significance to our traditional notions of economic well-being and access to life chances. More important, wealth . . . captures inequality that is a product of the past, often passed down from generation to generation."[21] Thus, wealth confers privilege along multiple, mutually reinforcing dimensions.[22]

Stratification in terms of wealth—as opposed to income—is problematic because it hardens and stabilizes such advantages into an enduring class structure. While there is some intergenerational continuity of income, the stability of wealth levels across generations is far higher.[23] This is because wealth comes with special economic and political privileges that enable the wealthy to protect and increase their assets better than others.[24] For example, wealth provides well-being in the form of a safety net, offering the freedom to take risks and recover from missteps that might derail the lives of less wealthy individuals.[25] In addition, wealth enables individuals and families to ride out economic declines, and even to profit from them by buying investments at rock-bottom prices while others are strapped for cash. This, in turn, generates new income and additional inequality. As C. Wright Mills put it in his mid-twentieth-century classic *The Power Elite*, "Wealth not only tends to perpetuate itself, but . . . tends also to monopolize opportunities for getting 'great wealth.'"[26]

This self-perpetuating aspect of wealth, particularly in its relation to income, is often overlooked in discussions of inequality. As the data indicate, even income inequality itself is driven not so much by paychecks as by wealth put to work as capital. Specifically, economic research has found that for the most part, "the extremely large incomes of the income-richest are the realized capital gains from the sales of shares or other assets."[27] But while wealth generates income, it is more difficult for income to generate wealth.[28] Although it is possible to acquire wealth based purely on labor income, those cases are exceptional; examples might include sports stars or entertainers.

In light of this, economist Thomas Piketty recently observed that "wealth also generates income and . . . wealth originating in the past automatically grows more rapidly, even without labor, than wealth stemming from work, which can be saved."[29]

The 1 percent

As an example of the relative significance of wealth and income, consider the following illustration from the United States. Federal Reserve data show that the average annual income of the top 1 percent of earners is $1.38 million; however, what makes this group really extraordinary is that their wealth (net worth) exceeds their income by more than an order of magnitude, averaging $16.45 million per household.[30] In contrast, the median American household has a net worth of about $64,000—just a bit larger than its median income of $53,000, and lower than the median household wealth measured at any other point in the past fifty years.[31] While it is possible to amass a fortune through careful saving, the evidence suggests other sources for the wealth of the 1 percent: more than 75 percent of their net worth derives from ownership of financial instruments (such as stocks and bonds) and real estate (not including their primary residences).[32]

In other words, what makes the 1 percent extraordinary—and extraordinarily problematic—is not just their compensation from work but their ownership of assets that boost their incomes and multiply their wealth at a rapid pace. Thus, the top 1 percent in the United States have captured 17 percent of the nation's income but 35 percent of its wealth.[33] Not only does wealth inequality represent double the problem that income disparities do in terms of magnitude, but the wealth gap is growing much more rapidly.[34] Indeed, one recent estimate shows that the wealth gap doubled between 2003 and 2013.[35]

The implications of this were underscored by the financial crisis of 2008 and the extreme inequality of the subsequent recovery. In contrast to the vast majority of Americans, who still have not fully recouped their losses from the crisis, the wealth of the 1 percent has grown steadily since 2008, at an annual rate of 9 to 18 percent.[36] In 2015 the wealth of this group reached a record-high $15 trillion.[37] The members of the Forbes 400 list of the wealthiest people in the United States are now 45 percent wealthier than they were in 2007.[38]

A similar pattern holds elsewhere in the world. Globally, wealth is concentrating at an extraordinary rate, such that 1 percent of the world population now controls half of its wealth.[39] More generally, the total population of high-net-worth individuals has continued to grow steadily, along with their fortunes, in the postcrisis years. There are now about 14.6 million individuals in the high-net-worth category worldwide, and their wealth amounts to just over $56 trillion—triple the GDP of the United States, and greater than the sum of the world's fifteen largest national economies.[40]

Inheritance

Current levels of economic inequality are problematic not just because a small group of individuals are disproportionately wealthy *now*. The future implications offer additional reason for concern: what will happen to all this wealth when its current owners pass away? In the United States, it is estimated that between $10 trillion and $41 trillion of private wealth will be transferred through inheritance in the next three decades.[41]

While scholars disagree on the exact amount, there is convergence on the most important point: virtually all of the wealth will go to a tiny percentage of the population, while the vast majority—80 percent—will inherit nothing.[42] The proportion of American households that receive an inheritance has been shrinking over the past several decades, and the dollar amounts of the transfers have become dramatically skewed: the wealthiest 1 percent of households now inherit an average of $2.7 million, while those with the median level of household wealth inherit an average of $34,000.[43]

Elsewhere in the world, the differential in the magnitude of inheritances remains roughly similar.[44] In Western Europe, the sums transferred through inheritance are smaller than in the United States—an estimated €100 billion to €150 billion annually in Germany, for example—but are similarly restricted to a tiny elite.[45] Moreover, the significance of that windfall for the life chances for Europeans has been increasing since the 1970s.[46] This is largely due to the ownership structure of many of Europe's largest corporations: most are "closely held" by the founding families rather than selling shares on the open market, meaning that through inheritance, "such families end up controlling considerable portions of their countries' economies."[47] As Jens Beckert has written in his analysis of inherited wealth worldwide, this phenomenon has implications far beyond the economic: wealth transfers "allow for the intergenerational continuity of social positions, they stabilize spheres of affiliation and thus the social structure of society, and they counteract the vagaries of success in the marketplace."[48]

This pattern of ownership and intergenerational transfer has also played a significant role in shaping inequality in de-

veloping countries, such as China, Russia, and the resource-
rich nations of Africa. In those countries, private fortunes are
growing more rapidly than anywhere else in the world, and—
unlike in the West—they are largely unchecked by state interventions. Much of that wealth has fled offshore: recent estimates
suggest that about 30 percent of African private wealth and
more than 50 percent of Russian wealth is held in Switzerland
and other tax havens.[49] The OECD has recently urged such
countries to implement more aggressive taxation regimes and
higher rates of redistribution in order to slow the harmful economic and social effects of dynastic formations.[50] Given the
extreme wealth inequality that already exists in developing
countries and their lack of basic infrastructure, public policy
organizations have warned that further dynastic concentration
threatens to destabilize governments as well as markets.[51]

Worldwide, a major problem with the intergenerational
transmission of wealth is what it means for the future configuration of economic resources and political power. As one
legal scholar explained, "An elite, an upper class, is a class
that inherits. A lower class is a class that inherits nothing";
this makes the transfer of accumulated wealth "one of the
most vital and fundamental of all social processes."[52] This
observation is supported by the recent empirical findings of
Thomas Piketty and other economists, showing that intergenerational transfers have acquired a self-perpetuating momentum, avoiding the shirtsleeves-to-shirtsleeves pattern of
dissipation and replicating the conditions of inequality that
pertained during the Gilded Age.[53]

In the early nineteenth century, when the United States was
still very much under the influence of the Enlightenment-era

revolt against inherited wealth and privilege, Alexis de Tocqueville wrote of the country as a place where wealth "circu-
lates with inconceivable rapidity, and experience shows that it
is rare to find two succeeding generations in full enjoyment
of it."[54] Equal opportunity, democratic participation, and entrepreneurial activity, in Tocqueville's account, were all closely
connected to this pattern of dynamic, temporary economic
inequalities.

Thus, when some people earn more than others—even a
lot more—that does not necessarily constitute a threat to
democracy or capitalism.[55] The trouble arises when those
inequalities become stabilized, interfering with the processes
of meritocracy and individual achievement that underpin
the kind of thriving capitalist democracy Tocqueville described. Indeed, centuries of political philosophy singled out
inheritance of wealth as a major threat to social development.
Thinkers including Rousseau, Mill, Bentham, and Tocqueville advocated eliminating or tightly limiting the right of
inheritance so as to prevent the reestablishment of the concentrations of political and economic power that the revolutions
of the eighteenth century sought to demolish.[56] The *Communist Manifesto* put "abolition of the right of inheritance" at
number three on a list of the ten steps necessary to realize "the
forcible overthrow of the whole extant social order."[57]

Hostility to inherited wealth, far from being a radical idea,
was the mainstream in political and social thought long after
the Enlightenment. Indeed, many societies implemented laws
specifically designed to limit inheritance rights in the name of
preserving justice, meritocracy, and democracy.[58] As recently
as the mid-twentieth century, U.S. president Franklin Roosevelt spoke openly of "malefactors of great wealth" and warned

that "the transmission from generation to generation of vast fortunes by will, inheritance, or gift is not consistent with the ideals and sentiments of the American people. . . . [They] amount to the perpetuation of great and undesirable concentration of control in relatively few individuals over the enjoyment and welfare of many, many others." With these words, Roosevelt persuaded Congress to increase taxation of inheritances among the nation's wealthiest citizens. But as one legal scholar put it recently, "Nobody uses this language today."[59] When Roosevelt gave that address to Congress in 1935, only 8 percent of tax professionals (mostly accountants and lawyers) opposed an inheritance tax; by 1994, the proportion of those in opposition had more than tripled.[60] This was part of a broad change in public sentiment that led to the U.S. inheritance tax being repealed entirely (although temporarily) in 2010, and an ongoing effort in Congress to repeal it permanently.[61] Similar changes occurred elsewhere in Western countries as part of the neoliberal turn of the 1980s. For example, in the United Kingdom, observers noted that the "reduced redistributive ambitions of successive governments" was a major factor in that country's growing wealth inequality.[62]

Within the relatively short span of a few decades, the moral valence attached to wealth—particularly enduring, inherited wealth—changed radically, diverting attention and resources away from the upper ends of the inequality spectrum.

The role of wealth management

As part of this neglect, questions of agency have remained almost totally unexamined. For example, Piketty's observation about the sharp increase in the impact of inheritance on stratification patterns after decades of declining significance has not yet led to systematic inquiry into the actors who made this happen. To the extent that research has been conducted into the causal forces behind wealth inequality, it has focused on public policy and taxation institutions.[63] To be sure, these are important factors. But there remains an irreducible element of agency in these developments that has not been explored: we still lack a coherent account of the key actors involved, as well as their methods and motives. In the rare instances when these issues have been considered at all, wealthy people themselves have been identified as the key actors. This is despite recent evidence that undermine that narrative, such as media coverage of the 2012 presidential campaign of Mitt Romney, which revealed that his $250 million personal fortune was held in a complex global web of trust funds managed by a private banker at Goldman Sachs: "His Goldman investments are handled by Jim Donovan, who . . . gave Mr. Romney's trusts access to the bank's own exclusive investment funds and helped him execute an aggressive and complex tax-deferral strategy known as an 'exchange fund' in 2002. (Since 2003, most of Mr. Romney's money has been held in blind trusts, meaning that he no longer makes many of his own investment decisions.) According to tax returns released this week, the family's three principal trusts earned more than $9 million from various Goldman Sachs investment vehicles in 2010."[64] Even though this news made the front page of the *New York Times* and named the individual in charge of Romney's wealth management plan—as well as underscoring Romney's detachment from the process— this did not stimulate efforts to examine the role of professionals in creating economic inequality. But as this book has attempted to show, wealth managers deserve a great deal more attention in this respect than they have so far received from scholars or journalists. Inquiry into the sources of inequality should explore the " 'placeless' international forms of expertise . . . [that are] providing a foundation for a new kind of cosmopolitan power elite."[65]

It is particularly suggestive that the global concentration of wealth in recent years has been marked by an upswing in the indicators of wealth management activity. For example, the amount of wealth held offshore has surged by 25 percent since 2008, and there has been a dramatic increase in the use of shell corporations during that time.[66] These shifts appear to have made wealth managers' clients richer than ever: while there has been an overall decrease in the *number* of clients, there has been a significant rise in the *amount* of assets under management, and the increase has been particularly pronounced among fortunes of $50 million or more.[67] In other words, there are fewer clients, but they are much wealthier than before. Through the work of wealth managers, ultra-high-net-worth individuals are prospering and inequality is growing.[68]

Finally, Piketty and colleagues have shown that the economic significance of inheritance began its resurgence in the 1980s, coinciding roughly with the professionalization of wealth management. Anecdotally, several participants in this study highlighted the same time frame in their comments as the moment when they saw patterns of wealth changing. For example, when asked to identify major trends in the wealth management industry, Neal—the English practitioner working in the Cayman Islands—replied, "Increasing wealth inequality . . . Extremely wealthy people are able to structure their affairs in such a way that they are able to pay much less tax than they would if my work and my industry didn't exist. And once you get a head start growing wealth, that lead is going to keep growing, progressive taxation and redistributive policy notwithstanding. It becomes increasingly difficult with time to reverse these inequalities, short of revolution." This observation points up a unique insight offered by this study: while other work on wealth inequality starts with structures, this research sheds light on the people who create the structures. In large quantitative analyses of inequality, the role of individual or collective agency is often obscured. As one historical review of wealth and inheritance put it, "money makes money" not because accumulation is natural or inevitable but because "rich people . . . can afford the best investment advisers, the best accountants, the best lawyers."[69] Thus, to understand the sources of conflict and change around inequality, it is crucial to examine the actors who shape the larger institutions.

Creating dynastic wealth

A defining characteristic of dynastic wealth is that it endures and becomes "relatively indestructible" through legal practices and structures.[70] In the past, those practices took the form of entail, primogeniture, and trusts; now, through the innovations introduced by wealth managers, there are many new ways of achieving wealth protection. A variety of structures can be deployed, onshore or offshore, depending on clients' circumstances and their constellation of assets, constraints, and goals. In general, the structures allow wealth managers to achieve three things, as shown in Figure 5.1:

1. To limit dissipation of the client's income (whether from labor, wealth, or both) that may occur as a result of taxes, debts, or penalties; the goal is to maximize the amount of income left over as surplus

2. To steer part of that surplus toward investment opportunities for high growth with low risk—investments not necessarily managed personally by the wealth manager, but arranged through his or her intervention

3. To ensure that the client's wealth passes to subsequent generations with minimal transaction costs and maximum opportunity to grow undisturbed by family conflicts or other forces of dissipation

Once these conditions are implemented, it sets in motion a kind of perpetual moneymaking machine. Wealth grows, protected by trusts and offshore vehicles, generating more income, feeding more economic resources into the system. In the words of Tocqueville, "The machine once put in motion will go on for ages, as [it] . . . unites, draws together and vests property and power in a few hands; it causes an aristocracy, so to speak, to spring out of the ground."[71]

The power of these structures and strategies is such that they can create dynastic wealth even when there is no intention to do so on the part of clients or wealth managers. As one study observed: "Families can acquire a dynastic character in spite of explicit intentions, merely because of the *dynastic bias* built into the conventionalized process of giving structure to private wealth. . . . In such cases, dynasties have largely been fashioned by the professional work of fiduciaries, whose basic resource has been the trust instrument and its legal traditions."[72] The implication is that as soon as one gets a wealth manager involved in the care of one's fortune, that sets in motion conditions conducive to the growth of enduring and rapidly multiplying inequality. Figure 5.1 illustrates the mechanisms through which professional intervention makes this possible. The following sections analyze each of the mechanisms individually.

Limit income dissipation, increase surplus

As soon as a client receives income, whether from labor, investments, or rents, it becomes a target for taxation, as well as for seizure in payment for debts and penalties. Professional intervention at this stage of building a fortune is focused on preventing losses. Chapter 4 detailed methods for reducing taxation through the use of trusts and offshore vehicles, as well as for making a client's fortune inaccessible to creditors, divorcing spouses, or litigants. In addition to these methods, many wealth managers take the extra step of acquiring an "opinion letter" from an accountant or a lawyer, certifying that the techniques used to avoid tax or debts are legal, in the professional's judgment. These opinion letters run to about a hundred pages and cost $50,000 to $75,000 to obtain. In wealth management practice, they function as a sort of "get out of jail free" card. As one report concluded, "The real value of opinion letters is as a shield from government penalties."[73] Such penalties are normally waived, even if a particular strategy for "income defense" is found to be illegal, on the premise that the client relied in good faith on expert advice.

Direct surplus toward high-profit, low-risk investments

As the use of opinion letters indicates, protection from risk plays a significant role in growing surplus income into a dynastic fortune. Indeed, a common denominator of the growth strategies that wealth managers devise for their clients is that they are "deliberately structured to eliminate virtually all investment risk."[74] This flies in the face of the economic theories underpinning modern capitalism, in which financial rewards come only to those who accept risks.[75] That is the basis of the entrepreneurial ideal, and of the legitimacy historically accorded to great fortunes.

But one of the things the wealthy can do better than others is hedge their risks. This occurs on a number of fronts simultaneously, from the use of legal fig leaves such as opinion letters and the sheltering of assets in judgment-proof Cook Islands trusts, to the choice of a diversified portfolio of investments.[76] Having all one's eggs in a single basket, financially speaking, makes one's wealth very vulnerable to economic downturns. Those whose wealth is spread among stocks and bonds, real estate, art, and cash are in a much better position to withstand market declines—or even take advantage of them. For example, during the 2008 financial crisis, high-net-worth individuals lost money temporarily on their stocks and bonds, but most had plenty of other assets that held their value and allowed them to buy when everyone else was selling. Malik, a New York–based wealth manager, said in an interview shortly after the crisis that "the super-rich seem to be getting richer, and they're bargain hunting. I had a colleague call me yesterday asking me to help an ultra-high-net-worth client buy a couple of department stores."

This points up a third way in which wealth managers help their clients grow their wealth: steering them toward exclusive investment opportunities not available to the general public. This may take the form of a private exchange of art, houses, and other assets, as described by Michael in Guernsey (see Chapter 3). There are also numerous high-return investment opportunities in finance that are exclusive to high-net-worth individuals. For instance, wealth managers can direct their clients' assets to "dark pool" investment funds—a private trading system in which prices are invisible to the public and participation is by invitation only—and hedge funds, which are limited by law to accept as investors only those with a net worth of $5 million or more.[77]

These private investment opportunities are lightly regulated, particularly in offshore jurisdictions. This offers privacy for the transaction participants and lower transaction costs compared to the open market, providing more room for profit.[78] This last point is crucial, and often overlooked: one way to get rich and stay that way is to keep transaction costs to a minimum. As the well-known American mutual fund manager Bill Miller is known for saying, "Lowest average cost wins."[79] That is, the way to make the most money—to "win"— isn't just by earning the highest returns but also by minimizing costs. This is consistent with the observations of the Nobel Prize–winning political theorist Douglass North, who argued that transaction costs are the most significant determinant of wealth (and poverty) worldwide.[80]

Thus, among the privileges afforded to those who work with a wealth manager is the ability to grow one's wealth at minimal cost and with minimal risk. This conservative approach to growth may earn wealth managers the disdain of

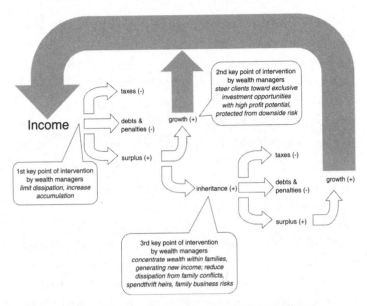

Figure 5.1. The "perpetual-motion machine" of wealth inequality.

investment bankers and others in finance (see Chapter 2), but it has proven very effective in helping clients retain and expand their wealth over the long term. This strategy of limiting costs and risks played a vital role in the unequal recovery from the 2008 financial crisis. According to U.S. Federal Reserve data, the economic crash of 2008 destroyed 38.8 percent of the wealth held by the median American family, and recovery from this blow has been "particularly slow."[81] In contrast, the wealthiest Americans lost far less, then experienced a quick recovery followed by rapid, robust growth of their fortunes. From 2008 to 2009, the median wealth loss was 6.4 percent for the richest 10 percent of Americans—about one-sixth of the effect felt by the median family in the United States.[82] Those ranked on the Forbes 400 list of the wealthiest Americans experienced declines amounting to a 19 percent loss in the total wealth held by those on the list—half of what the median American family lost.[83] Having more wealth on hand than most others when the crash hit meant that high-net-worth individuals could buy up stocks, real estate, and other assets, so that when the recovery occurred, they profited more than any other group. As a study of the Forbes 400 concluded, "The easiest way to make money is to begin with money."[84]

Concentrate wealth within families

Ensuring the transmission of fortunes from one generation to the next, with as few losses as possible, has historically been one of the chief tasks and specialties of wealth managers.[85] This goes back to the medieval origins of trusts and trusteeship, in which the sole function of the trustee was to hold and transfer ownership of land to the settlor's designated heir. In the twenty-first century, this activity comes with a host of new demands, but the process of succession remains a core task for professional wealth managers and a key point of intervention in making wealth endure over time.[86]

As with the other intervention points shown in Figure 5.1, ensuring the continuity of wealth means reducing risks and transaction costs that might dissipate the fortune, as well as creating conditions for its growth. This starts with ensuring a smooth, low-cost transition from one generation to the next. The more wealth that can be preserved in this way, the more easily it multiplies itself. As Piketty has shown empirically, "People with inherited wealth need save only a portion of their income from capital to see that capital grows more quickly

than the economy as a whole. Under such conditions, it is almost inevitable that inherited wealth will dominate wealth
amassed from a lifetime's labor by a wide margin, and the
concentration of capital will attain extremely high levels."[87]
Thus, the wealth manager's mandate to preserve clients' assets includes succession planning of some sort, which serves
to reduce transaction costs and the risk of dissipation.

The prime directive in this effort, perhaps surprisingly, is
usually not to benefit their heirs but to preserve the fortune for
its own sake. To be sure, heirs derive many personal advantages
from inheriting wealth. But on closer inspection, many of these
benefits are by-products of strategies designed to serve the interests of the family fortune and contribute to its continuity over
time. For example, being the beneficiary of a trust fund may
improve not just individuals' economic position but their social
status as well. As the poet and playwright John Dryden once
wrote, in a sly reference to the way wealth enhances marriage
prospects, "All heiresses are beautiful."[88] But in this respect,
the trust also benefits the family fortune by making a beneficiary "fit" to marry among other wealthy people.[89] This makes
possible an age-old technique for consolidating and growing
family wealth and power: "The great families intermarry among
themselves and, in a veritable collective alchemy, they produce
the miracle of the multiplication of the loaves, in every form of
capital."[90] At the same time, trusts and other structures can
protect the family wealth from divorce and other forms of
family conflict that can dramatically increase the transaction
costs associated with succession of an estate.[91]

By the same token, legal scholars have noted that the tax
benefits accorded to trusts don't accrue to trust beneficiaries:

they are still subject to income taxes on distributions they receive from the trust. Instead, the tax savings go to "the disembodied ancestral legacy—the trust."[92] Similar observations have been made about the spendthrift trust, which serves primarily to protect a family fortune *from* its heirs and any debts or penalties they might incur. As the interview data from Chapters 3 and 4 suggest, heirs sometimes are the biggest threats to the continuity of a family fortune, and wealth managers guard against them accordingly.[93] In this sense, the inheritance plan is put in place specifically to reduce the risks represented by the beneficiaries, rather than being constructed with their interests in mind. As one wealthy Bostonian observed of his nineteenth-century Brahmin contemporaries: "Immense wealth had been accumulated in Boston in the first sixty years of the republic; instead of trusting their sons and sending them out at their own risks . . . they distrusted their ability . . . and had them all trusteed."[94]

It is a truism in sociological theory that organizations seek above all else to survive.[95] This observation is as applicable to the organizational structures created by wealth managers as it is to corporations and government agencies. So when professionals intervene to organize the transmission of wealth through inheritance, they are usually acting not on the basis of the client's generosity but rather in the interests of the system—to perpetuate wealth for its own sake. As one study put it, "Inter-generational altruism is rare, legacies of precaution being more frequent than legacies of transmission."[96] In so-called old-money families, this is made explicit. The heirs to the Rockefeller fortune, for example, have written about the ways it was impressed upon them that their inheritances represented a burden and a duty rather than a gift.[97] Paraphrasing

Bourdieu, one study summed up the practical meaning of inheritance as follows: "The individual is inherited in a way by his inheritance, snatched up by the duty to assume the transmission from which he benefits but of which he, in turn, is obliged to assure the succession."[98]

Beyond the client: broader impacts of wealth management on inequality

As all this implies, discussion of wealth management's impact on inequality is really a discussion about the impact of *dynastic wealth*, which—particularly in the modern era—endures not on its own but only through the intervention of professionals. The scope of this impact is significant, affecting the distribution of both economic and political resources within societies. In this sense, wealth management influences social structure, supporting class stratification as well as shaping democracy and culture. The following sections address each of these impacts in greater detail.

Economic impact

Wealth managers' work exacerbates economic inequality in two ways: through keeping wealth tied up in families, and through tax and debt avoidance, which shifts the costs of business and government to the nonwealthy. Inheritance, while it does not completely eliminate economic mobility, impedes it considerably. The purpose of inheritances, particularly when they are held in trust, is to stabilize concentrations of capital, rather than letting it reenter the market for use by others. Max

Weber made this point in his discussion of the Islamic version of the trust, called the *vakf*. Weber observes that although the *vakf* is supposed to consolidate capital for charitable purposes, its use as a means of transmitting wealth through inheritance served mainly to create a rentier class: "The very persistent immobilization of accumulated wealth in the form of *vakfs* was of very great importance for the economic development of the Orient . . . which used accumulated wealth as a source of rent, not as acquisitive capital."[99] Later scholarship has been more explicit, pinning centuries of underdevelopment in the Middle East specifically on the institution of the *vakf*, which "locked vast resources" away from the market and from applications that could have enhanced the region's human capital.[100]

Scholars of the Enlightenment era observed a similar drag on economic development from the use of trusts, entail, and other traditional European means of keeping wealth within families over the long term. As a result, a major legacy of that period was the elimination of many inherited privileges, from titles of nobility to hereditary land claims.[101] Even the most liberal market enthusiasts recognized that these feudal practices posed a threat to the advancement of commerce and innovation by reducing the mobility of wealth itself. And with the recent resurgence of inherited wealth as a major factor in economic inequality, we have seen a corresponding decline in the movement of individuals through the class structure.[102] The result is "substantial immobility" in both wealth and income, particularly at the bottom and the top ends of the economic spectrum.[103] This has not eliminated opportunities for individuals' fortunes to rise or fall on the merits of their contributions—the major justification of the unequal distribution of wealth—but it has reduced mobility considerably. "For the most part," one study concluded, "meritocracy is superimposed on inheritance rather than the other way around—effects produced by merit or luck occur within the context of effects produced by differential inheritance."[104]

Wealth managers' contribution to this trend includes not only the effectiveness with which they ensure the continuity of family fortunes but also their skill in helping clients avoid taxes and debts. The use of trusts, along with other tools for tax avoidance such as offshore corporations, makes those who do not use trusts poorer and often reduces the public services available to them—services such as education, health care, and infrastructure that might otherwise help them to be upwardly mobile. Wealth managers' tax avoidance strategies shift the fiscal burdens of the state downward, imposing a surcharge on those who are unable to afford (or unwilling to use) such strategies. In the United States, estimates of this surcharge vary between 7 and 15 percent in additional taxes to cover the $35 billion underpayment by the wealthiest Americans.[105] Similarly, the United Kingdom is believed to lose £100 billion annually as a result of tax avoidance, with tens of thousands of the country's wealthiest individuals paying little or no income tax.

To stem the tide of capital flowing out to offshore jurisdictions in search of tax breaks, onshore governments have been cutting their tax rates, particularly on income from investments. So wealth managers' use of offshore strategies on behalf of their clients has a doubly negative effect on inequality, depriving states of revenues in two ways: through the success of their legal tax avoidance strategies and through the downward pressure this creates on statutory tax rates onshore. To compensate for these revenue losses, governments must either increase taxes on those least able to avoid them or cut public services that might offset the impact of inequality on life chances.[106] In both cases, the poor are made poorer by these strategies, just as the rich are made richer by them.

This has ominous long-term implications for human capital and national development. Drastic cuts in public services are occurring now in Greece, Spain, and other EU countries where massive levels of tax avoidance by the wealthiest citizens depleted government coffers prior to the financial crisis.[107] These tax deficits have been directly attributed to the intervention of wealth managers, who continually "innovate new techniques of evasion and avoidance."[108] As underfunded states crumble, the most able and talented citizens often leave, and those left behind are ripe to be "tempted by nationalist solutions, ethnic divisions, and the politics of hatred."[109] Thus tax avoidance and rising inequality creates a threat to democracy itself.

Finally, the use of trusts to avoid paying debts and penalties also increases the costs of debt and other transactions for others. As one legal scholar explained, "Abolition of the rule against perpetuities and the rise of asset protection trusts . . . benefit trust users, both settlors and beneficiaries, as well as trust service providers, by shifting burdens to trust non-parties: beneficiaries' creditors, taxpayers, and the general population. . . . Perpetual trusts are also likely to contribute to the preservation of the current distribution of society into classes, increasing the likelihood that the descendants of today's wealthy class will be members of the wealthy class of a hundred or two hundred years hence. In sum, perpetual trusts increase the externalities consequent on trust use. They exacerbate socioeconomic inequality."[110] In particular, asset protection trusts and perpetual trusts (described in Chapter 4) deepen inequality by providing special protections and privileges to those who need it the least: the very rich, who can afford trusts in the first place.

This inequality reverberates through the economic system to create further disadvantages for those who are not wealthy. For example, in response to the losses imposed on them by the use of asset protection trusts, banks and any other entity that offers financing (such as car or appliance dealerships) can raise the costs of borrowing. This increase in transaction costs has the largest impact on the least wealthy members of society, deepening their indebtedness and making upward mobility increasingly difficult to attain.[111] Many of the changes that have made trusts more effective as shields against the obligations of debt and taxes were spearheaded by wealth managers' activity in the political sphere.

Political impact

The effects of wealth management on political inequality are both direct and indirect. The direct impact includes the involvement of STEP and individual practitioners in lobbying legislatures and drafting laws to advance the interests of high-net-worth individuals. Wealth managers have been instrumental in "a succession of developments in the law that uniquely serve the interests of the very wealthy."[112] These include repeal of the rule against perpetuities and the development of the asset protection trust, mentioned in Chapter 4. Another well-known instance of this political activity by wealth managers occurred in the British Virgin Islands, where a law permitting a new trust structure known as VISTA (see Chapter 3), designed to attract high-net-worth clients from Asia, "was drafted by a Society of Trust and Estate Practitioners (STEP) committee headed by Chris McKenzie, the founding chairman of STEP's BVI branch."[113]

In addition to such formal interventions by STEP, individual wealth managers are often asked to collaborate in creating new financial laws offshore, as part of what Simon—an English fiduciary working in Singapore—called the strong "informal relationship between regulators and professionals." As a recent example, he noted, "the Monetary Authority of Singapore just sent me their draft trust law for comments before it was released to the public." David, the English lawyer working in Hong Kong, says that the governments he has worked with are even more direct about their desire to cater to the interests of the wealthy, via their professional representatives: "In Hong Kong, the law is very profession-driven: the professions tell the government what laws need to be made."

Wealth management thus contributes to political inequality by magnifying the "voice" and influence of the most economically privileged members of society. In addition to direct involvement in lawmaking, wealth managers contribute indirectly to political inequality by nurturing the fortunes that enable clients to influence elections and public policy—and to escape the consequences if they don't like the results. In this sense, the use of "aggressive planning techniques (tax-driven and otherwise) that are used by the very wealthy to secure and grow a fortune for untold generations to come" can become "enormously consequential for the health of a democratic polity."[114]

Wealth leads to outsize political influence because political participation is a "luxury good," available primarily to those who are not totally consumed with providing life's necessities and who can afford to pay others to care for their homes or children while they vote or engage in organizing activities.[115] In addition, the affluent are thought to be more easily mobilized to political engagement because they have more at stake in the daily decisions of their government, such as tax policies.[116] In many countries, wealth offers the opportunity to buy political influence. In corrupt regimes, this takes the form of bribery. But even where bribery is uncommon, such as in the United States, campaign contributions offer elites a legal and effective means of exerting political clout: "wealthy donors are responsible for a vastly disproportionate percentage of the funds that fuel federal elections."[117] This is a phenomenon driven by multimillion-dollar donations from private individuals, not from corporations. This pattern of disproportionate influence by the wealthy in politics is extremely widespread. A recent review of world economic and political history, covering thousands of years across Europe, Africa, and the Americas, suggests that the biggest danger of wealth inequality is not economic but rather capture by elites of the political system. The "vicious circle" of mutually reinforcing economic and political power is not driven by the income of those elites; rather, "their wealth forms the basis for the continuation of their power."[118]

In addition to wealth managers providing clients with the means to exert more than their fair share of influence over the political process, they also give high-net-worth individuals a way to escape political consequences and accountability. Thus the wealthiest Americans favor cutting the national old-age health care and pension programs (Medicare and Social Security), which are funded through federal taxation; after all, they are unlikely ever to need such public services or to experience any negative effects from those programs being cut.[119] Despite their preferences being diametrically opposed to those of the vast majority of Americans (who want both programs expanded), the wealthy have made these service cuts a key political issue in the 2016 presidential campaign because—as a recent study concluded—they are "extremely active politically" and "exert more political influence than their less fortunate fellow citizens do."[120] In other words, wealth trumps the will of the people.

Similarly, the wealthy in Brazil have shaped public policy in such a way that the country's tax code favors them dramatically, at the expense of the middle class. This occurred even under the left-wing populist regime of Luiz Inácio Lula da Silva.[121] But when insufficient government revenues meant that the roads in the major cities began to crumble and policing became dangerously inadequate, Brazil's elites did not use their political influence to remedy the situation; instead, many purchased private helicopters and employed full-time pilots to get them safely from home to work and school.[122] Their fortunes, carefully husbanded by wealth management professionals, permit them to live "in a world apart," in which they need not experience the consequences of policies and laws that benefit them at the expense of others.[123]

Most important, contemporary wealth management plans provide the richest members of society with anonymity and secrecy—both scarce in the Internet era, and increasingly valuable in light of protest movements such as Occupy Wall

Street. The use of trusts and offshore vehicles don't just make it difficult to collect taxes, debts, and penalties; they cloak political and economic privilege in a strategic veil of privacy. Individual clients can remove that veil at will, such as when making charitable donations; otherwise, their identities are obscured from public view, keeping them largely safe from opposition or accountability.

Perhaps the most significant political issue is what wealth managers' skillful use of trusts and other structures has done for the high-net-worth population as a group, by reducing public awareness of their concentration of economic power and its implications. As one legal expert put it: "The chief contribution of the trust concept has, broadly speaking, been to help in masking the extent of inequality within society. It does so by obscuring the link between private property—a key source of power—and its ultimate owners."[124] Partly as a result of wealth managers' success in keeping this information under wraps, a recent study found that Americans underestimate the extent of wealth inequality in the United States by 42 percent.[125]

STEP and changing views of inequality

STEP and individual wealth managers are well aware of their contributions to economic and political inequality. "How do you feel about preserving the wealth of the few at the expense of the majority?" asks one of STEP's training manuals for the basic credentialing course.[126] With regard to tax avoidance, the organization proudly positions wealth management as a defender of entrepreneurs against "confiscatory" and misguided welfare state politics.[127] Throughout STEP's publications, one finds statements such as the following, excerpted from the TEP course text on accounting: "Onerously high, some may say unethical, tax demands to finance generous government spending clearly act as a chill upon the entrepreneur as a creator of wealth; whereas, on the other hand, the poor may then be caught in the poverty trap and rely on state welfare handouts rather than engage in productive work."[128] In other words, STEP, as an organization, rejects the application of any negative meaning to its members' role in facilitating legal tax avoidance. On the contrary, it frames this work as a justified and even noble defense of capitalism, free markets, and competition—a position that has been largely successful in fending off governmental challenges to tax avoidance practices.[129]

However, the same accounting textbook from which the quotation above was taken also paints an unexpectedly ambivalent portrait of the profession's clientele. Just one page after this vigorous ethical defense of tax avoidance, the text goes on to say of the wealthy hypothetical entrepreneur facing "unethical" levels of taxation, "If he feels strongly enough, the individual can always opt out of the tax system and emigrate. However, few wish to go to that extreme. They want to stay in the country that they regard as home, but pay less tax. *They want to have their cake and eat it.*"[130]

The TEP course text on trust law offers a similarly mixed message about the use of asset protection trusts to help clients make their wealth debt-proof and judgment-proof. In one of the few instances where the notion of ethics is mentioned in any of the STEP training books, the text acknowledges that "there is inevitably an ethical tension involved in advising a prospective settlor who desires genuine asset protection planning."[131] While these two examples by no means offer an indictment of debt dodging or tax avoidance, they may reflect some uneasiness on the part of the profession with respect to its role in the "massive organized attempt by the richest and most powerful to take advantage of collective goods on a scale rarely seen."[132]

This ambivalence was reflected in the interviews I conducted with practitioners. All were acutely aware of the bad reputation that taints their profession in the public eye, particularly in connection with their facilitation of tax avoidance. Strangely, there was no defensiveness—either from individual practitioners I interviewed or in the STEP literature—concerning inheritance. This may reflect the widespread backlash in recent decades against ideals of equitable distribution of wealth and power, as well as the esteem accorded to all forms of "success," regardless of whether it is earned or inherited.[133] In contrast, issues of taxation and tax avoidance elicited enormous response from practitioners. Their mixed feelings on the subject lined up with the ambivalence evident from the TEP course texts.

Several shared the anger of the BVI practitioner mentioned in the appendix to Chapter 1, who expressed outrage at the profession being "vilified" and his clients painted as "immoral for not paying as much tax as some people think they should." These individuals viewed public criticism of tax avoidance as a personal injustice: a slur against their good name and good work. But many others took a dispassionate view, treating the negative perception of their activities as misguided or naive rather than malicious. Some argued, as STEP did, that tax avoidance is simply a rational response to irrational and illegitimate rules. Mark, the English practitioner based in Dubai, said, "We all believe in taxes in civilized society; they provide essential services. But it is theft by another word. When taxes get ridiculous, as they do at times, the tax avoidance industry arises." By far the most colorful rationale, however, came from Louis, the reserved and aristocratic practitioner in London. He turned the image of the rapacious tax avoider on its head by comparing his clients to harmless but sensible squirrels:

> Social democracy is creating too big demands on the wealth creators. That must be obvious to you in academia. You can't get voted in now unless you support massive entitlement programs, because too many people receive them. With the result that governments now need an ever-increasing share of GDP from the producers to fulfill their promises. So naturally the wealth creators, like squirrels collecting their nuts, are scaling back; they're saying to themselves that they don't want to collect as many nuts next year, because the government just takes them away. . . . It's nature, people don't like the fruits of their labors taken away so arbitrarily. The squirrel says, "You know what, I did pretty well last year and stashed all my nuts in that tree, but the government knows where I live and took them all away. So I'm going to bury them in the woods where no one will find them and go occasionally when no one is looking to collect them." This leads wealth creators to engage in the shadow economy, and so forth.

In other words, from Louis' perspective, the world's wealthiest people aren't benefiting from the exploitation of legal loopholes or free-riding on honest taxpayers. On the contrary, as he sees it, the wealthy are the ones being exploited. Louis and some of his colleagues see themselves as acting to mitigate this injustice. This point of view is reminiscent of one legal scholar's observation on the social impact of dynastic trusts: "Concentrating and guaranteeing property-power not only fails to impose moral obligations on the powerful, but actually encourages us to think of moral obligations owed to them."[134]

On the other hand, a significant minority of practitioners expressed some queasiness about growing wealth inequality and their own position in an "ethical gray area"—a realm of activity that is formally legal but socially illegitimate.[135] They not only were aware of their profession's reputation for doing financial "dirty work" but seemed to see that reputation as being at least partly deserved.[136] Trevor, a South African practicing in Panama, lamented having to engage in activities that "give honest people a bad name," adding: "I can understand how people outside the industry think of what we do as evil and Machiavellian." Neal, the English wealth manager working in the Cayman Islands, said with some resignation, "You've got to totally be able to suspend your own personal sense of ethics in this work." He added that he encourages his clients to engage in philanthropy, partly undoing some of the social damage done by the tax avoidance he facilitates: "It's the lack of tax paying here [offshore] that is contributing to society falling apart, so I encourage clients to make lots of charitable contributions, because that's what creates the safety net." Similarly, Elias—a Panama City practitioner who spent his university days campaigning for the rights of indigenous and impoverished Panamanians—said he engaged in a kind of informal "consciousness raising" with clients to offset or undo his work in helping them avoid taxes. In interactions with high-net-worth individuals, he tells them about Panama not only as a tax haven but also as a country divided by extreme economic inequality: "I talk about poverty in my presentations to clients, and people say, 'Are you a communist or something?' . . . When I talk about Panama, I acknowledge that our economy is booming, but also that 25 to 30 percent of our people live in poverty. I talk to people about Amartya Sen and Joseph Stiglitz. A lot of people think that's weird for someone working in the deepest part of capitalism."

Asking wealthy individuals to acknowledge inequality is not necessarily good for business. But, like Neal's efforts to encourage philanthropy among his clients, Elias' discourses on poverty seem designed to counter the "bad people doing bad things" reputation of their profession, and to resolve some of the moral ambiguities attendant upon the changing social views of wealth and wealth management.

Conclusion

As the French sociologist Rémi Clignet has written, a major challenge facing the study of inequality is "to ascertain *who* makes things endure and *how*."[137] This chapter has addressed the challenge by specifying how an elite professional group makes clients' fortunes endure, shaping broader patterns of resource distribution in the process. To understand how this occurs, it is first essential to appreciate the distinctive role of wealth, as opposed to income, in social stratification. Using the key tools described in Chapter 4—trusts, foundations, and offshore corporations—wealth management professionals intervene at three crucial points in their clients' asset accumulation cycles. First, the professionals minimize dissipation due to taxes, debts, and penalties, maximizing the surplus available for further growth. Second, wealth managers give their clients access to exclusive opportunities to reap significant profits at low risk. Third, carefully managed succession processes keep the wealth concentrated in a few hands, so that it can continue to grow undisturbed. The result is a kind of perpetual-motion machine of wealth creation: rather than allowing wealth to evaporate over three generations via the "shirtsleeves to shirtsleeves" pattern, these structures preserve and compound advantages over time.

Political power, exercised both by wealth managers and by their clients, blocks the development of laws and policies that might interfere with this wealth concentration and its broader consequences. The exercise of this power includes lobbying onshore governments, writing new laws offshore, and influencing elections in an effort to protect and enhance these accumulation strategies. The effect is not only to make the rich richer but also to undermine meritocracy, mobility, and political voice for others.

Wealth management practitioners are acutely aware of their contributions to inequality but vary widely in their moral interpretations of this role. Some are quite defensive or conscience-stricken, while others express confidence that they have justice and common sense on their side. Although wealth management is not well known and is generally overlooked by scholars and journalists, what little public awareness has developed around the profession is negative. Somewhat surprisingly, this opprobrium has centered around just one part of the professionals' involvement in wealth concentration: tax avoidance. Their contribution to inequality by means of facilitating inheritance is largely ignored, in part because of shifts in the public discourse about economic success and its justifications.[138] Exposing these areas of contradiction, omission, and ambivalence about inequality is one of the major benefits of studying a profession operating, as the Panamanian wealth manager Elias put it, "in the deepest part of capitalism."

Wealth Management and the State

THE RELATIONSHIP OF WEALTH MANAGEMENT TO STATES AND
their legal systems is surely one of the most distinctive features
of the profession. Historically, the professions have been
thought of as beholden to states: dependent upon government
licensing to legitimate professional credentials and authority,
as well as to create the markets for professional practice.[1] This
relationship is so strong that some social scientists define the
state itself in terms of its power to shape employer-employee
relations, as well as the institutions of work training and education. As a classic study explained, "The prime contingency
of professionalism is the state and its policies."[2]

This remains the case for many professions, such as law and
medicine, which one cannot practice without a state-issued li-
cense, and then only within certain state-defined boundaries.
But while other professions have traditionally depended on
the state to ratify and legitimate their power, wealth management stands in a different position. Unlike doctors and lawyers,
wealth managers have never depended upon the state for
licensing or other forms of permission to practice. While the

wealth management profession has historical roots in the United Kingdom and a professional society based in London, it grants credentials recognized worldwide, based on a paradigm that is fundamentally transnational. Although many wealth managers hold state-issued credentials in law or accounting, those are not prerequisites for practitioners. It is still possible to be a success in the profession without any state licensing or even a STEP credential. Examples in this book include Dieter, the German nobleman who enjoyed a thriving career without any formal qualifications beyond a high school diploma, and Nick, the former boatbuilder who found his way into the profession by crewing on America's Cup yachts (see Chapter 3).

Perhaps because of this unusual independence from state authority, the work of wealth management thrives by exploiting states' power—sometimes opposing it, sometimes supporting its development in particular directions. This does not mean that wealth managers are anti-state or anti-law. They have no reason to be: in fact, it would be counterproductive to dismantle state structures, because "creative compliance" is the main source of their power as experts, and the basis for their remuneration.[3] The maze of laws created by the Westphalian nation-state system, along with the paucity of international laws governing wealth and its movement, provides plenty of opportunities to create the autonomy clients desire. As Bruce, the American wealth manager working in Switzerland, defined his job, "It's all about playing cat and mouse with tax authorities around the world." Practitioners' skill lies in using state institutions, often playing them against one another, to serve clients' best interests. Their work highlights, and often exacerbates, the "lack of existing regulatory capacity at the global level"—that is, the absence of effective institutions to address gaps and conflicts in national laws with regard to global capital flows.[4]

Examining the relationship between states and wealth managers ties into ongoing debates about the extent and consequences of globalization, known as "one of the most vexed issues in all of social science."[5] On the one hand, there is recognition of a profound change occurring in the configuration of state power. Some view this as the end of the Westphalian system: "A key feature of the current epoch is the supersession of the nation-state as the organizing principle of capitalism. . . . [T]ransnational or global space is coming to supplant national spaces."[6] But "globalization skeptics" see this as excessively pessimistic about the role of the state.[7] In particular, they point to lack of coordination in the international financial system as indicating that the forces of economic globalization pose a weak challenge to the power of the state. Their viewpoint, however, may miss the development of a different kind of coordination: one based not on hard law and formal institutions but on the diffusion of professional practices, which directly and indirectly influence the laws and policies of states. Instead of producing the global convergence in financial regulations that many expected, the agency of professionals such as wealth managers has resulted in expansion of gaps and conflicts.[8] This benefits the professionals and their clients, while bringing mixed results for others.

To be sure, this process began not with wealth managers but with the states themselves loosening capital controls and making their currencies fully exchangeable, setting the institutional groundwork for the international mobility of wealth. From this followed increased international mobility of wealthy *people*, undermining a system of state authority based primarily on a fixed subject: that is, individuals who consistently inhabit a specific space within a well-defined jurisdiction.[9] Allowing capital and its owners to be more mobile gave rise to one of the novelties of globalization: "the 'lifting out' of social relations from local contexts of interaction and their restructuring across indefinite spans of time-space."[10] This contributed to the creation of an international elite, as hypermobile as their capital. As a result, wealth managers were able to expand their jurisdiction globally, increasingly specializing in cross-border transactions.

As transnational actors, wealth managers have come to play a key role in several key areas of conflict and change with respect to the nation-state system. These include challenges to the relevance of states' authority and geographical boundaries, the influence of wealthy families as competitors with state power, and the impact of international finance on developing countries, particularly in former colonial states.

Sovereignty, borders, and the purpose of the state

Conceptually, the wealth management industry draws its legitimacy and raison d'être from a very limited theory of the state. As a practical matter, the profession depends upon treating government as having a narrowly defined constellation of aims and authority. One of the textbooks for the TEP credential summarizes this view of the state as follows: "A broad aim of any government is to attract business, and to expand its economy, for the benefit of the country and its people as a whole. Thus, so far as financial services are concerned, each jurisdiction is able to mould its own legal system in such a way that makes it attractive to foreign investment."[11] Compare this with the words of the world's oldest constitution in continuous use—that of the Commonwealth of Massachusetts, which subsequently inspired the language of many national constitutions.[12] It reads: "Government is instituted for the common good; for the protection, safety, prosperity and happiness of the people; and not for the profit, honor, or private interest of any one man, family, or class of men."[13] In the view of STEP and many wealth management professionals, these two views of the state do not conflict: attracting business and foreign investment is a central part of looking after the common good, including the prosperity and happiness of the people. As Chapter 5 showed, wealth managers contribute to this effort by helping states create laws that appeal to the interests of high-net-worth individuals. In this way, they act very much in the service of the state.

But at the same time, wealth managers' advisory role in contemporary jurisdictional competition often leads to driving tax rates and regulatory restrictions down to a minimum. Wealth managers further limit state revenues through the use of trusts, foundations, and other vehicles, which make it difficult and costly for states to collect the taxes that *are* owed (see Chapter 4). This is problematic because taxation provides the funding for public services such as schools and roads— elements of the "common good" that states are supposed to ensure. Tax revenues fund regulation and other state activity, so that without tax, there is no state.[14] As the philosopher Edmund Burke once wrote, "The revenue of a state is the state."[15] In this regard, helping states reduce or eliminate taxes in order to make themselves more attractive to foreign investors would seem tantamount to helping those states cut their own throats.

Some within wealth management would argue, however, that states that follow the tax-cutting approach to jurisdictional competition can recoup their losses by other means. In this view, wealth managers help states regain some of the fiscal power they lost decades previously because of outdated policies and unintended consequences. As political scientists have pointed out, "The traditional architecture of the tax state was based on the assumption that all taxable events have a clearly identifiable place in space."[16] Compounding this is a model of property taxation based on registered ownership of land and other immovable or hard-to-move goods. Now that most private (and corporate) wealth is financial and fungible, modern states are handicapped by the difficulty of establishing ownership and tax responsibility.

Public policy has yet to catch up with reality when it comes to movable wealth. As Thomas Piketty wrote recently of tax avoidance, "This is the problem of modern nations: they still live with a system to register property that was conceived more than two hundred years ago."[17] If anything, this understates the problem. Not only have state policies failed to keep up with changes in the nature of wealth, but many states have voluntarily relinquished their power to tax effectively. Beginning in the 1950s and 1960s, many countries began removing limits on the convertibility of their currency and the amounts that could be taken outside national boundaries; some, such as the United Kingdom, were also active in encouraging the development of the offshore industry.[18]

In other words, there is an argument to be made that many of the states complaining about harmful international tax competition, particularly from offshore financial centers, are culpable in the creation of the problem. Their responsibility is a matter of both omission (failing to keep their taxation models current) and commission (relaxing currency controls and sponsoring the development of the offshore system). To many wealth management practitioners, this gives the OECD and other institutions seeking to crack down on tax avoidance the air of hypocrisy. Louis, one of the London-based wealth managers, remarked that "on the one hand, they are pro–free trade in Brussels, but they are desperate to stop it. Governments were used to pulling the strings, but now they're bankrupt and they are dependent upon the wealth creators. That really is the crux of the matter. And you've got people in Brussels desperate that there is tax leakage all over the place—that they can't control people's mobility in an era of increasingly easy jet travel, lack of border controls, et cetera."

This conflict has been particularly heated in the aftermath of the 2008 financial crisis and the subsequent euro zone banking crisis, both of which have left governments scrambling for tax revenue and eager to crack down on tax avoidance. The fiscal shortfall is so pressing that crisis-stricken countries such as Spain and Cyprus have ramped up efforts to persuade high-net-worth individuals—primarily from Russia, China, and the Middle East—to change their citizenship.[19] In return for making investments and paying tax in their new homelands, these wealthy individuals automatically get EU passports, avoiding the lengthy and uncertain bureaucratic process to which the nonwealthy are subject.[20] While legal, such cash-for-passports programs have been attacked by the European Commission as undermining the legitimacy of state authority.[21]

Other countries have taken even more extreme measures to shore up their treasuries in the face of rampant tax avoidance. For example, both Germany and the United Kingdom have paid millions to obtain stolen data: records taken illegally from private banks in Switzerland and Liechtenstein, detailing the names, addresses, and offshore holdings of wealthy clients, some of whom have illegally dodged their tax obligations.[22] However—like the sale of citizenship—this strategy has put state legitimacy and state solvency on a collision course. Although pursuing errant taxpayers on the basis of stolen data has brought a fiscal windfall to some governments, it has also led to accusations that those governments are themselves "immoral and criminal" in betraying their duty to uphold the role of law.[23] For example, when Germany paid about $5 million for data that quickly led to collection of more than $30 million in back taxes, the move was denounced in the domestic press and brought a stinging rebuke from neighboring Denmark, whose tax minister called the move an "advanced form of handling stolen goods."[24]

Some wealth managers believe their services to states offer a way out of the conflict between solvency and legitimacy. By facilitating capital mobility and by advising governments on how best to attract the business of high-net-worth individuals, wealth managers argue, they can help states compensate for tax losses through other economic channels. An empirical study in the United States seems to support this idea. When some U.S. states began abolishing the rule against perpetuities—a move that allowed trust funds to be exempted from certain federal taxes—each state that eliminated the rule attracted an additional $6 billion in trust assets, leading to an average 20 percent increase in business. While this did not raise tax revenues in these states, putting more assets under management increased the amount of fees and other rents that could be collected by the states' financial firms and financial professionals.[25]

Drew, the Canadian wealth manager based in London, argued that this phenomenon also obtains at the international level. Drew's law firm regularly advises the U.K. Parliament on legislation affecting the firm's high-net-worth clients. This work has included legal changes directed at making the country a particularly attractive place for high-net-worth foreigners to shelter their wealth tax-free, especially through the use of property investments. Said Drew, "The British economy has for twenty years been based on the inflation of property values. That's why the country is competing so hard to attract ultra-HNWIs, because those people—even if the country can't tax them—buy up the huge properties as tax shelters, and that in turn pumps up property values for everyone. And when people see their home values going up, they feel secure, and when they feel secure, they spend, and that keeps the wheels of the economy turning." The idea, according to Drew, is that the fortunes of the foreign investors who buy property in London will end up benefiting the United Kingdom economically through their (or their family's) consumption of goods and services, as well as payment of sales taxes, property taxes, and so forth. That counts as a win in the zero-sum calculus of jurisdictional competition, in which the "motive of these states is to draw rent surpluses from the income that would otherwise accrue" to other states.[26] Therefore, Drew and his colleagues advise governments on how best to capture those rents.

But does the jurisdictional competition benefit residents and citizens of the United Kingdom who are not wealthy or involved in the financial services industry? Drew's consumption-of-goods-and-services argument may not hold because many of the tax-sheltering properties owned by foreigners remain unoccupied; there is no one "home" to buy groceries or employ a full household staff.[27] And while the purchases of London real estate by high-net-worth individuals from abroad has indeed pumped up property values, this has made the city nearly unaffordable for everyone else.[28] According to one estimate, residential property valuations in London increased by 49 percent between 2009 and 2012— five times more than the growth of property values in the United Kingdom as a whole. While this is good news for those who already own London real estate, this development is widely viewed in the domestic press as a foreign "invasion."[29]

This unbalanced impact—beneficial to property owners, damaging to others—may reflect a long-standing institutional bias in the way wealth managers influence legislation. For example, some members of Drew's firm act as "Parliamentary Agents," an enormously powerful position that historically has been used to advance the interests of the wealthiest members of British society. As Drew explained, "England has fourteen Parliamentary Agents in total—[many] of them work here. PAs draft legislation and critique it; they speak in Parliament on behalf of legislation, and they are the only nonmembers allowed to address Parliament. The fourteen positions are fixed and hereditary. Where it became incredibly profitable to have Parliamentary Agents was during the railway building era—you'd get a monopoly and statutory right to certain firms to expropriate government lands and build a railway from here to Scotland. This is how private fortunes got made in the nineteenth century."

This historical role of the Parliamentary Agent is more than a matter of lobbying, as STEP does, or having the ear of a particular politician, like the London wealth manager James, who was friendly with the prime minister's father-in-law (see Chapter 3). It actually gives an institutionalized voice, at the highest levels of government, to the representatives of the richest members of society. While that once meant representing the landed gentry and railroad barons of the United Kingdom, the Parliamentary Agents at Drew's firm—and others—now typically act as a voice for the interests of high-net-worth individuals from *outside* the country.[30] One recent report on wealth management in London claimed that the profession "is not especially interested in the UK; it exists to serve 'EMEA,' a land known only to bankers: Europe, the Middle East, and Africa."[31]

Dynastic wealth as a challenge to state authority

By giving a powerful voice in lawmaking and policy to a transnational clientele, professionals are effecting a change in the balance of power between states and the wealthy. This is driven not only by direct interventions in the creation of legislation but also by the scale of accumulation that wealth management makes possible. Mark, the English practitioner in Dubai, said that as a result of skillful wealth management in the region, individuals there had become richer than anywhere else in the world: "You're into hundreds of billions of private wealth—the Dubai ruler's younger brother admitted under questioning in London court to having assets of $19 billion. That's literally equivalent to the GDP of small countries, or even European countries." In fact, that figure is more than the GDP of Malta, an EU member state, as well as fifty-one other countries elsewhere in the world.[32]

This kind of economic power gives wealthy individuals and families an unusual degree of leverage in their dealings with the countries where they place their wealth under management. For example, it has been reported that in Jersey, "superwealthy people . . . can actually negotiate the tax rates they pay" by sending their wealth managers to arrange secret deals with island officials.[33] Although Jersey's top tax bracket is set at only 20 percent, private agreements allow some wealthy individuals to pay just a fraction of the island's already low statutory rates, or to avoid paying any tax at all. The state's revenue losses from these deals have been offset in part by rising consumption taxes; partly as a result of this tax shift, 45 percent of the island's full-time residents say they have trouble paying their bills each month.[34]

The search for "freedom from democratic restraint" by the world's wealthiest people does not stop with having laws bent or made in their favor.[35] In extreme cases it means ignoring laws and state authority altogether while the state turns a blind eye. Erika, a German national who worked for Greenpeace before becoming a wealth manager in Zurich, was particularly troubled by her wealthiest clients' view of themselves as "above nationality and laws." Asked to give an example of what she meant by this, Erika related the story of an in-person consultation with a client who seemed to have found a way to ignore the laws of multiple countries with no negative consequences. The client was so powerful that he was able to extend this immunity from the law to Erika and her boss, at least for the duration of time they were working for him:

> I had to fly outside Europe with the CEO of my company to meet a client. I had switched handbags and left my passport in the bag at home. The client had sent a limo to take us to the airport in Zurich, and a private plane to take us to him. So at the airport, I discovered I didn't have my passport and told the CEO I had to go home to get it. He said, "Don't worry about it." I said, "But we're leaving Europe; I need my passport." And he said, "Really, you don't need it; you don't need to go home." So I figured okay, if the CEO tells me twice not to go get my passport, I won't press the issue, and if I get detained and stuck at the airport, so be it. So we get on the plane in Zurich, and no one checked our documents. And then when we arrived at the client's location, there was just a limo waiting to take us directly to him. Nobody asked for our passports, even when we returned to Switzerland on the client's jet. The CEO was right. These people, our wealthiest clients, are above the law. . . . It's potentially very dangerous.

As wealthy and powerful as such individuals are, they still seem to require the services of professionals like Erika. When queried about this, Erika responded that while her firm didn't make clients wealthy to begin with, it served them in other ways: by ensuring that their fortunes were protected from lawsuits, divorces, disappointed heirs, and other forces of dissipation, and by carefully guarding the clients' privacy at the same time. "They come to [our firm] for discretion and loyalty," Erika concluded.

Wealth's impact on political economy

By helping clients amass and maintain private fortunes that in some cases rival the GDP of whole nations, wealth management professionals are changing how states behave—sometimes to the detriment of state power itself, as well as to the rights and well-being of the states' residents and citizens. For example, in Jersey, the island's success in becoming a wealth management center has driven up prices for land, goods, and services, leading to significant weakening of tourism and agriculture as contributors to the island's economy.[36] This makes the country less self-sufficient economically and more vulnerable to financial downturns elsewhere in the world. Indeed, single-minded devotion to offshore finance seems to be catching up with Jersey. Its years of being a "miracle of plenty"—a low-tax welfare state—have led to a "black hole" of a budget deficit. With no alternative economic base left, the government is planning to lay off staff and cut benefits to the neediest members of the population, such as pensioners and children.[37]

The success of wealth management in freeing its clients from state authority also undercuts the overall legitimacy of that authority: if some individuals are above the law, refusing to accept everything from tax regulations to border controls, why should anyone else subject themselves to those constraints?[38] In Jersey, this crisis of state legitimacy has meant that "half those born on the island choose not to live there anymore and voting rates have plummeted as the majority of Jersey's people say they no longer trust the government or the island's judiciary."[39] But the response to such distrust has been apathy rather than resistance. This phenomenon is not unique to Jersey: in fact, the recurrence of this pattern in offshore financial centers—the hollowing out of civil society, combined with the destructive monoculture of the economy—has been dubbed "the finance curse."[40]

This was not lost on the wealth management practitioners interviewed for this study. Many wondered openly about the impact that the success of their profession might be having on society at large, and particularly on the nonwealthy. Paul, an English wealth manager practicing in Dubai, said of the tax breaks he negotiated for his internationally mobile clientele, "It becomes a vicious circle because the tax burden then increases on the people who are *not* mobile, and they get resentful and try to think up ways to avoid their taxes." In the Cook Islands, a chance encounter with a prosperous local fisherman offered me some insight into native residents' view of the wealth management industry and its impact on the nation. "They're why everyone calls us the 'Crook Islands' now; they've got our government in their pockets," he said. "I hate what they've done to my country."

Wealth managers might therefore be said to have a leading role in creating a new "political economy of wealth," not only shaping how state power is used (or not used, as in Erika's example) but also influencing the kinds of constituencies to which states respond. Most surprising is that the intervention of wealth management professionals seems to shift states' attention toward the interests of entities who are unable to vote for them, at the expense of those who can. Louis, the London-based practitioner, described the contours of this configuration of power: "I think what people fail to realize is that governments are now just little parishes. Who do you think is more powerful—Procter & Gamble or the government of France? P&G, of course. They can set down their business anywhere in the world they please. *And high-net-worth individuals are the same way.* Governments know that to some extent, so you've got people moving around the world in response to things like tax incentives offered by the U.K. or the U.S. or wherever." The tax incentives Louis spoke of are frequently the creation of professionals just like him (see Chapters 4 and 5). This affects politics by influencing the mobility patterns of the ultra-wealthy. As one recent study put it, "Tides of financial capital flow around the world in response to small changes in these kinds of incentives."[41]

The individuals Louis had in mind are a group whose wealth makes them, for all practical purposes, "citizens of the world." They have a passport, or maybe several, but they can renounce or acquire citizenship at will, because of their economic power. In fact, recent crackdowns on offshore tax avoidance have resulted in a record number of citizenship renunciations.[42] Just like firms that give up their onshore incorporation in order to reincorporate offshore and save on taxes, an increasing number of high-net-worth individuals have responded to states' efforts to impose the duties of citizenship by fleeing the "sovereign national cage."[43] In a process usually directed by wealth managers, high-net-worth individuals simply acquire a more convenient citizenship, usually in low- or no-tax jurisdictions.[44] Thus, through the intervention of professionals like Louis, high-net-worth individuals gain many of the same tools for avoiding tax and regulation as multinational corporations, and therefore the ability to amass power rivaling that of nation-states.

Croesus unbound

The power struggle between states and their wealthiest citizens is nothing new. Since the first trustee helped a feudal lord evade the king's tax and inheritance laws, the forebears of the wealth management profession have played a central role in the struggle (see Chapter 2). In the nineteenth and twentieth centuries, the nascent wealth management profession not only helped keep its clients rich but also provided the template for the power elite in its relationship to society and the state. In particular, institutions developed to preserve dynastic wealth became the models for legitimating the ongoing domination of wealthy families in societies that had nominally dedicated themselves to meritocracy, capitalism, and equal opportunity. The trust and the fiduciary role "supplied an ideology of moral leadership by upper-class institutions and their personnel in a democratic polity and market economy . . . in which the upper class serves as a fiduciary to society."[45] This kept a small cohort of families at the head of the institutional triad of family, market, and state despite broad political and economic changes that would seem to threaten their dominance.

In some cases, this was effected by opening elite family institutions to the public. Organizations that had once served as an independent power base for wealthy families, providing them some autonomy from state control, were later deployed for "structural expansion of the fiduciary role" into functions previously carried out by the state, such as banking, education, and health.[46] The models provided by the trust structure and its fiduciaries provided the means for wealthy families to challenge states in the provision of these major institutional services. The influence of dynastic wealth on states made this surprisingly easy to achieve. For example, in the United States, the wealthy have long been permitted to create their own banks, in the form of an "unregulated or 'lightly regulated' trust company."[47] This is the how the Bessemer Trust and the Rockefeller Trust (now Rockefeller & Co.), which originated to serve the Phipps and Rockefeller families alone, subsequently became major wealth management firms directing $150 billion in assets from clients worldwide.[48]

Perhaps surprisingly, contemporary wealth management advice is quite explicit in encouraging high-net-worth families to continue in this vein, developing institutions that rival those created by states or markets. A 1997 book frequently referenced by participants in this study as the "bible" of the profession advises families that preserving their fortunes requires "the creation and practice of a system of representative governance," preferably constituted as a republic.[49] *Family Wealth:*

Keeping It in the Family was written by a second-generation wealth manager and is often quoted by other books on wealth management.[50] Many participants in this study said they bought the book in bulk to give to clients, in order to educate them about the strategy of long-term wealth preservation.

This strategy involves having high-net-worth families create written constitutions to govern themselves, and to form representative assemblies that meet regularly to make joint decisions on the management of familial wealth and institutions. These include a "family bank," which "provides means for a family's wealth to be leveraged by making loans available to family members on terms not available commercially."[51] The loans are to be subject to formalized conditions, such as providing a business plan, and are to be awarded based on "their contribution to the family's long-term wealth preservation plan."[52] In other words, families are advised to create institutions that mirror those provided by the state or the market, but with a crucial difference: the family institutions are designed with the sole purpose of making those particular families wealthier over time. The result is a "private welfare regime" that competes with the state not only by offering services to a single family but also by permitting sufficient accumulations of wealth and sufficiently enduring institutions to engage in public-facing activities.[53]

These activities include philanthropy, which has been by far the most effective and popular means of competing with the state, and institutionalizing the interests of high-net-worth individuals in the public sphere. Philanthropy not only allowed trusts to endure forever—before the widespread repeal of the rule against perpetuities, charitable trusts were always exempt—but also allowed wealthy families to create institutions that posed a significant challenge to the ideology and legitimacy of the state. At the head of philanthropic trusts, elites and their agents (the wealth managers) could "become private fiduciaries, not of family fortunes, but of the public order in general."[54] The effects were sometimes very positive: many of the world's leading universities, museums, and hospitals bear the names of wealthy benefactors who created these institutions by means of philanthropic trusts or foundations.

On the other hand, wealthy families—aided by wealth managers—have also created institutions that intentionally compete with the policies and programs of elected governments and other public governance structures. In the United States, the belief that "big government" has failed or that private programs are more effective and efficient than their public sector counterparts has led some high-net-worth families and individuals to use philanthropic trusts and foundations to address social problems such as education and poverty, without public accountability and often with mixed results.[55] In less developed countries, wealthy philanthropists have stepped into what they see as a governance gap, bypassing the public sector in the belief that it is incompetent or inefficient. This has created the perception in some developing states that a kind of neoimperial agenda is being advanced in the guise of charity. For example, sponsorship of malaria research by the Bill and Melinda Gates Foundation has been characterized as a "cartel" that undermines national institutions in developing countries, with "dangerous consequences on the policy-making process in world health."[56]

Development and the postcolonial conundrum

To questions this chapter might raise about whether wealth managers support or undermine state authority, all the answers seem to be yes; the impact depends on which states are involved, and when. For some states, engaging with wealth managers to maximize their jurisdictions' appeal to high-net-worth individuals can be lucrative. In particular, the parameters of interstate tax competition tend to favor the smaller countries because "small countries have little domestic tax base to lose but a lot of foreign tax base to win."[57] For such countries, lowering or eliminating taxes may not cost them much in economic terms. On the contrary, attracting the custom of high-net-worth individuals can turn an "economic backwater"—as the British Virgin Islands were described up until the mid-1970s—into a financial center.[58] The BVI, which eliminated most taxes and created an innovative law to help international businesses avoid tax in their home jurisdictions, now hosts 40 percent of the world's offshore business, representing hundreds of billions of dollars in corporate and private wealth.[59] However, as will be explained below, this economic surge has been a mixed blessing for the local people of the BVI, who have seen their tax burden increased and their democratic process compromised.

Wealth management, globalization, and postcolonial development

If global financialization is "a decidedly Anglo-American phenomenon," that is due in large measure to the impact of trusts and the fiduciary role, which spread with the expansion of the British Empire in the eighteenth and nineteenth centuries.[60] As a direct result of colonialism, the trust and the concept of trusteeship—core tools of the wealth management profession—diffused into the legal systems of every imperial territory. The remnants of that framework can still be observed in today's leading offshore financial centers, most of which are current or former British territories, including Singapore, Hong Kong, the Channel Islands, Bermuda, the Cayman Islands, and the British Virgin Islands. As one scholar put it nearly a century ago, "Wherever the Common Law penetrates, it carries with it its younger sister Equity along with the whole apparatus of Trusts and the distinction of legal and equitable ownership."[61]

These former colonial jurisdictions are now where many innovations in the law and tools of wealth of management are taking place.[62] In a sense, many of the independence movements of the 1950s and 1960s simply led to ex–colonial states becoming unofficial colonies of global finance, led by the former imperial powers. Prior to their independence, many colonies were used by imperial elites to shelter their wealth from taxation in their home countries.[63] Once the colonies were separated politically from the imperial powers, elites found themselves in need of new tax shelters, particularly since onshore marginal tax rates at the time could be upward of 90 percent.[64]

Perhaps unsurprisingly, postcolonial policy then focused on developing those new countries as international finance and free trade centers, whose primary attraction would be their low tax rates combined with their legacy legal systems from the European powers. Elites' fiscal motivations dovetailed nicely with the prevailing political sentiments of the time. Several former imperial states, notably the United Kingdom and the Netherlands, were "uncomfortable in their anachronistic role as colonial masters and . . . support[ed] offshore aspirations" of their former colonies.[65]

Building the financial sector, which required little infrastructure compared to other industries, was seen as the quickest way to develop the colonies and make them self-sufficient economically. Trevor, who now runs a wealth management practice in Panama City, played a leading role in this process: "I was sent by the British government to Turks and Caicos in 1969 to look at the financial service laws and establish a financial services commission. Part of my remit at that time was, 'These islands are costing the British taxpayer a fortune, so we want you to encourage offshore banking and offshore corporations to develop economic independence there.'" The Turks and Caicos became politically independent in the mid-1970s, and the territory now reaps 30 percent of its GDP from the financial services sector.[66]

For small countries with few other options for economic self-sufficiency, becoming a provider of wealth management services looks like a very attractive shortcut to economic independence. As a result, many offshore governments act not only as regulators of their financial services industry but also as builders of that industry, to promote the economic well-being of their countries. Thus, a financial regulator in the Seychelles—a native Seychelloise—described how her agency created the infrastructure to make the island more competitive in the international arena: "Yes, we are trying to grow and develop the industry. . . . [W]e do it through an agency we created, the Seychelles Institute of Management. The teachers there include regulators. . . . Like STEP, the Institute offers a foundation certificate in the offshore business world to teach locals about the industry." Strategies like this have helped to make the Seychelles the richest country in Africa.[67] The island's success in the offshore business, and the pride some indigenous people have in this achievement, suggests why the OECD's efforts to blacklist tax havens engaged in "harmful tax competition" were criticized as "fiscal colonialism" and "economic imperialism."[68]

The more that capital becomes globally mobile, the greater advantage small postcolonial states derive from enforcing their territorial boundaries and sovereign independence. For instance, the geographical remoteness of the Cook Islands is a major factor in its appeal as the leading jurisdiction for asset protection trusts. That location, plus its strategic detachment from the web of international treaties that once made Switzerland a financial powerhouse enable it to rebuff international pressure with impunity and provide it with an unbroken record of success (see Chapter 4). Location makes it possible for the Cooks and other remote tax havens to make good on the possibilities offered by sovereignty, the most important of which is the authority to recognize no laws but their own. As the case of land-locked Switzerland shows, states that are more centrally located sometimes find geographical convenience a liability: it can enmesh them in the international legal and financial system, making it easier to bend them to the will of external forces.

Panama, a former colony of Spain, and later under partial control of the United States, now exercises its sovereign rights on a basis similar to that of the Cook Islands. Its distinctive geographical characteristics give it the ability to withstand pressures from the OECD and the United States to curtail its involvement in the tax haven business. As Nick, an Englishman who now works as a wealth manager in Panama City, explained: "The OECD threatens to blacklist countries that don't share tax information, but . . . Panama has leverage. It has something called the Retaliation Act—allowing the country to use economic leverage to fight back against attacks. In practice, that means shutting down the Canal. This is especially important with the U.S., which has had a Big Brother relationship with Panama for more than a century. So Panama has a credible threat to use against strong-arming from the OECD and America: the country can shut down the economy of the U.S. East Coast if they want." This institutionalized resistance to international pressure—in the form of the Retaliation Act—comes out of a distinctively postcolonial mindset, one that treats engagement with offshore finance and the wealth management profession as an assertion of political independence and national pride.

Many wealth managers who participated in this study saw themselves as playing a vital and very positive role in the economic development of former colonies. They described their work as a private-sector counterpart to the mission of international development agencies. Steve, one of the English wealth managers based in Hong Kong, was dismayed that this aspect of the profession was so poorly understood: "Without our profession, there wouldn't be the large pools of capital available to fuel economic development. So many of us, if not all, see our work as primarily about helping people—not just our clients, but more generally by helping maintain capital flows for investment and economic growth. But we can't get this message out effectively. We have, by the nature of our work, cultivated privacy and discretion, so the profession is totally unprepared to respond to the claims being made about us and about the industry. . . . [W]e cannot win publicly, let's face it."

It was not only white Europeans such as Steve who voiced this perspective. Wealth managers who were natives of the countries where they practiced expressed similar views. For example, Arjun—a native Mauritian of Indian ancestry—said that he was puzzled by the "negative image" of the profession and its offshore activities. Without wealth managers promoting the tax treaty between Mauritius and India, and helping clients use it, he said, "maybe India wouldn't have gotten the investment it has gotten in the last ten years." Jin, a former law professor now practicing wealth management in his native Hong Kong, made a similar observation about the impact of his work. By helping wealthy Hong Kong families get wealth offshore, to be invested in African natural resources and the New York Stock Exchange, "we provide an efficient workaround so that our country can develop economically while our institutions catch up; we don't want to wait generations for our economy and political system to mature while the world passes us by."

However, this narrative of positive contributions to postcolonial economic development is undercut by evidence from the many former colonies that have not entered the business of wealth management and offshore financial services. Such countries have frequently been driven into further financial hardship by their elites' use of tax havens abroad. For instance, capital flight from Nigeria—a former British colony—has cost the country more than $300 billion in lost tax revenues, a sum that would pay the nation's foreign debts several times over.[69] More than one-quarter of Nigeria's $82 billion in private wealth is currently located in just two places: British real estate and Swiss bank accounts.[70]

This is consistent with larger patterns in global capital flows. Most of the world's new wealth is being created outside of Europe and North America, but much of it ends up in those traditional centers of wealth management activity.[71] In this way, wealth management helps undermine some developing states while assisting elites in those countries to develop independent "power bases" offshore—ensuring the growth of their private fortunes at the expense of their less fortunate countrymen.[72]

Hacking sovereignty

One of the less appreciated paradoxes of globalization is that while wealth managers help make offshore financial centers "zones of ultra-freedom" for international capital, the countries themselves are "often highly repressive places."[73] Some have compared the situation that of the U.S. naval base at Guantanamo Bay, saying that offshore is to the former colonial powers as the Cuban site is to the United States: such locales allow sponsoring countries to "do offshore what is illegal onshore."[74] Like the overseas "black sites" where illegal U.S. operations have been conducted in the war on terror, "tax havens have the protection and support of the major countries that sponsor them, but sufficient independence for their sponsors to claim that they are not their responsibility and hence are beyond their control."[75] For instance, the Cayman Islands were instrumental in making possible the Iran-Contra affair of the 1980s, in which the United States routed the proceeds of illegal arms sales to Iran through Cayman accounts to fund an illegal war in Nicaragua.[76] This is the political equivalent of the economic "shell game extraordinaire" mentioned in Chapter 1.[77] In addition to serving as "secrecy jurisdictions" for wealthy individuals and families, offshore financial centers offer plausible deniability to some onshore states— like the United States in the Iran-Contra affair, or in the more recent scandal over "extraordinary rendition" of suspected terrorists—which contributes to the growth of "non-locatable structures of domination."[78] A counterpart of economic globalization, this constellation of power between offshore and onshore governments in many ways reinscribes colonial relations without any of the formal mechanisms. It therefore lacks even the degree of accountability and responsibility that once characterized the relationship of governing powers to their colonies.

Of course, the phenomenon of the captured state raises a question: captured by whom? The answer seems to be that the state has been captured not necessarily by former colonial governments but by a "transnational class" that includes high-net-worth individuals, with elite professionals such as wealth managers acting as their agents. The professionals gain the cooperation, or at least the acquiescence, of local elites through quid pro quo. For example, R. Allen Stanford (of the "Baby Mama Trust" discussed in Chapter 4) essentially bought the Caribbean island of Antigua by making "loans" to the government: this meant that in return for providing $30 million to build a hospital, for which the political leadership could take credit publicly, Stanford received numerous legal and economic concessions. Ultimately, Stanford's personal wealth swelled to $2.2 billion—nearly double the GDP of Antigua itself—and he became the second-largest employer on the island, as well as the owner of its primary newspaper. In return, Antigua's native political elites enriched themselves and held on to political power by seeming to spread largesse (covertly funded by Stanford) to the public.[79]

In scenarios such as these, state power increasingly serves the interests of people who are neither residents nor citizens of the state, and "there is little to no risk that democratic politics will intervene and interrupt the business of making (or taking) money."[80] In practice, the political climate of offshore financial centers means that the rights of local people are often curtailed when they interfere with the preferences of transnational capital and its representatives. In addition, inquiry and transparency are discouraged through the use of detention, deportation, and threats to journalists and researchers.[81] And when all else fails, local elites can play the imperialism card, claiming that any questions about undue influence of the financial industry on their country's politics and economy are an affront to their agency as citizens of an independent nation. This rhetorical strategy proved highly effective in staving off the OECD's attempt to blacklist some offshore financial centers in the early part of this century.[82]

Much the same way a computer connected to the Internet can be hacked to send out spam or spread viruses under remote direction—usually without the awareness of the computer's owner—the evidence from tax havens suggests that states can be hacked so that they become instruments of foreign elites. This process has been described more formally as follows: "A transnational bourgeoisie exercises its class power through a dense network of supranational institutions and relationships that increasingly bypass formal states, and in conjunction, through the utilization of national governments as territorially-bound juridical units (the interstate system), which are transformed into transmission belts and filtering devices."[83] The British Virgin Islands—which is now one of the world's leading offshore finance centers—offers a vivid case study of this phenomenon.

A captured state?

In 1984, the British Virgin Islands passed the International Business Corporation (IBC) Act, which radically transformed the offshore financial industry and catapulted the BVI into its current position as one of the leading tax havens in the world.[84] How the law came into being makes for an interesting illustration of the relationship between states, as representatives of the local public interest, and wealth management professionals, as the representatives of the narrower set of interests belonging to high-net-worth individuals from around the world. The IBC Act was created in response to the United States' cancellation of its double-taxation treaty with the BVI, a change that threatened to bring about a dramatic downturn in the islands' economy. But the act was not drafted by the legislators of the BVI itself. Instead, "the bulk of the work was done by . . . a tax barrister from London," with help from "a

Wall Street lawyer."[85] The law was written in the "record time" of six months; the BVI's lawmaking body then passed a special resolution allowing the act to become law in one day.[86] This prevented any public debate from taking place. In fact, one of the government ministers present said explicitly, "I do not see the need for any debate."[87] And thus a piece of legislation written primarily by English and American professionals became law in the BVI with no input from members of the public.

The STEP literature portrays this kind of legislative process as an advantage of working with small offshore states: "Being small and tightly focused on finance allows jurisdictions to amend laws and rules quickly, taking advantage of changes in the financial industry. Large diversified economies must consider and negotiate with many varied interests in order to make any changes."[88] Considering and negotiating with varied interests might be considered a sign of a healthy and functioning democracy. But such a process also takes time and raises uncertainty about outcomes, creating uneasiness among foreign investors.

The BVI's readiness to remove such inconveniences can be measured in part by its willingness to subsume its own culture and institutions to the preferences of some high-net-worth individuals. In 1988 an Australian accountant working in Hong Kong "begged, bullied or cajoled (history does not record which)" a BVI government official to open up the country's corporate registry office on August 8 so that Chinese clients could incorporate BVI companies on what was for the Chinese a supremely lucky date: 8/8/88.[89] Ordinarily, all government offices would have been closed on that day as part of the country's annual three-day celebration of the abolition of slavery. But the offshore business created new priorities for the islands, superseding the importance once accorded to recognizing their freedom from one of colonialism's most pernicious institutions. That this maneuver took place through coordination between professionals based in two former British colonies illustrates the workings of what some have described as a new form of stealth imperialism, embodied in "Britain's empire of tax havens—from Gibraltar to Jersey, from the Cayman Islands to the British Virgin Islands—on which the sun never sets."[90]

In subsequent years, to protect the interests of the wealth management industry and its clients, the BVI has repeatedly rebuffed requests for information from onshore states conducting tax evasion and criminal investigations. The BVI is not unique in this respect: as Chapter 4 discussed, this practice is also common in the Cook Islands. But unlike the Cooks, the BVI has signed a number of treaties pledging to exchange information with other jurisdictions about its offshore clientele. In spite of these agreements, "few foreign requests actually lead to the real beneficiaries being identified. Fifty-nine French requests have gone unheeded."[91]

Thus the BVI government's postcolonial development strategy could be described in lay terms as making the country as hospitable as possible for the wealth management industry and its clients—even if that means abandoning the country's own institutions and treaties. In addition to the political implications of this strategy, it inevitably shapes economic and cultural conditions for locals. On the one hand, the offshore finance business makes them better off than their neighbors:

British Virgin Islanders are said to "enjoy a standard of living far higher than on other Caribbean islands."[92] At least 60 percent of the country's GDP comes from offshore finance; Sherman, a local practitioner, said the figure was 70 percent.[93] Much of this is directly attributable to the IBC Act. The legislation has proved so appealing to foreign high-net-worth individuals and firms that the BVI has captured a 40 percent market share of the offshore business globally, including at least $615 billion in IBC assets.[94] In light of the islands' success, the language of the IBC Act has been "copied (often verbatim) by other jurisdictions seeking to build finance industries."[95]

Yet local people cannot use the laws and services they provide to foreigners: for instance, no BVI International Business Corporation is permitted to trade or conduct business with any citizen of the islands. And when personal and corporate income taxes were abolished in 2004, in order to make the BVI even more attractive for potential IBC users, another law that same year shifted the fiscal burden of the state downward. Since passage of the Payroll Act of 2004, each local paycheck has been docked 8 percent. Even more telling, the most powerful and best-paid jobs in the offshore industry are still dominated by white male expats from the United Kingdom, North America, and South Africa.[96] Thus opportunities for local people to gain upward mobility are highly constrained within the offshore industry by nationality, gender, and race.

In every office where I conducted interviews in the BVI— as well as in the Seychelles and many other tax haven islands—the client-facing jobs were almost completely dominated by white men from English-speaking countries, while the back-office work was done by local people of color, mostly women. Constance, an Afro-Caribbean lawyer who is unusual in occupying one of those client-facing jobs in the BVI, said that "the industry is run internationally and run by international people—English or South African. Something like 80 to 90 percent of those involved in the trust industry are English. So at least one of my colleagues would describe it as a recolonization." In a nod to the leading role of missionaries in colonial history, Constance added, "With the English people who come out here to practice, they are bringing STEP with them in a sort of evangelical way."

In another indication of whose interests are being served by the inroads that wealth management has made in the BVI, a recent eyewitness account from a high school in the capital city included the following dialogue between a teacher and her young students—all people of color, judging from the accompanying photo:

> "The Virgin Islands aim to protect the secrecy and assets of investors who base their companies here," the students chant with one voice.
>
> "Who collects taxes?" Scatliffe-Edwards [the teacher] asks. "Governments, isn't that right?"
>
> "Yes!"
>
> "Do people like paying taxes?"
>
> "No!"
>
> "So don't they have the right to choose to pay their taxes wherever they're lowest?"
>
> "Yes!"
>
> "Freedom of choice is a citizen's fundamental right," she concludes professorially. "And they're right to choose the Virgin Islands."[97]

This dialogue occurs within the context of a course on finance, but the ideological elements seem designed to "hack sovereignty" by making the voting public of the BVI less likely to develop a critical perspective on the offshore financial industry and its impact on their society. So while the country remains a democracy in formal terms, its democratic process appears to be distorted by the power of wealth management and its clientele.

Conclusion

The events leading to the passage of the IBC law in the British Virgin Islands offer a useful glimpse into the effects of globalized wealth on state power. They also show how power relations associated with the colonial era can be reinscribed through offshore finance and the work of wealth managers. The role of expatriate professionals in writing the law and the collaboration of BVI officials in getting it passed without debate illustrate the observation that onshore and offshore are not opposing forces, but rather "mutually dependent and relative spaces."[98]

The case of the IBC Act also brings to the fore a question implicit throughout this chapter: who benefits from such uses of sovereignty and professional expertise? As Chapter 1 mentioned, professions have historically been expected to justify their own privileges in terms of "the special importance of their work for society and the common weal."[99] Likewise, democratic legislatures, such as that of the BVI, are supposed to represent the will and best interests of all the country's citizens. To be sure, the islands benefit economically from their role in offshore finance—to the tune of more than half the revenues coming into government coffers each year. But their democracy, and even their educational system, seems to be unduly influenced by wealth managers who represent clients with no connection to the islands and no real stake in the well-being or development of their people.

These dual effects of the profession on offshore states may account for the love-hate relationship wealth management can engender among the locals of those countries. On the one hand, the profession brings with it economic prosperity, at least in the short term, but on the other hand, the price it demands in return seems to include surrender of many key institutions. In the long run, states that accept this Faustian bargain can end up economically bereft and politically dysfunctional if their benefactors fall on hard times: Antigua, for example, lost 10 percent of its GDP and 25 percent of its tourism revenues "overnight" after Allen Stanford's financial fraud collapsed.[100] Recent reports suggest that Jersey is similarly endangered as its offshore finance industry declines. Its economy is said to be "heading for bankruptcy," and its political, educational, and social institutions have been severely weakened by reliance on offshore finance.[101] Whether these nations can recover after giving away so much to the service of transnational wealth remains to be seen.

As one scholar of the offshore world put it, "Globalization is taking place . . . not at the expense of the state or sovereignty—it is taking place at the expense of popular sovereignty."[102] This could equally well characterize the continued challenge that wealthy families pose to state authority, overriding publicly accountable institutions to create their own models of governance through philanthropic trusts. These efforts gain their legitimacy, as well as their organizational effectiveness, through the model of fiduciary management of trusts—the precursors to today's wealth management profession. Contemporary wealth managers continue this tradition by advising their clients on creating their own banks and other tools that provide wealthy families with zones of autonomy from state authority, as well as the capital to mount a meaningful challenge to state institutions.

Yet these activities have by no means made the nation-state irrelevant. Instead, through the agency of actors such as wealth management professionals, state power has been "hacked" so that it serves the interests of people who are neither residents nor citizens. In offshore states that are nominally democracies, contributions to the common good are secondary outcomes of laws and policies primarily oriented to the owners of transnational capital. To the question of whether wealth management enhances or undermines state power, the answer seems to be both, depending upon what is most advantageous to individual practitioners, their clients, and their profession. Such instability of alliances seems to be a norm of globalization, along with the increasing divide between the super-rich and everyone else. As one recent study put it, "Modern plutocracy is just a set of ever-shifting alliances among rich organizations and individuals whose interests overlap sufficiently for them to find it useful to cooperate from time to time, as well as compete."[103]

To be sure, competition has long been part of the international political economy. But until fairly recently, a measure of state power was the ability to *repress* contenders.[104] What has changed in the contemporary setting is that co-optation, rather than repression, seems to be the dominant dynamic. Instead of an open struggle for dominance, the agents of transnational elites (with wealth managers playing a leading role) are executing one silent, bloodless coup after another. Particularly offshore, this process of state capture seems to be proceeding with great success.

Onshore, there may be more reason for optimism. A recent study reports Israel's success in co-opting wealth management professionals and using them to crack down on illegal activity—including tax evasion—by high-net-worth individuals. Lacking the personnel necessary to track down all of Israel's tax evaders, the Israeli Revenue Authority persuaded the government to create legislation altering the cost/benefit calculus for both professionals and their clients. Clients now have fewer incentives to work with foreign wealth managers, while Israeli practitioners can now profit from ensuring tax compliance as much as they once profited from facilitating avoidance. The study concludes, "Regulators thus split apart the usual coalition of advisors and their clients, creating in its stead a pro-compliance coalition of advisers and regulators."[105]

Whether these innovations can be adapted to other national contexts remains to be seen. Some argue that Israel is a special case due to traditionally high levels of social solidarity; others point out that recent opinion polling among Israelis shows that social solidarity is "quite low," particularly when it comes to economic inequality and measures to combat it.[106] The latter suggests that Israel may indeed offer a useful precedent for some onshore states seeking to stop tax leakage from their boundaries.

‹ **7** ›

Conclusion

"THE SECRET POINT OF MONEY AND POWER," WROTE JOAN
Didion, "is neither the things that money can buy nor power
for power's sake . . . but absolute personal freedom, mobility,
privacy."[1] The crucial insight of this book is that professionals
make these goals attainable. That is, their application of a
particular form of financial-legal expertise to money management provides freedom, mobility, and privacy to the high-net-
worth individuals of the world. Wealth managers secure and
maintain these privileges for their clients through the strategic
use of trusts, foundations, and corporations. Tracing the development of these practices in the making of a global profession
has been one of this book's main objectives.

Another has been to examine the implications of wealth
management for social organization. I contend that this form
of professional work has an impact far beyond its small client
base of high-net-worth individuals. The data suggest that,
given the size of the capital flows they control and their role
in legislative processes, wealth managers wield significant
influence on social institutions—including families and

markets—and on broader patterns of social structure, such as inequality. These professionals are often at the forefront of conflict and change in these areas of social life, since their work straddles the boundaries of public and private spheres, linking dynastic formations to the worldwide political economy.

By directing the placement of the largest private fortunes in the world, wealth managers influence the whole "institutional triad" of markets, states, and families. In the economic realm, they have contributed to modern finance taking its current multiterritorial form, creating what has been termed a new era of "fiduciary capitalism."[2] The complexity of the international financial markets works in favor of the profession and is one reason that it has been so politically active: both to assert its jurisdictional claims and to exploit the conflicts and gaps among the laws of individual nation-states. As one study of the professions pointed out, "Simple problems and obvious solutions are not conducive to the monopolization of expertise."[3] Wealth management thrives on the legal and organizational intricacies of moving clients' fortunes around the world; to accomplish this, practitioners have become institutional innovators, adapting old financial structures to new conditions and even (re)writing the laws of some jurisdictions.[4]

Yet the workings of wealth management, as well as its impact on social organization, have passed largely unnoticed by scholars. I will try to rectify the omission by drawing out the implications of this professional practice for major issues of social, economic, and political interest. The remainder of this chapter reviews the ways that a better understanding of wealth management can provoke new insights on inequality, the family, globalization, the professionalization process, and state authority. I will conclude with comments on the future of wealth management and recommendations for policy makers.

Contributions to theory and research

Inequality

Inequality is rightly a topic of intense contemporary discourse, and for the first time in generations, scholarly research is shifting its focus toward the upper end of the stratification spectrum.[5] This study builds on that momentum and moves the debate forward in two ways: first, by shifting attention from income to wealth, and second, by offering a finer-grained understanding of agency in the development of stratification systems—that is, explanations of who makes inequality happen, and how.

All the available data indicate that inequality based on wealth is of far greater magnitude than that based on income and that, thanks to the kind of interventions outlined in Figure 5.1, wealth inequality is multiplying itself at a much faster rate.[6] And yet, for a variety of reasons outlined in Chapter 5, we know very little about this problem. This book has argued for a revaluation of the role of wealth in stratification research, on the grounds that it captures far more of what really matters about inequality than income does. While income may fluctuate from year to year, wealth stabilizes. Wealth also provides the basis for long-term investments in education, housing, health care, and other factors that can have profound, multigenerational effects on individuals' positions in the social structure. Finally, wealth can be inherited; as Thomas Piketty and others have shown, the importance of inherited wealth for locking in positions of socioeconomic privilege has grown significantly in recent years.[7] Even economists who study income inequality acknowledge that the significance of their findings lies partly in how income shapes wealth accumulation over time.[8] Showing precisely how professionals nurture and expand wealth inequality—against the forces of dissipation and the "shirtsleeves to shirtsleeves" pattern—has been a major theme of this book.

By examining the interventions of wealth managers in their clients' fortunes, the study has provided an unusually detailed look at the workings of agency in producing larger patterns of stratification. While other research on inequality has focused mainly on structures, this study has examined people who create those structures. As one historical review of wealth and inheritance put it, "money makes money" not because accumulation is natural or inevitable but because rich people can afford the best investment advisers, the best accountants, and the best lawyers—in short, the best suite of wealth management professionals.

This book contends that to understand the dynamics of inequality, it is crucial to examine the actors who shape the larger institutions. Doing so required a long-term investment in "immersion ethnography," as described in the appendix to Chapter 1. In quantitative analyses of inequality, the role of agency is often obscured. But by undergoing the wealth management training course over two years and then "following the money" and the professionals around the world to eighteen different countries, I was able to piece together the intricate web of actions and interactions that underpin the macro structure of global wealth stratification.

One implication the study holds for future research is the significance of inheritance as a mechanism in the growth of inequality. While the special privileges of the rich in terms of tax avoidance and investment advice get the bulk of scholarly and popular attention, this study suggests that these only set the stage for the most structurally significant event: the intergenerational transmission of wealth. By turning one generation's surplus (created perhaps through tax avoidance and special investment opportunities) into a dynastic fortune, wealth managers contribute to the hardening of class divisions over time. Using trusts, offshore firms, and foundations, professionals can ensure that inequality endures and grows in a way that becomes difficult to reverse short of revolution. These resulting concentrations of private wealth, in turn, enable high-net-worth individuals to continue shaping the future in their favor by "buying" the versions of political and economic organization most favorable to themselves.

The degree to which professional intervention has succeeded in reconcentrating wealth in a handful of powerful families is in some ways suggestive of a return to feudal conditions—albeit without the noblesse oblige that once imposed a sense of responsibility on elites to feed, house, and clothe those living under their rule. It is not just the extent of wealth concentration but the way it has been achieved that so strikingly blends the medieval and modern. Trusts, of course, not only survived the Middle Ages but have come to play a vital role in contemporary global finance, both for private individuals and for public corporations.[9] More surprisingly, legal-financial innovations within the traditional trust structure, led by wealth managers themselves, have mainly served to create new pathways to stratification structures that, if not feudal, hark back at least to the Gilded Age.[10]

For example, the Special Trusts Alternative Regime law of 1997 in the Cayman Islands offers a modern route to reestablishing entail and primogeniture, the centuries-old practices ensuring that land and other assets would be passed down within families, indivisibly, to an heir designated by the settlor—usually the firstborn son.[11] While these practices are now illegal in most onshore states, STAR trusts offer wealthy families a contemporary workaround: assets held in the trusts are "locked in," meaning that beneficiaries have no right to sell them, and often cannot challenge the terms of the trust in court.[12] The major difference between STAR trusts and the medieval trust is that while the latter could contain only family lands, the former can contain any kind of asset, including stocks, bonds, and—most commonly now—family businesses.[13] But like the heir to a landed estate in centuries past, the beneficiary of a STAR trust is bound to a perpetual family dynasty under highly specific terms, making him "inherited in a way by his inheritance" rather than the other way around.[14]

Families

The case of STAR trusts points up a paradox of wealth management vis-à-vis the family as a social institution: as professionals, wealth managers represent the sort of expert authority described by Max Weber, but their work serves to reproduce

within the families they serve the kind of tribal solidarity ana-
lyzed by Émile Durkheim. In some cases this may mean providing recognition for interpersonal ties that are meaningful
to clients but which may have no legal standing, such as relationships with other adults not bound by marriage, or with
children born out of wedlock. Through the use of trusts, offshore corporations, and foundations, those relationships can
be acknowledged economically—for example, through a lifetime income, provision for living expenses, or an inheritance.
Some social scientists, particularly in anthropology, argue that
such transfers define the bonds and boundaries of a family
more powerfully than any legal distinctions.[15] In this way,
wealth management unites what Weber once called opposing
"value spheres": the rational-calculative world of formal organizations and money with the socioemotional world of human
relationships.[16]

To preserve family fortunes against the many forces of dissipation requires multigenerational coordination, usually organized by professionals rather than family members. The
professional's authority to lead the family in this way derives
from "a claim to service or stewardship, not to the ongoing and
individual interests of particular persons . . . but to the Durk-
heimian whole that is more than the sum of its parts."[17] This
ideal of stewardship, of course, is itself a medieval holdover,
originating in the management of a feudal lord's household.[18]
Similarly, the family "whole" as an organizing principle of social life hails from the pre-Enlightenment era, before the triumph of individualism.[19]

So as far as families are concerned, wealth management
uses the tools of modern finance to create something that is

fundamentally at odds with modernity. This poses a challenge to contemporary social scientific theories of the family, which focus on fragmentation, diversity, and rapid structural change.[20] At least among the families of their clients, wealth managers do everything possible to encourage stability and a collectivist orientation.[21] This reorientation of self within family, as opposed to self as free agent, is reinforced institutionally through means such as the creation of a family system of governance or a family bank, as described in Chapter 6. Ultimately, this collides two forms of organization that are ordinarily thought to stand in opposition to each other: bureaucracy and the family. As wealth managers encourage clients to assimilate forms borrowed from the modern corporation, the families take on "characteristics of formal organization which are usually assumed to be antithetical to kin-based groups."[22] How this alters family dynamics remains to be explored in future research.

Globalization

In addition to suggesting revisions to current models of family life, this study implies a new way of looking at globalization. In particular, it extends recent work on the role of professionals as key agents of global change by foregrounding the micro level of interactions with clients, peers, and policy makers.[23] The data from this study are to some extent consistent with the predictions made by globalization scholars since the late 1990s to the effect that professionals would step into the role of adjudicators and institution makers in the transnational arena.[24] Where conflicts of laws and regulatory voids have arisen in global transactions, professional innovation—mainly in finance and law—has held the system together.

But those predictions were based on a view of professional activity as collective action by organizations, such as firms or professional societies; further, that action was expected to be strategically planned around "critical projects."[25] This view of profession-led globalization, while validated to some extent in empirical research, has left a persistent gap in knowledge about the role of agency, particularly when it comes to the "linkages between micro-processes and institutions."[26] This study addresses that shortcoming by positing globalization as a process that occurs in part through the improvisations of individual actors—particularly those in privileged positions, like elite professionals. The data reviewed in the previous chapters exemplify the observation that "global arenas and global processes are created from below."[27] Among the most significant insights offered in the book is that "below" begins at the level of interpersonal interactions, such as those between wealth managers and their clients, peers, and policy makers.

By offering a relational analysis of global phenomena—that is, an analysis focused on individual actors and encounters—this study offers to globalization research a more nuanced examination of the dynamics of institutional change. While previous research has acknowledged that "the global does not exist outside of its relationship to, or more specifically its incarnation in, local practices," most studies of transnational institutions neglect the interpersonal level.[28] There is widespread agreement that professionals play a significant role in global institutional change, but few models exist of how this occurs outside the context of action by professional societies and other organizations.[29]

Even studies that have looked at individual-level interactions and agency leave many important questions unanswered, such as whether all global change led by professionals must be "a conscious and systematic project."[30] While most current research assumes this to be the case, the data presented in this book suggest that invention and improvisation play a very significant role in global change. For example, Chapter 3 offers several accounts of wealth managers' off-the-cuff innovations in the form of "indigenizing" the Anglo-Saxon trust for clients in Saudi Arabia and China.[31] Relating the trust to the life of Mohammed isn't just an inspired piece of salesmanship but also a way of effecting globalization: in this case, persuading a client in the modern Middle East to adopt a medieval English institution, thereby disseminating it to a completely different cultural and historical context.

This view of globalization highlights improvisation as an important but often neglected aspect of professional activity.[32] In general, professional work resists standardization: nonroutine problem solving is a defining characteristic of this type of work.[33] The need for flexibility and adaptability is deepened by globalization, as actors are confronted by the intersections of diverse legal, economic, and cultural systems. Under these conditions, which are the norm in wealth management, "novel institutional complexity" demands nearly continuous incremental innovations.[34] As the practitioners interviewed for this book explained, their innovations are provoked by clients'

demands for solutions to specific problems. Whether that results in the expansion of a local institution such as the trust
to the global arena or in a change to the legal system of an
entire country, the catalytic events occur through interpersonal interactions.

This suggests the need for a relational analysis of the dynamics of globalization. Concretely, this means treating the
social world as a set of "dynamic, unfolding relations" instead
of as a world of fixed rules that give rise to structures in a programmatic and orderly fashion.[35] A relational perspective is
distinct from interactional analysis, which understands social
actors as fixed analytical givens, as well as from network theory,
which focuses primarily on the structures and "mechanistic"
properties of interpersonal ties.[36] Most important with regard
to institutional change, relational analyses allow for emergence, change, and improvisation. A relational view allows us
to analyze aspects of professional work often neglected in institutional theory, particularly the strategic, inventive uses of
indeterminacy and expert knowledge.[37]

If, as some have observed, institutional theory needs a
better analysis of agency in professional settings, the relational
perspective supported by this study offers a means to achieve
those aims.[38] This is a particularly noteworthy problem given
the significance of globalization to institutional change dynamics. The literature on globalization has pointed up the
role of professionals in creating "successfully globalized local
institutional solutions," including "globalized localisms" such
as the Wall Street legal firm and the trust.[39] But we must turn
to relational theory for an account of agency—specifically, the

micro-level processes that "allow the dis- and re-embedding of practices" from one set of national and institutional contexts to another.[40]

In summary, the theoretical model suggested by this study extends understanding of professionals' impact on globalization by foregrounding the role of situated improvisation as a source of institutional change. This addresses a neglected dimension of agency in institutional theory, which has too often privileged intentionality and foresight to the exclusion of contingency and invention.[41] Contemporary professional service contexts require "practical-evaluative improvisations" in which "actors develop and realize their interests" not through planning but through practice.[42] This is particularly true in the international realm, in which professionals face novel institutional configurations in the form of laws, professional rules, cultures, and norms meeting across jurisdictions.[43] In such cases, the narrow construction of institutional agency as based on "standardized interaction sequences" or "established procedures" excludes important realms of professional activity.[44]

Professionalization

The relational perspective developed in this study also provides new insights for the literature on professionalization. This is the study of the origins of the professions: the circumstances under which they arise, along with the actors, events, and institutions that give each profession its distinctive form. As the late German sociologist Norbert Elias theorized in his famous treatise on officers in the British navy, professions de-

velop from "a process of trial and error in which people attempt to match occupational techniques or institutions and
human needs. Every single step in this direction is executed
by individuals. Yet the process as such, the genesis and development of a profession, or of any other occupation, is more
than the sum total of individual acts. It has a pattern of its
own."[45] Elias' model, which acknowledges the exploratory
and iterative qualities of professional work, is consistent with
the improvisational focus of the relational perspective. Ultimately, he writes, what makes a set of practices into a profession is the hardening of these trial-and-error techniques into
institutions. This not only institutionalizes forms of work but
also creates "institutionalized sets of human *relationships*,"
consisting of "specialized social functions which people per-
form in response to specialized needs of others."[46]

Wealth management provides an unusual opportunity to
observe this institutionalization process in real time. As
Chapter 2 describes, the professionalization of wealth managers is still in progress, having begun quite late compared to
that of lawyers and accountants. For example, while the legal
and accounting fields had established professional societies
and credentialing practices by the early- to mid-1800s, wealth
management did not reach those milestones until well over a
century later.[47] By the time the Society of Trust and Estate
Practitioners held its inaugural meeting in 1991, globalization
and financialization were in full swing, giving the profession
some of its distinctively modern features, such as an international orientation.[48] This is quite different from related professions, which have tended to be deeply embedded in the local
conditions of their emergence.[49]

Two other unusual aspects of the professionalization of wealth management suggest interesting new directions for social scientific theory and research. First, there is the history of resistance to wealth management becoming professionalized in the first place; second, the seemingly conflict-free integration of practitioners with middle- or working-class origins, in contrast to the pattern of other professions. The implications of these distinctive features will be discussed below.

Resistance to professionalization. Wealth management is far from the only case of an amateur undertaking becoming professionalized: creative occupations such as interior design and cooking are also notable examples of this pattern.[50] But wealth management does represent one of the few instances in which professionalization was met with active resistance. As Chapter 2 showed, this resistance was sustained both culturally and institutionally, both formally and informally. To reiterate the famous dictum of eighteenth-century legal scholar Francis Sanders, the work that we now know as wealth management was perceived as "a burden upon the *honor* and *conscience* of the person intrusted [the trustee], and not [to be] undertaken upon mercenary motives."[51] Institutionally, this custom was upheld by the courts: wealth managers were barred from receiving a salary for their work, except in cases where a "compensation clause" was added to the instructions they received from clients.[52] Only in the twenty-first century—as of the creation of the U.S. Uniform Trust Code and the U.K. Trustee Act of 2000—has the law recognized the professionalization of wealth management by independently affirming practitioners' right to receive a salary for their work.[53]

Some similarities to this unusual pattern of resistance to professionalization can be observed in the realm of sport. As with wealth management, change appears to have been driven by a combination of technological innovation and globalization. The process was played out dramatically in the case of the Olympic Games. As with wealth management, amateurism in sport was long considered a safeguard of honor and gentlemanly behavior, as instantiated by the upper classes. Founded by the Baron Pierre de Coubertin in the 1890s, the Games were based around a "rigid, restrictive and aristocratic" code that held professionals in suspicion.[54] The amateurs-only rule was enshrined as a bylaw in the Olympic Charter until 1988, and it not only excluded professionals from participating in the Games but also allowed the International Olympic Committee to disqualify anyone who was merely *considering* turning professional.[55]

This amateur ideal in sport is thought to have given way under the increasing frequency of international competition and the significant increase in performance capacity that advances in medical technology made possible. Ever higher levels of sporting achievement were facilitated by the growing sophistication of devices for measuring athletes' metabolism, heart and lung function, and movements.[56] As performance expectations ratcheted upward, mass media brought top athletes to a wider audience than ever, giving them celebrity status and dramatically increasing the profits generated by their performances.[57]

While the professionalization of wealth management shares some aspects of this pattern—particularly in terms of the roles of technology and globalization—in other ways it remains a unique story. Unlike athletes, wealth managers never attained celebrity status and never experienced the lure of star athletes' salaries. For wealth managers, the "great leap forward" in compensation was simply that the norms and laws shifted so that they were allowed to be compensated at all, without damage to their reputations. If anything, earning the kind of money that professional athletes do would cast doubt on their trustworthiness as fiduciaries. This is particularly true now, when technology makes it easy to price-shop for financial information and professional services, creating downward pressure on wealth managers' fees.[58]

Entry and social class. In some respects, the history of wealth management parallels Norbert Elias' account of recruitment to the officer corps in Britain's Royal Navy. For centuries, entry into wealth management was barred to all but members of the upper classes; in matters of trust, "gentlemen wished to have their money . . . dealt with by gentlemen."[59] This foregrounded the role of cultural capital, and the highly specific set of interpersonal norms described in Chapter 3, such as avoiding direct discussion of money.

By the same token, the Royal Navy described in Elias' meticulously researched study was dominated by noblemen. Only they were permitted to become officers, even if they lacked the most basic seamanship skills. In fact, they were discouraged from acquiring any technical competencies at sea: "Gentlemen could not learn the art and craft of a seaman without feeling that they had lowered themselves in the eyes of the world."[60] Over time, this strict division between gentlemen and "tarpaulins" (the nickname for sea captains who were not to the manor born) softened, so that two separate classes of officers developed in parallel: while nominally equals at sea, they remained profoundly at odds everywhere else. The rivalry and friction between the two classes of officers was prolonged over centuries, their antagonism so heated that solutions to the problem were debated among the leading government officials of the time.[61]

This conflict between social rank and professional position does not seem to have arisen in wealth management, despite the increasing entry of practitioners from working- and middle-class backgrounds. For example, Nick—the Englishman whose origins as a shipbuilder and yacht crew member would have marked him as a tarpaulin in Elias' terms—does not seem to have been held back in his professional career by his working-class origins. Nor did any of the other participants in this study who emerged from similar backgrounds, such as Sherman and Elaine, who both started off as low-level bank clerks without university educations before entering the profession.

I propose that financialization opened up wealth management to recruitment from social groups beyond the "gentlemen" class. While the profession is still dominated in many ways by white men of Anglo-Saxon origin, as Table 1.1 suggests, the entry of people from the middle and working classes—as well as that of women and people of color—does not seem to have generated the kind of resentment Elias documented among naval officers of different backgrounds. This may reflect broader social changes, such as financialization, that demanded more technical expertise of wealth managers. For example, as clients' wealth became more fungible, and more of it consisted of stocks and bonds rather than land, wealth managers had to master a suite of new financial-legal skills: even if they hired outside advisers, they themselves had to possess enough knowledge in those areas to be selective about the expert advice they took on clients' behalf.

This is not to say that the need for cultural capital has been eliminated: as Chapter 3 shows, the ability to embody trustworthiness in the idiom of wealthy clients remains an essential skill. But the addition of new technical dimensions to the demands on wealth managers seems to have opened the paths of recruitment to a wider range of backgrounds than was the case for centuries. In this sense, the professionalization of wealth management is a story of modernity and the ascendance of expertise and achievement over ascription and social class.[62]

In summary, through Elias' model we can understand the professionalization of wealth management as a process that began with techniques designed to meet the needs of a small group of individuals—originally, wealthy English landowners. While wealth managers still serve a relatively small client base of high- and ultra-high-net-worth individuals, the past 180 years have seen a gradual development of institutions out of those relationships. This process has coincided with other world-historical changes, such as globalization and financialization, which have given wealth management two of its distinctive characteristics. These include an openness to technically skilled entrants, regardless of their social class origins (but provided they can master the behavioral norms expected by their elite clients), as well as an unusually broad conception of professional jurisdiction, which treats national boundaries as a resource to be exploited rather than as a limiting factor.

Political economy

As the previous chapter showed, wealth management has an unusual relationship to state authority, enjoying a degree of independence unknown to most other professions. The work of wealth managers often has an ambivalent effect on states, bolstering their power in some respects and undermining it in others. On the one hand, the profession has championed the strategic uses of state sovereignty, helping some jurisdictions— both onshore and offshore—make their laws more attractive to high-net-worth individuals. This has brought significant revenue to many states in the form of fees from financial services to the wealthy, or via other means, such as generating property tax payments.

On the other hand, by detaching wealthy individuals and their fortunes from state power, wealth management has damaged the legitimacy of government in the eyes of many and eroded popular sovereignty.[63] This suggests that the profession may be driving a new political economy of wealth, in which states respond not to the will of voters but to the "stateless superrich."[64] The data presented in this book suggest that to some extent, many countries are already more receptive and accessible to wealth managers, who are acting on behalf of the world's richest people, than they are to elected representatives from their own governments. Thus the multiple instances described in Chapter 6 of wealth managers persuading governments to override national laws and institutions in conflict with the interests of high-net-worth individuals. At a minimum, a state system that might be called the "parasitic twin" of the Westphalian model seems to have emerged, partly through the work of these elite professionals.

These observations link wealth management to classic questions in social scientific theory about the sources and legitimacy of state power, as well as the role of elites in society. The implications for research and policy are detailed next.

The stateless super-rich. As the previous chapters have shown, laws that are supposed to apply to all residents of a country can be made irrelevant to high-net-worth individuals through the interventions of wealth managers. To an extent, wealth has always provided this kind of freedom to elude state authority; in 1909, G. K. Chesterton wrote: "The poor man really has a stake in the country. The rich man hasn't; he can go away to New Guinea on his yacht. The poor have sometimes objected to being governed badly; the rich have always objected to being governed at all. Aristocrats were always anarchists."[65]

What has changed in the intervening century is the increasing ease with which the rich can detach themselves from unwanted governance. It no longer requires a yacht or a trip to New Guinea. Thanks to developments such as cash-for-passport programs, the legal constraints to which wealthy people are subject can be altered almost as easily as the regimes affecting their fortunes. Put another way, the increasingly fungibility of citizenship and residency obligations has followed the increasing fungibility of capital: as it became easier to move wealth around the world to enjoy the most favorable conditions, it also got easier to manipulate the state affiliations of the wealthy themselves. As a result, without breaking any laws, legal compliance can essentially be made voluntary for the rich, through the interventions of wealth managers; court orders and family obligations can be avoided and art can be moved around the world in contravention of patrimony laws, all without sanctions.

Anyone can be an outlaw, but it is a special privilege to defeat the spirit of the laws without violating them formally. For the price of employing a wealth manager, some elites can achieve this condition, and also enjoy the benefits of laws written specifically with their interests in mind. As Chapters 3 and 6 detailed, the wealth management profession increasingly provides its international high-net-worth clientele with an institutionalized voice at the highest levels of government, in countries where those clients may not actually reside.[66]

By giving a powerful voice in lawmaking and policy to a transnational clientele, professionals are effecting a change in the balance of power between states and the wealthy. This power distorts political processes, particularly in the small countries that have sought postcolonial independence through involvement in offshore finance. And because the exercise of this power usually involves reduction or elimination of the tax burden borne by the wealthy, states lose further legitimacy by becoming financially unable to provide services and regulate for the common good.

Furthermore, the stateless super-rich themselves cannot be prevailed upon to pay taxes, and not just for reasons of economic self-interest. Since they belong nowhere in particular and can move at will (much like global corporations), ideological appeals to patriotism or civic duty are meaningless. If anything, countries now seem to consider themselves fortunate to have the rich within their ambit, if only temporarily.

By detaching clients from allegiance and obligation to any particular state, wealth managers weaken those individuals' need (and perhaps willingness) to submit to *any* laws, anywhere. As social scientists have known for generations, being a law-abiding citizen depends on a sense of membership in a collective. From that group membership comes acceptance of and adherence to rules: "a sense of rights and obligations derived from an identity and membership in a political community and the ethos, practices and expectations of its institutions."[67]

The success of wealth managers in freeing their clients from state authority, as well as the decreasing legitimacy of state authority this has created, may account in part for the decline of the "old money" ethic among the rich. The sense of obligation to public service and to model civic behavior has sometimes been mocked as a false front or derided as *noblesse oblige*, but it had real consequences.[68] Testaments to this period in which the wealthy still belonged somewhere are still readily observable in in forms such as the thousands of public libraries built by Andrew Carnegie, or of the interstate highway and Internet systems, created in the decades following World War II by a federal government that was able to impose—with little resistance by elites—a top marginal tax rate of 70 to 90 percent.[69]

Several policy directions have been proposed to address this problem of waning civic obligation and dwindling regard for state authority among the stateless super-rich. At one extreme, American policy makers have sought to reimpose state power with an iron hand, punishing high-net-worth individuals who relinquish their citizenship. U.S. consular fees for renunciation have been hiked by 442 percent in recent years (making them twenty times higher than the average for developed countries); if that doesn't provide a sufficient deterrent, several of those former citizens have been barred from reentering the country.[70] At the other extreme, some observers argue that it is better to acquiesce to the crumbling of the Westphalian system by giving up on the notion of citizenship altogether. A recent book of policy scholarship proposes "abolishing borders and transforming all human beings into citizens of the world."[71] The seriousness with which this proposition has been greeted suggests how deeply impaired the centuries-old world system of states, sovereignty, and citizenship has become, partly thanks to the work of wealth managers.

A new state system? Picking up on this theme, recent work by economist Gabriel Zucman has argued that the offshore financial system has grown to be such a threat to the old Westphalian order that it calls into question the future of states themselves. His argument is based primarily on tax avoidance, which he calls "theft pure and simple."[72] By allowing taxpayers to steal from their governments to the tune of $200 billion in worldwide lost tax revenue each year, Zucman argues, wealth managers facilitate the economic hobbling of the state system overall.

Zucman focuses on the case of Luxembourg, where nearly half the country's production benefits foreign individuals and organizations. Such a space, he says, is more like a free trade zone than a country, particularly since the local living conditions are in "accelerated decline" for everyone except the wealth managers, who reside there temporarily.[73] Others have made a similar point about Jersey: thanks to the economic and political dominance of wealth management, it is no longer really a sovereign state in any meaningful sense (see Chapter 6 for details). Existing in what one reporter called the "enchanted inbetween," Jersey can claim all the privileges of sovereignty without providing the benefits and protections of that status to the majority of its citizens.[74] In any ordinary sense of the term, Jersey "is not a country"; rather, it is "45 square miles of self-governing ambiguity."[75] Such cases, in Zucman's view, raise the question "What is a nation?"[76] His research suggests that the fault lines appearing in the state system as a result of offshore finance are potentially creating new forms of state power that bode very ill for the nonwealthy.

This study supports Zucman's line of thinking and adds three novel components on which to build future research. First, as emphasized above, this book offers more specificity about sources of agency in the undermining of the traditional state system. The data from participants in this research confirms Zucman's claims about the significance of the offshore states in this process, but they make the additional contribution of showing that wealth managers are key actors in this process. The offshore system is of course not self-managing: it is manipulated, directly and indirectly, by actors such as elite professionals. In the case of wealth management, this agency includes writing the laws of offshore states and enjoying privileged informal access to the leaders of government, both onshore and off.

Second, the evidence from this study suggests that much more than lost tax revenues is undermining the Westphalian state system. To a greater extent than Zucman's work, this study emphasizes the decline in states' political legitimacy as a result of offshore activity. The offshore world has created zones of lawlessness: not just in regard to tax laws but with respect to *all* laws. As some observers have already noted, there is an "anarchic" aspect to wealth management, with the result that the locales where this activity takes place—whether that is offshore, on Wall Street, or in the City of London—can seem surprisingly akin to the havens created by left-wing anarchists, such as pirate radio platforms.[77] Such comparisons are not just metaphorical. The anarchic effects of wealth management can be observed in the chaos unleashed in 2008, when bad debts and risks hidden from regulators in obscure offshore vehicles grew to unmanageable size and nearly destroyed the world financial system.

Less appreciated is the way that offshore has become a place where wealth managers are "happy to help anyone, from anywhere, avoid anything."[78] Whether that means avoiding taxes, dodging alimony payments, or getting around trade sanctions matters little. Instead, the significance of these zones lies in the evidence they provide us that the wealthy, and the elite professionals who serve them, have created a kind of parallel world of selective lawlessness: selective in that high-net-worth individuals can continue to enjoy the benefits of laws that suit their interests while ignoring laws that inconvenience them. Some might argue that it was ever thus. No doubt this is true to an extent. But the data from this study suggest that the problem has grown to an extent almost unimaginable previously; even in the feudal era, there were still authorities (such as the Roman Catholic Church in Europe) that retained a meaningful power to impose laws on even the wealthiest and most privileged of individuals. Today there no longer seem to be such authorities or such power. The high-net-worth individuals of the world are largely ungoverned, and ungovernable. It is this, even more than the emptying of state coffers, that poses the direst threat to the Westphalian system.

This brings us to the third and final contribution of this book to the study of states and political economy: the suggestion that a kind of parallel state system has arisen for the wealthy, a system that operates largely unnoticed except when it throws the world that the rest us inhabit into chaos. This system operates like a parasitic twin on the Westphalian model. In the biological realm, the medical literature defines this condition as one of "unequal and asymmetric twinning," in which the parasite is less developed than and dependent upon its host.[79] This seems an apt metaphor for the relationship of the offshore world to traditional states. But unlike with biological twins, the members of the parasitic political system extract resources through organized, systemic thievery; Zucman calls out for particular mention the "sinister trio of the Virgin Islands, Luxembourg and Switzerland," which cooperate by specializing in different components of the theft process.[80]

Perhaps most troubling about this system is that the parasitic twin has all the lawmaking powers of the host: the offshore nations have the same right to make their own rules, and to ignore those of other countries, as the sovereign states in the Westphalian system. But the aims of the parasite are totally different: rather than offering governance and public services to the populace at large, the parasitic system offers zones of state-sanctioned lawlessness that benefit only international elites. What this is doing to the Westphalian host system is similar in some respects to what e-commerce has done to bricks-and-mortar business, destroying it in a race to the bottom. The key difference is that while the benefits of e-commerce (both for business owners and consumers) are open to anyone with an Internet connection, the benefits of the parasitic state system are offered only to the world's wealthiest people. The coordinated extraction of capital from the host states and the undermining of their legitimacy makes life consistently worse for the vast majority of people while benefiting a tiny few.

The future of wealth management

This book has traced the development of wealth management from voluntary work undertaken by friends and kinsmen into a thriving form of expert power. Despite challenges from local and international authorities, the profession's fundamental independence from states has allowed it to grow by leaps and bounds, even as its mainstay activities—such as helping clients avoid taxes or maintain secrecy around their fortunes—come under attack. Many scholarly observers are skeptical that these attacks will make a meaningful impact, in part because the professionals have been so successful in consolidating clients' wealth. Widening economic inequality has multiplied the economic and political clout of high-net-worth individuals, increasing states' dependence on them as financial crises continue to shake world markets. As one study concluded, despite declarations to the contrary by the OECD and other international institutions, "financial secrecy and opacity are far from dead," and that means wealth management will continue to thrive.[81]

The practitioners interviewed for this study concur with the scholars' assessments. Constance, the native Caribbean wealth manager working in the British Virgin Islands said she was optimistic about the future growth prospects of the profession because "there will never be a shortage of wealth in the world . . . and there will always be a place for services to the very wealthy." Erika, the German wealth manager based in Zurich, took a similar view. Echoing the observation of Mark, the English practitioner in Dubai who compared his work to the provision of "extra-special bespoke service, just like suits," Erika said she expected that there would always be demand for wealth management, just "like there will always be a market for haute couture."

This is not to discount the global changes that affect the industry. For example, many of those interviewed for this study mentioned the decline in privacy and the increased costs of compliance as drivers of transformation in practice. Lynn, an Asian woman practicing in Panama City, said that "at the end of day, you're not going to be able to hide anymore. That and increased compliance are going to scare some clients off" wealth management services. But Elias, the native Panamanian practitioner, argued that new constraints would just lead to further financial-legal innovations and "another level of concealment for wealthy people."

Elias' prediction seems to be borne out by recent evidence indicating that national and international efforts to combat tax avoidance and other wealth management objectives have been sabotaged by "creative compliance."[82] For example, the European Union implemented the Savings Tax Directive in 2005 to combat tax evasion, but wealth managers immediately found a loophole—transferring clients' personal accounts, which were taxed under the directive, to accounts held in the name of shell corporations, which were not taxed. This move, while perfectly legal, undermined the intended effect of the law. After a decade, during which tax avoidance actually increased, the EU repealed the Savings Tax Directive. This policy failure has been laid by some directly at the feet of the European wealth management professionals who "deliberately, and on a large scale, torpedoed the savings tax directive."[83]

New opportunities for growth

So the game of "playing cat and mouse with tax authorities around the world," as one participant in this study described his work, seems unlikely to wind down anytime soon. In the meanwhile, the wealth management profession continues to grow in new directions. For example, Steve—an English wealth manager based in Hong Kong—predicted that mediation would be a major growth area for practitioners. He said this would come from an increase in what he called "generational and cultural disputes," driven by the use of trusts by people from countries governed by civil law or shari'a regimes, as well as the spread of concerns about privacy. As the Pritzker and Wyly cases demonstrated (see Chapters 1 and 4), the secrecy afforded by trust structures is undone when conflicts end up in court, making private arrangements a matter of public record. In consequence, Steve explained, "people are needed who can facilitate solutions without recourse to the courts. The idea is that trusts are private and people want to keep them private. Mediation can do that."

Several other practitioners suggested that the profession would grow by building on its unique expertise in facilitating complex multinational capital flows, both for private clients and for corporations. Unlike in the past, when the objective of these efforts was to avoid regulation, the novelty here will be in facilitating compliance and coordination. Carlos, an Argentinian practitioner, related the following story about a client with an account in Germany: "Deutsche Bank told one of my clients, 'If you don't prove to me that the assets in your account here have been declared to the [Argentinian] tax authorities, I'm going to close your account.' If the bank does that, they close the account and send you a check. Do you know what we do with checks here in Argentina? They become toilet paper." Under these circumstances, helping clients come into compliance with the law is the best wealth preservation strategy. This example is consistent with the recent research from Israel (mentioned in Chapter 6) suggesting that a changing cost-benefit analysis is turning an increasing number of wealth management professionals into international compliance specialists.[84] As Carlos concluded, "The future of the profession is . . . to help your clients move their funds from undeclared funds to declared status. The era of undeclared money is over."

While this sounds like a death knell for tax avoidance, it may simply usher in a new round of "creative compliance." Offshore financial centers contribute to the continuation of this practice. For example, in response to international demands to stem the flow of undeclared wealth through the creation of beneficial ownership registries, jurisdictions such as Belize and the Cayman Islands formally "complied." But while the registries exist, they remain inaccessible to the public and are available to law enforcement agencies only under special circumstances.[85] Such regimes make it possible for wealth such as like Carlos to place clients' wealth in structures that are nominally "declared" but which are in practice just as hidden as under the old system.

Another, less legally conflicted opportunity for growth has also presented itself: creating and managing complex international network of salary, pension, and insurance payments for corporations. As globalization drives growth in multinational projects and the expatriate labor force, this necessitates increasingly intricate transnational financial arrangements for staff.[86] An estimated 50 million people are currently working outside their home countries—a figure that has been growing steadily at about 2.5 percent annually since 2009.[87] Most of these workers are not the kind of high-net-worth individuals typically served by wealth managers, but their employers may manage pools of capital large enough to justify hiring a professional to manage a set of complex international pay arrangements. Paul, one of the English wealth managers I spoke with in Dubai, said that a typical scenario would involve

pension schemes and payroll schemes for international companies where they have employees all over the world—like in
the Sudan—and the payroll has to be organized centrally,
preferably from an offshore location for tax reasons. That's
because you'd have perhaps 20 different nationalities represented among your employees, and the employer is in yet another jurisdiction; if you pay someone who is a U.S. national
working in the U.K., you run into double-tax issues, the obligation to deduct tax at source or in some other way. But if you
pay the staff from an offshore, nil-tax jurisdiction, you avoid
the onus of dealing with all that regulation of different countries (which is always changing anyway). Instead, you put the
onus of the tax responsibility on the employee and you pay
them gross.

So even if the business of providing high-net-worth clients
with tax avoidance strategies and secrecy were to disappear,
the wealth management profession might continue to thrive
based on the increasing globalization of work and the transnational mobility of workers. The new direction would be in
turning the skills of wealth management to serve firms as the
client base, rather than private individuals and families. That
turn toward the bureaucratic and away from personal service
to wealthy clients may help the profession distance itself
from the damaging associations that have tarnished its reputation in recent years.

A new direction for policy

By now it is abundantly clear that direct efforts to curtail the
privileges of the super-rich have proven ineffective. The mo-

bility of wealth and its owners, coupled with the legal-financial skill of wealth managers, makes it all too easy to violate the spirit of the laws while adhering to them formally. In light of this, the major policy implication of this study is that political leaders interested in seeing elites pay their fair share of tax and otherwise submit to the rule of law should shift their attention away from the wealthy individuals and onto the professionals who serve them.

The problem for policy makers then becomes one of changing the incentive structure for the profession such that mediation of family disputes or the creation of complex international payroll schemes becomes a more attractive source of business than "creative compliance" with tax regulations and other laws. The goal would be to encourage wealth managers to apply their formidable legal, organizational, and financial skills in ways that are less harmful—or even beneficial—to states and societies. This would sidestep head-to-head battle with the power and expertise of the profession, since that strategy has also proven ineffective.[88] Instead, policy makers could seek to divert or redirect those resources, much the way engineers can divert the flow of powerful, flood-prone rivers so that the water serves communities rather than destroying them.

There seems to be some promise in this approach. This is suggested not just by recent empirical studies—such as the one carried out in Israel, described in Chapter 6—but by the ways that the wealth managers interviewed for this study see their profession developing into the future.[89] Given the institutional evolution of the profession and its remarkable independence from state control, it would be ironic to find the arc of wealth management bending at last toward alignment with a form of authority it has sought in so many ways to escape or combat.

Notes

1. Introduction

1. Charles Dickens, *Bleak House* (London: Penguin Classics, 2003 [1853]), 19.
2. George Marcus, "The Fiduciary Role in American Family Dynasties and Their Institutional Legacy," in George Marcus, ed., *Elites: Ethnographic Issues*, 221–256 (Albuquerque: University of New Mexico Press, 1983), 222.
3. Dickens, *Bleak House*, 540. See also Max Weber, "Bureaucracy," in Hans Gerth and C. Wright Mills, eds., *From Max Weber*, 196–244 (New York: Oxford University Press, 1946 [1922]), 233.
4. Marcel Mauss, *Essai sur le don* (London: Routledge and Kegan Paul, 1969 [1924]).
5. Pierre Bourdieu, *Outline of a Theory of Practice* (Cambridge, UK: Cambridge University Press, 1977).
6. James Hughes, *Family Wealth: Keeping It in the Family* (Princeton Junction, NJ: NetWrx, 1997), 119.
7. Michel Pinçon and Monique Pinçon-Charlot, *Grand Fortunes: Dynasties of Wealth in France*, trans. Andrea Lyn Secara (New York: Algora, 1998), 35.
8. Brooke Harrington, "Trust and Estate Planning: The Emergence of a Profession and Its Contribution to Socio-economic Inequality," *Sociological Forum* 27 (2012):825–846.

9. Ibid.

10. Jonathan Beaverstock, Sarah Hall, and Thomas Wainwright, "Servicing the Super-rich: New Financial Elites and the Rise of the Private Wealth Management Retail Ecology," *Regional Studies* 47 (2013): 834–849.

11. D. Maude, *Global Private Banking and Wealth Management: The New Realities* (Chichester, UK: Wiley, 2006).

12. Brooke Harrington, "From Trustees to Wealth Managers," in Guido Erreygers and John Cunliffe, eds., *Inherited Wealth, Justice, and Equality*, 190–209 (London: Routledge, 2012).

13. For "fiscal alchemists," see Peter Pexton, "Fast Forward: 2015," *STEP Journal*, April 2010. For "transaction planners," see John Langbein, "The Contractarian Basis of the Law of Trusts," *Yale Law Journal* 105 (1995): 630. For "income defense providers," see Jeffrey Winters, *Oligarchy* (Cambridge, UK: Cambridge University Press, 2011), 219.

14. Mark Del Col, Andrew Hogan, and Thomas Roughan, "Transforming the Wealth Management Industry," *Journal of Financial Transformation* 9 (2003): 105–113. See also Pexton, "Fast Forward."

15. Anton Sternberg and Michael Maslinski, "Trustees: The True Wealth Managers," *STEP Journal*, April 2008, 29.

16. Cap-Gemini, *World Wealth Report* (Paris: Cap-Gemini, 2014).

17. Entail is a restricted form of land ownership that prohibits sale or mortgaging of land as a condition of inheriting it; the heir to entailed land was thus more of a life tenant than an owner in the full sense of the term. Entail also limited possession of the land to specific people—usually the lineal descendants of the person who entailed the land in the first place. Among the lineal descendants, inheritance was often further restricted to the eldest male of the family, a practice known as primogeniture. For further discussion, see Jens Beckert, "The *Longue Durée* of Inheritance Law: Discourses and Institutional Development in France, Germany and the United States since 1800," *Archives of European Sociology* 48 (2007): 79–120.

18. Harrington, "Trust and Estate Planning."

19. Lawrence Friedman, *Dead Hands: A Social History of Wills, Trusts, and Inheritance Law* (Stanford, CA: Stanford University Press, 2009).

20. Ronen Palan, Richard Murphy, and Christian Chavagneux, *Tax Havens: How Globalization Really Works* (Ithaca, NY: Cornell University Press, 2010).

21. Robert Shiller, *Finance and the Good Society* (Princeton, NJ: Princeton University Press, 2012).
22. Michael Parkinson, *Trustee Investment and Financial Appraisal*, 4th ed. (Birmingham, UK: Central Law Training, 2008), 20.
23. Michael Parkinson, *Trust Creation: Law and Practice* (Birmingham, UK: Central Law Training, 2005), 220.
24. Stephane Fitch, "Pritzker vs. Pritzker," *Forbes*, November 24, 2003.
25. Graham Moffat, *Trust Law: Text and Materials* (Cambridge, UK: Cambridge University Press, 2009), 5.
26. Remi Clignet, *Death, Deeds and Descendants* (New York: Aldine de Gruyter, 1991), 29.
27. On professions and inequality, see Laura Hansen and Siamak Movahedi, "Wall Street Scandals: The Myth of Individual Greed," *Sociological Forum* 25 (2010): 367–374. See also John Heinz and Edward Laumann, *Chicago Lawyers: The Social Structure of the Bar* (Evanston, IL: Northwestern University Press, 1994). On "irreplaceable" actors, see Palan, Murphy, and Chavagneux, *Tax Havens*, 12.
28. Karen Ho, *Liquidated: An Ethnography of Wall Street* (Durham, NC: Duke University Press, 2009). See also Mitchel Abolafia, *Making Markets: Opportunism and Restraint on Wall Street* (Cambridge, MA: Harvard University Press, 1996).
29. Thorstein Veblen, *The Theory of the Leisure Class* (New York: Penguin, 1994 [1899]).
30. Jonathan Dunlop, "Healthy Competition," *STEP Journal*, April 2008, 31.
31. Cap-Gemini, *World Wealth Report*.
32. William Robinson, "Social Theory and Globalization: The Rise of a Transnational State," *Theory and Society* 30 (2001): 165.
33. James Davies, Rodrigo Lluberas, and Anthony Shorrocks, *Global Wealth Report* (Zurich: Credit Suisse, 2013).
34. Ibid.
35. Thomas Piketty, *Capital in the Twenty-first Century* (Cambridge, MA: Harvard University Press, 2014).
36. Melvin Oliver and Thomas Shapiro, *Black Wealth, White Wealth: A New Perspective on Racial Inequality* (New York: Routledge, 1995).
37. Palan, Murphy, and Chavagneux, *Tax Havens*, 12.
38. For the $21 trillion figure, see Heather Stewart, "Wealth Doesn't Trickle Down—It Just Floods Offshore, New Research Reveals," *The*

Guardian, July 21, 2012. For tax loss figure, see Gabriel Zucman, *The Hidden Wealth of Nations* (Chicago: University of Chicago Press, 2015).

39. Jonathan Beaverstock, Philip Hubbard, and John Short, "Getting Away with It? Exposing the Geographies of the Super-rich," *Geoforum* 35 (2004): 401–407.

40. Nicholas Shaxson, *Treasure Islands: Tax Havens and the Men Who Stole the World* (London: Random House, 2011).

41. Michael Cadesky, "A question of Legitimate Tax Policy," *STEP Journal*, March 2010. See also Marshall Langer, *Tax Agreements with Tax Havens and Other Small Countries* (London: STEP, 2005).

42. Gregory Jackson and Stephen Brammer, "Grey Areas: Irresponsible Corporations and Reputational Dynamics," *Socio-Economic Review* 12 (2014): 153–218.

43. Harrington, "Trust and Estate Planning."

44. Prem Sikka, "Accountants: A Threat to Democracy: The Tax Avoidance Industry Has a Veto on What Services the Government Can Provide," *The Guardian*, September 5, 2005.

45. Organisation for Economic Co-operation and Development (OECD), *Final Seoul Declaration* (Seoul, Korea: OECD, 2006), 4.

46. Carl Levin, "The US Tax Shelter Industry: The Role of Accountants, Lawyers, and Financial Professionals," statement before U.S. Senate Permanent Subcommittee on Investigations, November 18, 2003.

47. Dennis Jaffe and Sam Lane, "Sustaining a Family Dynasty: Key Issues Facing Multi-generational Business- and Investment-Owning Families," *Family Business Review* 17 (2004): 5–18; Fitch, "Pritzker vs. Pritzker."

48. Yoser Gadhoum, Larry Lang, and Leslie Young, "Who Controls US?" *European Journal of Financial Management* 11 (2005): 342.

49. Gerard Hanlon, "Institutional Forms and Organizational Structures: Homology, Trust and Reputational Capital in Professional Service Firms," *Organization* 11 (2004): 190.

50. Werner Conze and Jürgen Kocka, "Einleitung," in Werner Conze and Jürgen Kocka, eds., *Bildungsburgertum im 19. jahrhundert*, vol. 1: *Bildungssystem und professionalisierung in internationalen vergleichen*, 9–26 (Stuttgart, Germany: Klett-Cotta, 1985), 18.

51. Rachel Sherman, "'Time Is Our Commodity': Gender and the Struggle for Occupational Legitimacy among Personal Concierges," *Work and Occupations* 37 (2011): 81–114.

52. C. Wright Mills, *The Power Elite* (New York: Oxford University Press, 1956), 107.

53. Michael Luo and Mike McIntire, "Offshore Tactics Helped Increase Romneys' Wealth," *New York Times*, October 1, 2012.

54. Beckert, "The *Longue Durée* of Inheritance Law."

55. Talcott Parsons, *The Social System* (New York: Free Press, 1951).

56. Ian Hodder, *Çatalhöyük: The Leopard's Tale* (London: Thames and Hudson, 2006). See also Laurence Kotlikoff and Lawrence Summers, "The Role of Intergenerational Transfers in Aggregate Capital Accumulation," *Journal of Political Economy* 89 (1981): 706–732.

57. Karl Marx and Friedrich Engels, *The Communist Manifesto* (London: Penguin, 2004 [1848]), 222.

58. Jaffe and Lane, "Sustaining a Family Dynasty."

59. Timothy Colclough, "To PTC or Not to PTC," *STEP Journal*, November/December 2009, 51–53.

60. Friedman, *Dead Hands*.

61. Jason Sharman, *Havens in a Storm: The Struggle for Global Tax Regulation* (Ithaca, NY: Cornell University Press, 2006).

62. Daniel Bell, *The Cultural Contradictions of Capitalism*, 2nd ed. (London: Heinemann Educational Books, 1976). See also Joseph Schumpeter, "The Crisis of the Tax State," in Wolfgang Stolper and Richard Musgrave, eds., *International Economic Papers*, no. 4, 5–38 (New York: Macmillan, 1954 [1918]).

63. Bruce Carruthers and Terence Halliday, *Rescuing Business: The Making of Bankruptcy Law in Britain and the United States* (Oxford: Oxford University Press, 1998), 60.

64. Sigrid Quack, "Legal Professionals and Trans-national Law Making: A Case of Distributed Agency," *Organization* 14 (2007): 643–666.

65. Winters, *Oligarchy*, 222.

66. Friedman, *Dead Hands*.

67. Hughes, *Family Wealth*.

68. Schumpeter, "The Crisis of the Tax State."

69. Beckert, "The *Longue Durée* of Inheritance Law," 85.

70. Robert Miller and Stephen McNamee, "The Inheritance of Wealth in America," in Robert Miller and Stephen McNamee, eds., *Inheritance and Wealth in America*, 1–22 (New York: Plenum Press, 1998).

71. David Cay Johnston, "Dozens of Rich Americans Join in Fight to Retain the Estate Tax," *New York Times*, February 14, 2001.

72. Shaxson, *Treasure Islands.*

73. Adam Hofri, "Professionals' Contribution to the Legislative Process: Between Self, Client and the Public," *Law and Social Inquiry* 39 (2014): 96–126. See also George Marcus and Peter Hall, *Lives in Trust: The Fortunes of Dynastic Families in Late Twentieth-Century America* (Boulder, CO: Westview Press, 1992).

74. Michael Gilding, "Motives of the Rich and Powerful in Doing Interviews with Social Scientists," *International Sociology* 25 (2010): 755–777.

75. Laura Nader, "Up the Anthropologist: Perspectives Gained from Studying Up," in D. Hynes, ed., *Reinventing Anthropology*, 284–311 (New York: Pantheon, 1972), 302.

76. David Cay Johnston, "Costly Questions Arise on Legal Opinions for Tax Shelters," *New York Times*, February 9, 2003.

77. Marcus, "The Fiduciary Role."

78. Sharman, *Havens in a Storm.*

79. Robin Lakoff, "The Logic of Politeness: Or, Minding Your P's and Q's," *Papers from the Ninth Regional Meeting of the Chicago Linguistic Society*, 292–305 (Chicago: Chicago Linguistic Society, 1973).

80. Leah Goodman, "Inside the World's Top Offshore Tax Shelter," *Newsweek*, January 16, 2014. The details on Goodman's deportation and the ultimate removal of the U.K. travel ban can be found in the post "When Journalism Works," July 18, 2013, on Goodman's website, http://leahmcgrathgoodman.com/2013/07/18/when-journalism-works.

81. Brooke Harrington, "Immersion Ethnography of Elites," in K. Elsbach and R. Kramer, eds., *Handbook of Qualitative Organizational Research*, 134–142 (New York: Routledge, 2015).

82. Brooke Harrington, "The Social Psychology of Access in Ethnographic Research," *Journal of Contemporary Ethnography* 32 (2003): 592–625.

83. John van Maanen, "Observations on the Making of Policemen," *Human Organization* 32 (1973): 407–418.

84. Clifford Geertz, *The Interpretation of Cultures: Selected Essays* (New York: Basic Books, 1973).

85. Joseph Conti and Moira O'Neil, "Studying Power: Qualitative Methods and the Global Elite," *Qualitative Research* 7 (2007): 63–82.

86. Bourdieu, *Outline of a Theory of Practice*.

87. William Harvey, "Strategies for Conducting Elite Interviews," *Qualitative Research* 11 (2011): 431–441.

88. Philip Davies, "Spies as Informants: Triangulation and the Interpretation of Elite Interview Data in the Study of the Intelligence and Security Services," *Politics* 21 (2001): 73–80.

89. Max Weber, *Economy and Society* (New York: Bedminster Press, 1968 [1925]), 1:4.

90. Jens Beckert and Wolfgang Streeck, "Economic Sociology and Political Economy: A Programmatic Perspective," Working Paper 08/4, 2008, Max Planck Institute for the Study of Societies, Cologne, Germany.

91. Harrington, "The Social Psychology of Access." See also Brooke Harrington, "Obtrusiveness as Strategy in Ethnographic Research," *Qualitative Sociology* 25 (2002): 49–61.

92. For "world polity" approach, see John Meyer, John Boli, George Thomas, and Francisco Ramirez, "World Society and the Nation-state," *American Journal of Sociology* 103 (1997): 144–181. For states and classes approach, see Nicos Poulantzas, *State, Power, Socialism* (London: Verso, 2000). See also Theda Skocpol, *States and Social Revolutions: A Comparative Analysis of France, Russia, and China* (Cambridge, UK: Cambridge University Press, 1979).

93. Bruce Carruthers and Terence Halliday, "Negotiating Globalization: Global Scripts and Intermediation in the Construction of Asian Insolvency Regimes," *Law and Social Inquiry* 31 (2006): 521–584.

94. David Richards, "Elite Interviews: Approaches and Pitfalls," *Politics* 16 (1996): 200.

95. Robert Mikecz, "Interviewing Elites: Addressing Methodological Issues," *Qualitative Inquiry* 18 (2012): 483.

96. More information on credentials available in wealth management can be found on the website of the U.S. Financial Industry Regulatory Authority (FINRA) at http://apps.finra.org/DataDirectory/1/prodesignations.aspx.

97. Harrington, "Trust and Estate Planning."

98. Ann Ryen, "Ethical Issues in Qualitative Research," in Clive Seale, Giampietro Gobo, Jaber Gubrium, and David Silverman, eds., *Qualitative Research Practice*, 230–247 (Thousand Oaks, CA: Sage Publications, 2004).

99. This figure treats Hong Kong as part of the People's Republic of China, along with Shanghai, while Jersey and Guernsey are counted as separate countries—a status that reflects their history as the "last remnant" of the feudal state system that existed at the time of the Norman Conquest almost a thousand years ago. James Minahan, *The Complete Guide to National Symbols and Emblems* (San Francisco: Greenwood, 2009), 419.

100. Andrew Cook, James Faulconbridge, and Daniel Muzio, "London's Legal Elite: Recruitment through Cultural Capital and the Reproduction of Social Exclusivity in City Professional Service Fields," *Environment and Planning* 44 (2012): 1744–1762.

101. Bar Council, *Statistics: Demographic Profile of the Bar* (London: Bar Council, 2010). See also American Bar Association (ABA), *The Lawyer Statistical Report* (Chicago: American Bar Association, 2012).

2. Wealth Management as a Profession

1. Talcott Parsons, "The Professions and Social Structure," *Social Forces* 17 (1939): 457–467.

2. Steven Brint and Jerome Karabel, *The Diverted Dream: Community Colleges and the Promise of Educational Opportunity in America, 1900–1985* (New York: Oxford University Press, 1989).

3. Steven Brint, *In an Age of Experts: The Changing Role of Professionals in Politics and Public Life* (Princeton: Princeton University Press, 1994).

4. Harlan Stone, "The Public Influence of the Bar," *Harvard Law Review* 48 (1934): 1–14.

5. Eliot Krause, *The Death of the Guilds: Professions, States and the Advance of Capitalism* (New Haven, CT: Yale University Press, 1996).

6. Stephen Haseler, *The Super-Rich: The Unjust New World of Global Capitalism* (New York: Palgrave, 2000), 72. As Jens Beckert— director of the Max Planck Institute for the Study of Societies in Cologne, Germany—has pointed out in a personal communication, this characterization may do an injustice to the feudal era, since nobles of that period had some obligations toward their dependents; in contrast, the wealthy elites of today have few obligations, if any, toward those on the lower rungs of the socioeconomic ladder. The

more apt comparison may be to the unchecked exploitation of the Gilded Age of the late nineteenth and early twentieth centuries.

7. On Jersey and Guernsey, see James Minahan, *The Complete Guide to National Symbols and Emblems* (San Francisco: Greenwood, 2009), 419. On Liechtenstein, see Gwillim Law, *Administrative Subdivisions of Countries: A Comprehensive World Reference 1900 through 1998* (Jefferson, NC: McFarland, 2010), 220. On Malta and others, see Martin Lewis, "The Knights of Malta: Sovereignty Without Territory," *Geocurrents*, March 18, 2010.

8. Figures from Boston Consulting Group, *Global Wealth 2015: Winning the Growth Game* (Boston: BCG, 2015), www.bcg.it/documents /file190567.pdf. Quotation from Nicholas Shaxson, *Treasure Islands: Tax Havens and the Men Who Stole the World* (London: Random House, 2011). Shaxson is citing the words of Professor Maurice Glassman, of London Metropolitan University.

9. George Marcus and Peter Hall, *Lives in Trust: The Fortunes of Dynastic Families in Late Twentieth-Century America* (Boulder, CO: Westview Press, 1992), 64.

10. Eliot Freidson, *Professionalism: The Third Logic* (London: Polity, 2001).

11. John Langbein, "Rise of the Management Trust," *Trusts & Estates* 142 (2004): 52–57. See also John Langbein, "The Contractarian Basis of the Law of Trusts," *Yale Law Journal* 105 (1995): 625–675.

12. Frederic Maitland, *Equity: A Course of Lectures* (Cambridge: Cambridge University Press, 2011 [1909]), 23.

13. Anita Cervone, *Sworn Bond in Tudor England: Oaths, Vows and Covenants in Civil Life and Literature* (Jefferson, NC: McFarland, 2011).

14. A. Gurevich, "Representations of Property in the High Middle Ages," *Economy and Society* 6 (1977): 1–30.

15. Bernard Hibbitts, "Coming to Our Senses: Communication and Legal Expression in Performance Cultures," *Emory Law Journal* 41 (1992): 873–960.

16. John Austin, *Philosophical Papers* (Oxford, UK: Oxford University Press, 1961); Walter Beale, *Learning from Language: Symmetry, Asymmetry, and Literary Humanism* (Pittsburgh, PA: University of Pittsburgh Press, 2009).

17. R. B. Outhwaite, *The Rise and Fall of the English Ecclesiastical Courts, 1500–1860* (Cambridge, UK: Cambridge University Press, 2006).

18. R. J. Barendse, "The Feudal Mutation: Military and Economic Transformations of the Ethnosphere in the Tenth to Thirteenth Centuries," *Journal of World History* 14 (2003): 515.

19. Ibid.

20. Dan Terkla, "Cut on the Norman Bias: Fabulous Borders and Visual Glosses on the Bayeux Tapestry," *Word and Image* 11 (1995): 264–290.

21. Langbein, "The Contractarian Basis."

22. George Marcus, "The Fiduciary Role in American Family Dynasties and Their Institutional Legacy," in George Marcus, ed., *Elites: Ethnographic Issues*, 221–256 (Albuquerque: University of New Mexico Press, 1983), 231.

23. Trusts are not recognized by the civil law governing continental Europe, as well as much of South America and the Middle East; however, citizens of civil-law countries can (and often do) establish trusts in common-law jurisdictions. This will be explored at greater length in Chapter 4.

24. Chantal Stebbings, "Trustees, Tribunals and Taxes: Creativity in Victorian Law," *Amicus Curiae* 70 (2007): 3.

25. Frederic Maitland, *Selected Essays*, ed. Dexter Hazeltine, Gaillard Lapsley, and Percy Winfield (Cambridge, UK: Cambridge University Press, 1936), 175.

26. Langbein, "The Contractarian Basis," 638.

27. Barendse, "The Feudal Mutation."

28. Scott Waugh, "Tenure to Contract: Lordship and Clientage in Thirteenth-Century England," *English Historical Review* 101 (1986): 811–839.

29. Jason Sharman, *Havens in a Storm: The Struggle for Global Tax Regulation* (Ithaca, NY: Cornell University Press, 2006). This struggle endured for centuries, long past the Middle Ages; in the sixteenth century, for example, Henry VIII proposed the Statute of Uses to put elites' landholdings back within absolute royal control, and thus within the Crown's revenue system. We are now witnessing a similar back-and-forth between international governing bodies and global socioeconomic elites, in which ownership and taxation rights over primarily financial assets are at stake.

30. Tamar Frankel, "Cross-Border Securitization: Without Law, but Not Lawless," *Duke Journal of Comparative and International Law* 8 (1998): 258.

31. Alan Greenspan, commencement address delivered June 10, 1999, at Harvard University, Cambridge, MA, www.federalreserve.gov /boarddocs/speeches/1999/199906102.htm.
32. Roscoe Pound, *An Introduction to the Philosophy of Law* (New Haven, CT: Yale University Press, 1922), 236.
33. The medieval imprint continues to be visible in the language of trusts. For example, the notion of "indenture"—an instrument used by a lord to retain the services of an aide (Waugh, "Tenure to Contract")—carries over into the present-day "trust indenture." See, for example, the Trust Indenture Acts in U.S. law, which govern commercial trusts containing bonds and other debt instruments.
34. Michael Parkinson, *Trust Creation: Law and Practice*, 3rd ed. (Birmingham, UK: Central Law Training, 2005).
35. Frank Easterbrook and Daniel Fischel, "Contract and Fiduciary Duty," *Journal of Law and Economics* 36 (1993): 426–427.
36. Langbein, "The Contractarian Basis."
37. Francis Sanders, *An Essay on the Nature and Laws of Uses and Trusts, Including a Treatise on Conveyances at Common Law and Those Deriving Their Effect from the Statute of Uses* (London: E. & R. Brooke, 1791), 256, emphasis and spelling in original text.
38. American Bar Association, *Uniform Prudent Investor Act* (Chicago: ABA, 1994), www.law.upenn.edu/bll/archives/ulc/fnact99/1990s /upia94.pdf. Fiduciary administration of trusts is also governed by many subrules, including the duty to keep and render accounts, enforce and defend claims against trust assets, and minimize costs.
39. Despite their breadth, the rules remain meaningful and enforceable, as evidenced by the many successful lawsuits brought against trustees for breach of fiduciary duty; for several interesting cases, see John Harper, "The Ethical Trustee," *STEP Journal*, September 2010, 17.
40. Benjamin Cardozo, opinion in *Meinhard v. Salmon*, 164 N.E. 545 (N.Y. 1928), at 546.
41. Geoffrey Chaucer, *Canterbury Tales* (Mineola, NY: Dover, 1994 [1478]).
42. Langbein, "The Contractarian Basis," 638.
43. Langbein, "Rise of the Management Trust," 53.
44. The Bubble Act of 1720 forbade the creation of new joint-stock companies, except by royal charter. Passage of this law was intended to prevent the kind of speculation that that had led to the ruinous South

Sea Bubble earlier that year. Brooke Harrington, "States and Financial Crises," in Benedikte Brincker, ed., *Introduction to Political Sociology*, 267–282 (Copenhagen: Gyldendal Akademisk, 2013).

45. Michael Parkinson and Dai Jones, *Trust Administration and Accounts*, 4th ed. (Birmingham, UK: Central Law Training, 2008), 111.

46. Ibid.

47. Stebbings, "Trustees, Tribunals and Taxes."

48. Viviana Zelizer, "Payments and Social Ties," *Sociological Forum* 11 (1996): 481–495.

49. Bernard Rudden, review of *The Restatement of Trusts, Modern Law Review* 44 (1981): 610. See also John Langbein, "The Secret Life of the Trust: The Trust as an Instrument of Commerce," *Yale Law Journal* 107 (1997): 165–189.

50. Peter Hall, "Family Structure and Class Consolidation among the Boston Brahmins," Ph.D. diss., State University of New York at Stony Brook, 1973, 282.

51. Stebbings, "Trustees, Tribunals and Taxes," 7.

52. In this landmark case, a beneficiary of the McLean family trust (Harvard College) sued the trustee (Francis Amory) for having invested trust assets in stocks that lost money, thereby depleting the amount received by the beneficiary. The court sided with the trustee, stating that Amory—having been explicitly instructed by the trust instrument to invest in corporate stocks—had acted prudently and should not be blamed for the inherent instability of prices. See Samuel Putnam, "Harvard College versus Amory," *Journal of Portfolio Management* 3 (1976): 67–71.

53. Lawrence Friedman, *Dead Hands: A Social History of Wills, Trusts, and Inheritance Law* (Stanford, CA: Stanford University Press, 2009), 115.

54. Keith Macdonald, *The Sociology of the Professions* (London: Sage, 1995).

55. Marcus and Hall, *Lives in Trust*, 65.

56. Langbein, "Rise of the Management Trust."

57. Stebbings, "Trustees, Tribunals and Taxes," 4.

58. Jonathan Beaverstock, Philip Hubbard, and John Short, "Getting Away with It? Exposing the Geographies of the Super-rich," *Geoforum* 35 (2004): 401–407.

59. Jeffrey Winters, *Oligarchy* (New York: Cambridge University Press, 2011), 219.
60. Ibid.
61. Zygmunt Bauman, *Community: Seeking Security in an Insecure World* (Cambridge, UK: Polity, 2000). See also L. Sklair, "The Transnational Capitalist Class," in James Carrier and Daniel Miller, eds., *Virtualism: A New Political Economy*, 135–159 (Oxford, UK: Berg, 1997).
62. Marcus and Hall, *Lives in Trust*, 70. See also Marion Fourcade, "The Construction of a Global Profession: The Transnationalization of Economics," *American Journal of Sociology* 112 (2006): 145–194.
63. STEP, *STEP: The First Fifteen Years* (London: Society of Trust and Estate Practitioners, 2006), 1.
64. From remarks delivered at STEP South Africa conference, May 28, 2012.
65. Scott Devine, "Revealed: Incompetence and Dishonesty of Cowboy Will Writers," news release, STEP, January 26, 2011.
66. Ronen Palan, Richard Murphy, and Christian Chavagneux, *Tax Havens: How Globalization Really Works* (Ithaca, NY: Cornell University Press, 2010).
67. Sharman, *Havens in a Storm.*
68. Magali Larson, *The Rise of Professionalism: A Sociological Analysis* (Berkeley: University of California Press, 1977), 50.
69. Sigrid Quack, "Legal Professionals and Trans-national Law Making: A Case of Distributed Agency," *Organization* 14 (2007): 643–666. See also Royston Greenwood, Roy Suddaby, and C. R. Hinings, "Theorizing Change: The Role of Professional Associations in the Transformation of Institutionalized Fields," *Academy of Management Journal* 45 (2002): 58–80.
70. Peter Haas, "Introduction: Epistemic Communities and International Policy Coordination," *International Organization* 46 (1992): 1–35.
71. Jane Jenson and Boaventura de Sousa Santos, "Introduction: Case Studies and Common Trends in Globalizations," in Jane Jenson and Boaventura de Sousa Santos, eds., *Globalizing Institutions: Case Studies in Regulation and Innovation*, 9–26 (Aldershot, UK: Ashgate, 2000).
72. Greenwood et al., "Theorizing Change," 59.

73. Jennifer Palmer-Violet, "Championing the Cause," *STEP Journal*, October 2012.

74. Ward L. Thomas and Leonard Henzke, "Trusts: Common Law and IRC 501(C)(3) and 4947," 2003 EO CPE Text, U.S. Internal Revenue Service, Washington, DC, 2003, www.irs.gov/pub/irs-tege/eotopica03 .pdf.

75. Andrew Abbott, *The System of Professions: An Essay on the Division of Expert Labor* (Chicago: University of Chicago Press, 1988).

76. Randall Collins, *The Credential Society* (New York: Academic Press, 1979); John Heinz and Edward Laumann, *Chicago Lawyers: The Social Structure of the Bar* (Evanston, IL: Northwestern University Press, 1994).

77. David Sciulli, "Revision in Sociology of the Professions Today," *Sociologica* 3 (2008): 34.

78. Pierre Bourdieu and Loïc Wacquant, *Invitation to Reflexive Sociology* (Chicago: University of Chicago Press, 1992).

79. Karen Ho, *Liquidated: An Ethnography of Wall Street* (Durham, NC: Duke University Press, 2009).

80. U.S. Bureau of Labor Statistics, data for the category "Other Financial Investment Activities," which includes financial advisers and managers, 2013, www.bls.gov/oes/current/oes113031.htm.

81. Louise Story, "Executive Pay," *New York Times*, March 3, 2011.

82. Louise Story and Eric Dash, "Banks Prepare for Big Bonuses, and Public Wrath," *New York Times*, January 9, 2009.

83. Martin Williams, "Finance Industry Wages Rise Faster than Any Other Sector," *The Guardian*, February 26, 2013.

84. Philip Ruce, "Anti–Money Laundering: The Challenges of Know Your Customer Legislation for Private Bankers and the Hidden Benefits for Relationship Management ('The Bright Side of Knowing Your Customer')," *Banking Law Journal* 128 (2011): 548–564.

85. Tjun Tang, Brent Beardsley, Jorge Becerra, Bruce Holley, Daniel Kessler, Matthias Naumann, and Anna Zakrzewski, *Global Wealth 2013: Maintaining Momentum in a Complex World* (Boston: Boston Consulting Group, 2013).

86. McKinsey & Company, *Searching for Profitable Growth in Asset Management: It's about More than Investment Alpha* (New York: McKinsey, 2012).

87. Freidson, *Professionalism*, 17.

88. Michel Pinçon and Monique Pinçon-Charlot, *Grand Fortunes: Dynasties of Wealth in France*, trans. Andrea Lyn Secara (New York: Algora, 1998), 29.

89. Peer Fiss and Paul Hirsch, "The Discourse of Globalization: Framing and Sensemaking of an Emerging Concept," *American Sociological Review* 70 (2005): 29–52.

90. Patrik Aspers, *Orderly Fashion: A Sociology of Markets* (Princeton, NJ: Princeton University Press, 2010).

91. Vincent Manancourt, "Wealth Managers Are Having to Merge to Survive as Regulation Gets Tighter," *Financial Times*, September 19, 2014.

92. Deborah DeMott, "Internal Compliance Officers in Jeopardy?" *Australian Law Journal* 87 (2013): 451–454.

93. Ruce, "Anti–Money Laundering."

94. Joe Nocera, "The Good, the Bad and the Ugly of Capitalism," *New York Times*, March 16, 2012.

95. Richard Adams, "Goldman Sachs Senate Hearing: As It Happened," *The Guardian*, April 27, 2010.

96. Rudden, review of *The Restatement of Trusts*, 610.

97. Marcus and Hall, *Lives in Trust*, 71.

98. Indeed, if she had employed the Goldman model, she might have made more on the fees the client paid in order to place the disastrous trade, and even more by betting against him (taking a short position) than she could have by taking in his ordinary fees for wealth management. This is what Nocera ("The Good, the Bad and the Ugly of Capitalism") called "rip your eyeballs out" capitalism.

99. Barbara Reskin and Patricia Roos, *Job Queues, Gender Queues* (Philadelphia: Temple University Press, 1990).

100. Paul Oyer, "The Making of an Investment Banker: Stock Market Shocks, Career Choice, and Lifetime Income," *Journal of Finance* 63 (2009): 2601–2628.

101. STEP, "What Do STEP Members Do?" www.step.org/what-step-does, accessed October 6, 2014. The title and text of the note has undergone some minor changes since this chapter was written, but the emphasis on helping families remains.

102. Gregg Van Ryzin, "The Curious Case of the Post-9/11 Boost in Government Job Satisfaction," *American Review of Public Administration* 44 (2014): 59–74.

103. Robert Frank, "Another Widening Gap: The Haves vs. the Have-Mores," *New York Times*, November 15, 2014.
104. Peter Hall and George Marcus, "Why Should Men Leave Great Fortunes to Their Children? Class, Dynasty and Inheritance in America," in Robert Miller and Stephen McNamee, eds., *Inheritance and Wealth in America*, 139–171 (New York: Plenum, 1998).
105. Rachel Emma Silverman, "A Burden of Wealth: Family-Office Hunting," *Wall Street Journal*, January 3, 2008.
106. Robert Milburn, "Family Office Boom," *Barron's*, April 21, 2014.
107. Ibid.
108. Susan Cartwright and Nicola Holmes, "The Meaning of Work: The Challenge of Regaining Employee Engagement and Reducing Cynicism," *Human Resource Management Review* 16 (2006): 199–208.
109. Langbein, "The Contractarian Basis," 644.
110. Robert Clark, *Corporate Law* (New York: Aspen, 1986), 676.
111. Viviana Zelizer, "Circuits within Capitalism," in Richard Swedberg and Victor Nee, eds., *The Economic Sociology of Capitalism*, 289–321 (Princeton, NJ: Princeton University Press, 2005).
112. Lynne Zucker, "Production of Trust: Institutional Sources of Economic Structure, 1840–1920," *Research in Organizational Behavior* 8 (1986): 53–111.
113. Ibid., 100–101.

3. Client Relations

1. In one recent study, lawyers' relationships with clients were considered enduring if they lasted at least three years. Harris Kim, "Market Uncertainty and Socially Embedded Reputation," *American Journal of Economics and Sociology* 68 (2009): 679–701. A study of consumer behavior in financial services concluded that the vast majority (64 percent) of client relations with investment advisers lasted fewer than six years. Barry Howcroft, Paul Hewer, and Robert Hamilton, "Consumer Decision-making Styles and the Purchase of Financial Services," *Service Industries Journal* 23 (2003): 63–81.
2. John Langbein, "The Contractarian Basis of the Law of Trusts," *Yale Law Journal* 105 (1995): 661.

3. James Hughes, *Family Wealth: Keeping It in the Family* (Princeton Junction, NJ: NetWrx, 1997). See also George Marcus and Peter Hall, *Lives in Trust: The Fortunes of Dynastic Families in Late Twentieth-Century America* (Boulder, CO: Westview Press, 1992).

4. Max Weber, "Bureaucracy," in Hans Gerth and C. Wright Mills, eds., *From Max Weber*, 196–244 (New York: Oxford University Press, 1946 [1922]), 233.

5. Jessie O'Neill, *The Golden Ghetto: The Psychology of Affluence* (Milwaukee, WI: The Affluenza Project, 1997).

6. Michel Panoff and Michel Perrin, *Dictionnaire de l'ethnologie* (Paris: Payot, 1973), 259.

7. Donald Ferrin and Nicole Gillespie, "Trust Differences across National-Societal Cultures: Much to Do, or Much Ado about Nothing?" in Mark Saunders, Denise Skinner, Graham Dietz, Nicole Gillespie, and Roy Lewicki, eds., *Organizational Trust: A Cultural Perspective*, 42–86 (Cambridge, UK: Cambridge University Press, 2010), 44.

8. Nicholas Shaxson, *Treasure Islands: Tax Havens and the Men Who Stole the World* (London: Random House, 2011), 230.

9. Langbein, "The Contractarian Basis." See also Michael Parkinson, *Trust Creation: Law and Practice*, 3rd ed. (Birmingham, UK: Central Law Training, 2005).

10. Alison Wylie, "The Promise and Perils of an Ethic of Stewardship," in Lynn Meskell and Peter Pells, eds., *Embedding Ethics*, 47–68 (London: Berg Press, 2005).

11. O'Neill, *The Golden Ghetto*.

12. Jeffrey Bradach and Robert Eccles, "Price, Authority, and Trust: From Ideal Types to Plural Forms," *Annual Review of Sociology* 15 (1989): 108.

13. Scott Waugh, "Tenure to Contract: Lordship and Clientage in Thirteenth-Century England," *English Historical Review* 101 (1986): 825.

14. The Trusts (Guernsey) Law, 1989, Section 18.1, http://bpt-offshore.com/downloads/offshorelegislation/Guernsey/The-Trusts-%28Guernsey%29-Law1989.pdf, accessed April 11, 2015.

15. Marcus and Hall, *Lives in Trust*, 60.

16. Ibid., 70, emphasis added.

17. See Arlie Hochschild, *The Managed Heart: The Commercialization of Human Feeling* (Berkeley: University of California Press, 1983).

18. Langbein, "The Contractarian Basis."

19. Christian Stewart, "Family Business Succession Planning: East versus West," *STEP Journal*, January 2010, 27–29.

20. Erving Goffman, *The Presentation of Self in Everyday Life* (New York: Doubleday, 1956).

21. Gerard Hanlon, "Institutional Forms and Organizational Structures: Homology, Trust and Reputational Capital in Professional Service Firms," *Organization* 11 (2004): 205.

22. Madeline Levine, *The Price of Privilege* (New York: Harper, 2006).

23. John van Maanen and Ed Schein, "Toward a Theory of Organizational Socialization," *Research in Organizational Behavior* 1 (1979): 226.

24. Pierre Bourdieu, "The Force of Law: Toward a Sociology of the Juridical Field," *Hastings Law Journal* 38 (1987): 817.

25. Pierre Bourdieu, *Outline of a Theory of Practice* (Cambridge, UK: Cambridge University Press, 1977), 94. Italics in original.

26. Andrew Cook, James Faulconbridge, and Daniel Muzio, "London's Legal Elite: Recruitment through Cultural Capital and the Reproduction of Social Exclusivity in City Professional Service Fields," *Environment and Planning* 44 (2012): 1749.

27. Louise Ashley and Laura Empson, "Differentiation and Discrimination: Understanding Social Class and Social Exclusion in Leading Law Firms," *Human Relations* 66 (2013): 221.

28. Kathryn Haynes, "Body Beautiful? Gender, Identity and the Body in Professional Services Firms," *Gender, Work and Organization* 19 (2012): 490.

29. Liz McDowell, "Elites in the City of London: Some Methodological Considerations," *Environment and Planning* 30 (1998): 2135.

30. Michael Hogg, "Social Identity and the Group Context of Trust: Managing Risk and Building Trust through Belonging," in Michael Siegrist, Timothy Earle, and Heinz Gutscher, eds., *Trust in Cooperative Risk Management: Uncertainty and Scepticism in the Public Mind*, 51–72 (London: Earthscan, 2007).

31. Keith Macdonald, *The Sociology of the Professions* (London: Sage, 1995), 31.

32. Michael Useem, *The Inner Circle: Large Corporations and the Rise of Business Political Activity in the US and UK* (New York: Oxford University Press, 1986).
33. Marcus and Hall, *Lives in Trust*, 66.
34. Michel Pinçon and Monique Pinçon-Charlot, *Grand Fortunes: Dynasties of Wealth in France*, trans. Andrea Lyn Secara (New York: Algora, 1998).
35. Pierre Bourdieu, *Distinction: A Social Critique of the Judgement of Taste* (Cambridge, MA: Harvard University Press, 1994), 475.
36. Pete Mitchell, "Risky Business," *STEP Journal*, August 2011.
37. James Faulconbridge, Daniel Muzio, and Andrew Cook, "Institutional Legacies in TNCs and Their Management through Training Academies: The Case of Transnational Law Firms in Italy," *Global Networks* 12 (2012): 48–70.
38. Bourdieu, *Outline of a Theory of Practice*, 167.
39. Parkinson, *Trust Creation*, 33, emphasis added.
40. Ashley and Empson, "Differentiation and Discrimination."
41. Pierre Bourdieu, *The Logic of Practice* (Cambridge, UK: Polity, 1990).
42. Danny Quah, "The Global Economy's Shifting Centre of Gravity," working paper, London School of Economics, 2010, http://econ.lse.ac.uk/staff/dquah/p/2010.07-GE_Shifting_CG-DQ.pdf.
43. Suzi Dixon, "Singapore 'Could Be the World's Largest Offshore Finance Centre by 2015,'" *The Telegraph*, January 19, 2014.
44. Clifford Geertz, "The Bazaar Economy: Information and Search in Peasant Marketing," *American Economic Review* 68 (1978): 28–32.
45. John Langbein, "Questioning the Trust Law Duty of Loyalty: Sole Interest or Best Interest?" *Yale Law Journal* 114 (2005): 929–990.
46. Lusina Ho, *Trust Law in China* (Andover, UK: Sweet & Maxwell, 2003), 67.
47. Paul Zak and Stephen Knack, "Trust and Growth," *Economic Journal* 111 (2001): 295–321.
48. Patricia Doney, Joseph Cannon, and Michael Mullen, "Understanding the Influence of National Culture on the Development of Trust," *Academy of Management Review* 23 (1998): 601–620.
49. Ferrin and Gillespie, "Trust Differences," 44.
50. Jan Delhey and Kenneth Newton, "Predicting Cross-National Levels of Social Trust: Global Pattern or Nordic Exceptionalism?" *European Sociological Review* 21 (2005): 311–327.

51. Bruce Carruthers and Terence Halliday, "Negotiating Globalization: Global Scripts and Intermediation in the Construction of Asian Insolvency Regimes," *Law & Social Inquiry* 31 (2006): 530.

52. Chanthika Pornpitakpan, "The Effect of Cultural Adaptation on Perceived Trustworthiness: Americans Adapting to Chinese Indonesians," *Asia Pacific Journal of Marketing and Logistics* 17 (2005): 70–88.

53. Sami Zubaida, "Max Weber's *The City* and the Islamic City," *Max Weber Studies* 6 (2006): 111–118.

54. Max Weber, *Economy and Society*, vol. 2 (Berkeley: University of California Press, 1978).

55. Monica Gaudiosi, "The Influence of the Islamic Law of *Waqf* on the Development of the Trust in England: The Case of Merton College," *University of Pennsylvania Law Review* 136 (1988): 1231–1261. This raises a question: why don't contemporary Muslims use the *waqf* (also spelled *vakf*, which will be used throughout this text) instead of the trust structure for wealth management? One reason may be that wealth held in a *vakf* must ultimately be distributed for charitable purposes. Trusts are not limited in this way. They can be used for philanthropy but have much broader applications; in addition, they are more widely recognized internationally, which may make them more desirable in modern finance.

56. Max Weber, *From Max Weber: Essays in Sociology* (New York: Oxford University Press, 1946).

57. Cheris Chan, "Creating a Market in the Presence of Cultural Resistance: The Case of Life Insurance in China," *Theory and Society* 38 (2009): 300–301.

58. Langbein, "The Contractarian Basis."

59. Cap-Gemini, *World Wealth Report*, 2014, https://www.worldwealth report.com/download.

60. Simon Gray, "VISTA Trusts Allow BVI to Slough off Past and Attract Global Businesses," *The Lawyer*, January 17, 2005. See also Marcus Leese, "Settle Down," *STEP Journal*, February 2012.

61. Geert Hofstede, *Masculinity and Femininity: The Taboo Dimension of National Cultures* (Thousand Oaks, CA: Sage Publications, 1998).

62. Guido Mölleringa, "Leaps and Lapses of Faith: Exploring the Relationship between Trust and Deception," in Brooke Harrington, ed., *Deception: From Ancient Empires to Internet Dating*, 137–153 (Stanford, CA: Stanford University Press, 2009).

63. Chan, "Creating a Market."

64. Haynes, "Body Beautiful?"

65. Brooke Harrington, "The Social Psychology of Access in Ethnographic Research," *Journal of Contemporary Ethnography* 32 (2003): 592–625.

66. Macdonald, "The Sociology of the Professions," 188.

67. Kathryn Lively, "Client Contact and Emotional Labor: Upsetting the Balance and Evening the Field," *Work and Occupations* 29 (2002): 198–225. See also Erving Goffman, *Asylums* (New York: Doubleday, 1961).

68. Rachel Sherman, "'Time Is Our Commodity': Gender and the Struggle for Occupational Legitimacy among Personal Concierges," *Work and Occupations* 37 (2011): 81–114.

69. Pierre Bourdieu, *Language and Symbolic Power* (Cambridge, MA: Harvard University Press, 1999), 234.

70. Molly George, "Interactions in Expert Service Work: Demonstrating Professionalism in Personal Training," *Journal of Contemporary Ethnography* 37 (2008): 110.

4. Tactics and Techniques of Wealth Management

1. Jürgen Habermas, *The Theory of Communicative Action*, vol. 2, *Lifeworld and System: A Critique of Functionalist Reason* (Boston: Beacon Press, 1985).

2. Katherine Rehl, "Help Your Clients Preserve Values, Tell Life Stories and Share the Voice of Their Hearts through Ethical Wills," *Journal of Practical Estate Planning* 5 (2003): 17.

3. Norman Peagam, "Nine Centres Worth Finding on the Map," *Euromoney*, May 1989, 4–10.

4. Thorstein Veblen, *The Theory of the Leisure Class* (Oxford, UK: Oxford University Press, 2009 [1899]), 155.

5. Zygmunt Bauman, *Community: Seeking Security in an Insecure World* (Cambridge, UK: Polity, 2000).

6. Greta Krippner, "The Financialization of the American Economy," *Socio-Economic Review* 3 (2005): 173–208. See also Giovanni Arrighi, *The Long Twentieth Century* (London: Verso, 1994).

7. Philip Genschel, "Globalization and the Transformation of the Tax State," *European Review* 13 (2005): 53–71.

8. Jonathan Beaverstock, Philip Hubbard, and John Short, "Getting Away with It? Exposing the Geographies of the Super-rich," *Geoforum* 35 (2004): 401–407.

9. Michel Pinçon and Monique Pinçon-Charlot, *Grand Fortunes: Dynasties of Wealth in France*, trans. Andrea Lyn Secara (New York: Algora, 1998).

10. Stuart Turnbull, "Swaps: A Zero-Sum Game?" *Financial Management* 16 (1987): 15–21.

11. Graham Moffat, *Trust Law: Text and Materials* (Cambridge, UK: Cambridge University Press, 2009), 113.

12. U.S. Congress Joint Committee on Taxation, *Report of Investigation of Enron Corporation and Related Entities Regarding Federal Tax and Compensation Issues, and Policy Recommendations*, Report JCS-3-03 (Washington, DC: General Printing Office, 2003), 260.

13. Peagam, "Nine Centres."

14. Ibid.

15. Krippner, "The Financialization of the American Economy"; Arrighi, *The Long Twentieth Century*.

16. "Trawling for Business: The Gambia Looks to Join a Beleaguered Club," *The Economist*, August 24, 2013.

17. Brent Beardsley, Jorge Becerra, Federico Burgoni, Bruce Holley, Daniel Kessler, Federico Muxi, Matthias Naumann, Tjun Tang, and Anna Zakrzewski, *Global Wealth 2014: Riding a Wave of Growth* (Boston: Boston Consulting Group, 2014). See also Jorge Becerra, Peter Damisch, Bruce Holley, Monish Kuman, Matthias Naumann, Tjun Tang, and Anna Zakrzewski, *Shaping a New Tomorrow: How to Capitalize on the Momentum of Change* (Boston: Boston Consulting Group, 2011).

18. For the distribution of wealth among OFCs, see Beardsley et al., *Global Wealth 2014*. For the number of OFCs worldwide, see Ronan Palan, "Tax Havens and the Commercialization of State Sovereignty," *International Organization* 56 (2002): 151–176; see also Robert Miller, "Offshore Trusts: Trends Toward 2000," *Trusts & Trustees* 1 (1995): 7–10.

19. Michael Parkinson, *Certificate in International Trust Management*, 4th ed. (Birmingham, UK: Central Law Training, 2004).

20. Ibid, 11.

21. Nicholas Shaxson, *Treasure Islands: Tax Havens and the Men Who Stole the World* (London: Random House, 2011), 10, 8.

22. Palan, "Tax Havens and the Commercialization of State Sovereignty."

23. Ian Fazey, "World Banking System Is 'a Money Launderer's Dream,'" *Financial Times*, May 26, 1998.

24. Practitioners avoid involvement in illegal financial activities not only in consideration of personal and professional ethics but also because of the increasingly severe legal penalties imposed for facilitating such transactions; see Chapter 5.

25. Prem Sikka, "Accountants: A Threat to Democracy: The Tax Avoidance Industry Has a Veto on What Services the Government Can Provide," *The Guardian*, September 5, 2005.

26. Centre des Archives Économiques et Financières, *La bourse de Paris: Origines et historique, 1826–1926* (Paris: Éditions G. Gorce, 1926).

27. Alfred Fierro, *Histoire et dictionnaire de Paris* (Paris: Éditions Robert Laffont, 1999).

28. Palan, "Tax Havens and the Commercialization of State Sovereignty," 159.

29. Merritt Fox, "The Legal Environment of International Finance: Thinking about Fundamentals," *Michigan Journal of International Law* 17 (1996): 729.

30. Sigrid Quack, "Legal Professionals and Trans-national Law Making: A Case of Distributed Agency," *Organization* 14 (2007): 643–666.

31. Tamar Frankel, "Cross-Border Securitization: Without Law, but Not Lawless," *Duke Journal of Comparative and International Law* 8 (1998): 255–282.

32. Richard Deeg and Mary O'Sullivan, "The Political Economy of Global Finance Capital," *World Politics* 61 (2009): 731–763.

33. For first quotation, see Quack, "Legal Professionals," 653. For second quotation, see Frankel, "Cross-Border Securitization," 255.

34. Ibid.

35. David Leigh, Harold Frayman, and James Ball, "Offshore Secrets: British Virgin Islands, Land of Sand, Sea and Secrecy," *The Guardian*, November 25, 2012.

36. Michael Parkinson, *Diploma in International Trust Management: Trust Creation: Law and Practice*, 3rd ed. (Birmingham, UK: Central Law Training, 2005), 277.

37. Ibid, 276. For the remark about "confiscatory" taxation, see Miller, "Offshore Trusts," 9.

38. Shaxson, *Treasure Islands*, 230. Emphasis added.

39. Ibid. See also Jason Sharman, *Havens in a Storm: The Struggle for Global Tax Regulation* (Ithaca, NY: Cornell University Press, 2006).

40. Timothy Colclough, "To PTC or Not to PTC," *STEP Journal*, November/December 2009.

41. Christian Stewart, "Family Business Succession Planning: East versus West," *STEP Journal*, January 2010, 27–29.

42. Rosemary Marr, "Jersey: Riding the Tides of Change," *STEP Journal*, November 2014, 75.

43. Peter Wonacott, "As Reforms Stall, Calls Rise to Seize South Africa Farms," *Wall Street Journal*, June 21, 2011.

44. Shaxson, *Treasure Islands*, 25.

45. Transparency International, *Corruption Perceptions Index 2014*, www.transparency.org/cpi2014/results.

46. John Letzing, "Swiss Banks Say Goodbye to a Big Chunk of Bank Secrecy," *Wall Street Journal*, July 1, 2014.

47. Beardsley et al., *Global Wealth 2014*.

48. Martin Sixsmith, *Putin's Oil: The Yukos Affair and the Struggle for Russia* (New York: Continuum, 2010).

49. Jamil Anderlini, "Flood of Rich Chinese Settle in UK," *Financial Times*, January 13, 2015.

50. Rosa Prince, "Wealthy Foreigners Trade London Homes for New York," *The Telegraph*, July 1, 2014.

51. Louise Story and Stephanie Saul, "Stream of Foreign Wealth Flows to Elite New York Real Estate," *New York Times*, February 7, 2015.

52. Nicholas Shaxson, "A Tale of Two Londons," *Vanity Fair*, April 2013.

53. Ministry of Commerce, People's Republic of China, "Outward Investment and Cooperation Maintain Steady and Sound Development," press release, April 30, 2014, http://english.mofcom.gov.cn/article/newsrelease/significantnews/201405/20140500570450.shtml.

54. Keith Bradsher, "China to Crack Down on Tax Collection from Multinational Companies," *New York Times*, February 4, 2015.

55. Shaxson, *Treasure Islands*.

56. Megha Bahree and Deborah Ball, "Island Tax Haven Roils India's Ways," *Wall Street Journal*, August 29, 2012.

57. Leigh, Frayman, and Ball, Offshore Secrets."

58. Andrey Ostroukh and Alexander Kolyandr, "Russians Park Money in British Virgin Islands," *Wall Street Journal*, August 16, 2013.

59. Demetri Sevastpulo, "British Virgin Islands Suffers amid Push against Money Laundering," *Financial Times*, September 16, 2014.

60. Andrew Thorp and Simon Hudd, "The BVI Company in a Russian Context," *IFC Caribbean Review*, 2012, 34–35.

61. Quoted in Nicholas Shaxson, "Why Do Chinese Companies Flock to the BVI?" May 23, 2011, http://treasureislands.org/why-chinese -companies-flock-to-the-bvi.

62. Jennifer Holmes and Sheila Amin Gutiérrez de Piñeres, "Corruption: Is Dollarization a Solution?" in Kartik Roy and Jörn Sideras, eds., *Institutions, Globalisation and Empowerment*, 130–147 (Cheltenham, UK: Edward Elgar, 2006).

63. Nicolas Malumian, "Forced Heirship," *STEP Journal*, February 2011.

64. Robert Nozick, *Anarchy, State and Utopia* (New York: Basic Books, 1977).

65. David Sicular, "The New Look-Through Rule: W(h)ither Subpart F?" *Tax Notes*, April 23, 2007, www.paulweiss.com/media/104725 /subpartf04-may-07.pdf.

66. Kerry Hannon, "Family Foundations Let Affluent Leave a Legacy," *New York Times*, February 10, 2014.

67. Iris Goodwin, "How the Rich Stay Rich: Using a Family Trust Company to Secure a Family Fortune," *Seton Hall Law Review* 40 (2010): 467–516.

68. Hannon, "Family Foundations."

69. "Flat-Pack Accounting," *The Economist*, May 11, 2006.

70. Mark Wilson, "IKEA Is a Nonprofit, and Yes, That's Every Bit as Fishy as It Sounds," *Fast Company*, September 15, 2014.

71. "Flat-Pack Accounting."

72. Richard Orange, "IKEA Founder Pledges £1bn to Charity Following Nazi Past Revelations," *The Telegraph*, September 18, 2011.

73. Adam Hofri, "The Stripping of the Trust: A Study in Legal Evolution," *University of Toronto Law Journal* 65 (2015).

74. Dhana Sabanathan and Shu-Ping Shen, "A Brush with Death Taxes," *STEP Journal*, July 2014, 69.

75. Ibid.

76. Parkinson, *Diploma in International Trust Management: Trust Creation*, 279.

77. Parkinson, *Certificate in International Trust Management*, 109.

78. George Marcus and Peter Hall, *Lives in Trust: The Fortunes of Dynastic Families in Late Twentieth-Century America* (Boulder, CO: Westview Press, 1992).

79. Gary Watt, *Equity and Trusts Law Directions*, 4th ed. (Oxford, UK: Oxford University Press, 2014), 139, quoting Sir George Jessel.

80. Mark Trumbull, "The Tougher Terms Now Facing the Bankrupt," *Christian Science Monitor*, October 17, 2005.

81. Hofri, "The Stripping of the Trust," 24.

82. Leslie Wayne, "Cook Islands, a Paradise of Untouchable Assets," *New York Times*, December 15, 2013.

83. Hofri, "The Stripping of the Trust," 24.

84. Brief for Appellant Fannie Mae, *State of Minnesota v. Andrew C. Grossman*, State of Minnesota Supreme Court, dockets A10-1336 and A10-1505, 2011, http://mn.gov/lawlib//briefs/pdfs/a101336sca.pdf.

85. Leslie Wayne, "Unlocking the Secrets of the Cook Islands," International Consortium of Investigative Journalists, December 16, 2013, www.icij.org/blog/2013/12/unlocking-secrets-cook-islands.

86. Wayne, "Cook Islands, a Paradise of Untouchable Assets."

87. Rashneel Kumar, "Cook Islands on EU Blacklist," *Cook Islands News*, June 19, 2015, www.cookislandsnews.com/national/politics /item/52427-cook-islands-on-eu-blacklist.

88. Paul Southgate and John Lucas, *The Pearl Oyster* (Amsterdam: Elsevier, 2008), 333.

89. Ibid.

90. Douglas Martin, "Marc Rich, Financier and Famous Fugitive, Dies at 78," *New York Times*, June 27, 2013.

91. Cammie Fisher, "R. Allen Stanford Doesn't Face His Many Victims," *San Francisco Chronicle*, May 25, 2015.

92. Emile de Willebois, Emily Halter, Robert Harrison, Ji Won Park, and Jason Sharman, *The Puppet Masters: How the Corrupt Use Legal Structures to Hide Stolen Assets and What to Do about It* (Washington, DC: World Bank, 2011), 45.

93. Katia Savchuk, "Jury Finds Wyly Brothers Engaged in Fraud by Hiding Trades in Offshore Trusts," *Forbes*, August 5, 2014.

94. Joseph Guinto, "Sam Wyly's $550 Million Problem," *D Magazine*, February 2013.

95. Snejana Farberov, "Dallas Billionaire Who Used to own Michaels Arts and Crafts Chain Files for Bankruptcy One Year after $400M Judgment in SEC Fraud Case," *Daily Mail*, October 20, 2014.

96. Jonathan Kandell, "Baron Thyssen-Bornemisza, Industrialist Who Built Fabled Art Collection, Dies at 81," *New York Times*, April 28, 2002.

97. Marc Weber, "The New Swiss Law on Cultural Property," *International Journal of Cultural Property* 13 (2006): 99–113.

98. Mar Cabra and Michael Hudson, "Mega-rich Use Tax Havens to Buy and Sell Masterpieces," International Consortium of Investigative Journalists, April 3, 2013, www.icij.org/offshore/mega-rich-use-tax-havens-buy-and-sell-masterpieces.

99. George Marcus, "The Fiduciary Role in American Family Dynasties and Their Institutional Legacy," in George Marcus, ed., *Elites: Ethnographic Issues*, 221–256 (Albuquerque: University of New Mexico Press, 1983), 222.

100. Ibid.

101. See, for example, the Institute for Divorce Financial Analysts, which has certified more than 5,000 practitioners in the United States and Canada, according to its website, https://www.institutedfa.com.

102. Andrew Lynn, "Split-up Trusts," *STEP Journal*, December 2014.

103. Lorraine Wheeler, "Cases in Point," *STEP Journal*, April 2015.

104. John Heilprin, "Dmitry Rybolovlev: Most Expensive Divorce Costs Russian Billionaire £2.7bn," *The Independent*, May 20, 2014.

105. Frederic Maitland, *Selected Essays* (Cambridge, UK: Cambridge University Press, 1936), 157.

106. Francis Sanders, *An Essay on the Nature and Laws of Uses and Trusts, Including a Treatise on Conveyances at Common Law and Those Deriving Their Effect from the Statute of Uses* (London: E. & R. Brooke, 1791).

107. Joan Gunderson, "Women and Inheritance in America: Virginia and New York as a Case Study: 1700–1860," in Robert Miller and Stephen McNamee, eds., *Inheritance and Wealth in America*, 91–118 (New York: Plenum Press, 1998).

108. Adel Gonczi and Pamela Rideout, "Family Planning," *STEP Journal*, June 2013.

109. Julian Washington, "Keeping It in the Family," *STEP Journal*, April 2013.

110. See also Peagam, "Nine Centres."

111. Julian Washington, "Estate Planning: The New Era," *STEP Journal*, March 2014.

112. Katheryn Voyer, "Continuity the Trend Toward Equality: The Eradication of Racially and Sexually Discriminatory Provisions in Private Trusts," *William & Mary Bill of Rights Journal* 7 (1999): 944.

113. Parkinson, *Diploma in International Trust Management: Trust Creation*, 261.

114. Ibid.

115. Bonnie Steiner, "A Rock, a Hard Stone, and the Unknown," *STEP Journal*, December 2012.

116. Ibid.

117. Parkinson, *Diploma in International Trust Management: Trust Creation*.

118. Ibid., 336.

119. "Trawling for Business."

120. Frankel, "Cross-Border Securitization," 643.

121. Adam Hofri, "Professionals' Contribution to the Legislative Process: Between Self, Client, and the Public," *Law & Social Inquiry* 39 (2014): 96–126.

122. Shaxson, *Treasure Islands*, 42.

123. Austin Scott, "The Trust as an Instrument of Law Reform," *Yale Law Journal* 31 (1922): 457–458.

124. Except in New Zealand and Israel; see Hofri, "Professionals' Contribution."

125. Parkinson, *Diploma in International Trust Management: Trust Creation*.

126. Ibid. As an example, the flee clauses of many Bermudian trusts were triggered by the assassination of the island's governor in 1973. Keith Johnston, "A New Finance Centre Emerges," *STEP Journal*, February 2009.

127. Hofri, "The Stripping of the Trust," 25.

128. Robert Sitkoff and Max Schanzenbach, "Jurisdictional Competition for Trust Funds: An Empirical Analysis of Perpetuities and Taxes," *Yale Law Journal* 115 (2005): 356–437.

129. John Langbein, "The Secret Life of the Trust: The Trust as an Instrument of Commerce," *Yale Law Journal* 107 (1997): 165–189.
130. John Langbein, "The Contractarian Basis of the Law of Trusts," *Yale Law Journal* 105 (1995): 627.
131. Frank Easterbrook and Daniel Fischel, "Contract and Fiduciary Duty," *Journal of Law and Economics* 36 (1993): 427.
132. Hofri, "Professionals' Contribution." See also Brooke Harrington, "Going Global: Professions and the Micro-Foundations of Institutional Change," *Journal of Professions and Organizations* 2 (2015): 1–19.
133. Parkinson, *Diploma in International Trust Management: Trust Creation*, 327.
134. Donald Ferrin and Nicole Gillespie, "Trust Differences across National-Societal Cultures: Much to Do, or Much Ado about Nothing?" in Mark Saunders, Denise Skinner, Graham Dietz, Nicole Gillespie, and Roy Lewicki, eds., *Organizational Trust: A Cultural Perspective*, 42–86 (Cambridge, UK: Cambridge University Press, 2010).
135. Russell Clark, "Founding Father," *STEP Journal—Guernsey Supplement*, November 2012, 8–9.
136. de Willebois et al., *The Puppet Masters*, 47.
137. Ibid.
138. Brian McAlister and Timothy Yoder, "Advising Private Foundations," *Journal of Accounting*, April 1, 2008.
139. Richard Schmalbeck, "Avoiding Federal Wealth Transfer Taxes," in William Gale, James Hines, and James Slemrod, eds., *Rethinking Estate and Gift Taxation*, 113–163 (Washington, DC: Brookings Institution, 2001).
140. William Barrett, "Controversial Charity Files for Bankruptcy," *Forbes*, January 28, 2009.
141. Parkinson, *Diploma in International Trust Management: Trust Creation*, 5.
142. de Willebois et al., *The Puppet Masters*, 167.
143. Ibid.
144. Langbein, "The Secret Life of the Trust," 184.
145. Brooke Harrington, "States and Financial Crises," in Benedikte Brincker, ed., *Introduction to Political Sociology*, 267–282 (Copenhagen: Gyldendal, 2013).
146. Moffat, *Trust Law*.

147. Krippner, "The Financialization of the American Economy."
148. Hofri, "The Stripping of the Trust."
149. de Willebois et al., *The Puppet Masters.*
150. Michael Parkinson, *Diploma in International Trust Management: Company Law and Practice*, 5th ed. (Birmingham, UK: Central Law Training, 2006).
151. Ibid., 34.
152. Sicular, "The New Look-Through Rule."
153. Parkinson, *Certificate in International Trust Management.*
154. de Willebois et al., *The Puppet Masters*, 60.
155. Ibid.
156. Langbein, "The Secret Life of the Trust," 179.
157. de Willebois et al., *The Puppet Masters*, 88.
158. Parkinson, *Diploma in International Trust Management: Trust Creation*, 171.
159. Parkinson, *Diploma in International Trust Management: Company Law and Practice.*
160. Ibid., 261.
161. de Willebois et al., *The Puppet Masters*, 52.
162. Liz Moyer, "Private Trusts for the Very Rich," *Wall Street Journal*, December 14, 2014.
163. Colclough, "To PTC or Not to PTC," 51–53.
164. Goodwin, "How the Rich Stay Rich."
165. Colclough, "To PTC or Not to PTC," 53.
166. Parkinson, *Diploma in International Trust Management: Trust Creation.*
167. de Willebois et al., *The Puppet Masters*, 47.
168. Goodwin, "How the Rich Stay Rich," 468.

5. Wealth Management and Inequality

1. Emma Duncan, "Your Money, His Life," *Intelligent Life* (supplement to *The Economist*), September 2007, 73–79.
2. George Marcus, "The Fiduciary Role in American Family Dynasties and Their Institutional Legacy," in George Marcus, ed., *Elites: Ethnographic Issues* (Albuquerque: University of New Mexico Press, 1983), 227.

3. Thomas Piketty, *Capital in the Twenty-First Century* (Cambridge, MA: Harvard University Press, 2014). See also Arthur Kennickell, "Ponds and Streams: Wealth and Income in the US, 1989 to 2007," Federal Reserve Board Finance and Economics Discussion Series, Washington, DC, 2009, www.federalreserve.gov/pubs/feds/2009 /200913/200913pap.pdf. See also Melvin Oliver and Thomas Shapiro, *Black Wealth, White Wealth: A New Perspective on Racial Inequality* (New York: Routledge, 1995).

4. Ronald Chester, *Inheritance, Wealth and Society* (Bloomington: Indiana University Press, 1982), 128.

5. Carl Levin, "The US Tax Shelter Industry: The Role of Accountants, Lawyers, and Financial Professionals," statement before U.S. Senate Permanent Subcommittee on Investigations, November 18, 2003. See also Ronen Palan, Richard Murphy, and Christian Chavagneux, *Tax Havens: How Globalization Really Works* (Ithaca, NY: Cornell University Press, 2010).

6. Nicholas Shaxson, *Treasure Islands: Tax Havens and the Men Who Stole the World* (London: Random House, 2011), 28.

7. Kennickell, "Ponds and Streams."

8. Wojciech Kopczuk and Emmanuel Saez, "Top Wealth Shares in the United States,1916–2000: Evidence from Estate Tax Returns," *National Tax Journal* 57 (2004): 445–487.

9. James Davies, Susanna Sandström, Anthony Shorrocks, and Edward Wolff, "The World Distribution of Household Wealth," World Institute for Development Economics Research, Helsinki, Discussion Paper 2008/03, 2008, 17.

10. Santiago Budría, Javier Díaz-Giménez, José-Victor Ríos-Rull, and Vincenzo Quadrini, "Updated Facts on the US Distributions of Earnings, Income, and Wealth," *Federal Reserve Bank of Minneapolis Quarterly Review* 26 (2002): 2–35.

11. Sheelah Kolhatkar, "Inside the Billionaire Service Industry," *The Atlantic*, September 2006. See also Barbara Demick, "The 400 Richest: Many Folks Try to Stay Off List," *Philadelphia Inquirer*, October 7, 1990.

12. Heather Stewart, "Wealth Doesn't Trickle Down—It Just Floods Offshore, New Research Reveals," *The Guardian*, July 21, 2012.

13. Michel Pinçon and Monique Pinçon-Charlot, *Grand Fortunes: Dynasties of Wealth in France*, trans. Andrea Lyn Secara (New York: Algora, 1998), 8.

14. Michael Parkinson, *Certificate in International Trust Management*, 4th ed. (Birmingham, UK: Central Law Training, 2004), 9.
15. Simon Bowers, "Luxembourg Tax Whistleblower Says He Acted Out of Conviction," *The Guardian*, December 15, 2015; David Gauthier-Villars and Deborah Ball, "Mass Leak of Client Data Rattles Swiss Banking," *Wall Street Journal*, July 8, 2010; Max Seddon, "Panama Papers: Russian Cellist at Centre of $2bn Offshore Web," *Financial Times*, April 4, 2016.
16. Pinçon and Pinçon-Charlot, *Grand Fortunes*.
17. Blair Bowie and Adam Lioz, "Billion-Dollar Democracy: The Unprecedented Role of Money in the 2012 Elections," Demos.org, January 2013.
18. Davies et al., "The World Distribution of Household Wealth." See also Lisa Keister and Stephanie Moller, "Wealth Inequality in the United States," *Annual Review of Sociology* 26 (2000): 63–81.
19. Kennickell, "Ponds and Streams."
20. Thomas Shapiro, Tatjana Meschede, and Sam Osoro, "The Roots of the Widening Racial Wealth Gap: Explaining the Black-White Economic Divide," Research and Policy Brief, Institute on Assets & Social Policy, Brandeis University, Waltham, MA, 2013.
21. Oliver and Shapiro, *Black Wealth, White Wealth*, 3.
22. Shamus Khan, *Privilege: The Making of an Adolescent Elite at St. Paul's School* (Princeton, NJ: Princeton University Press, 2012).
23. Javier Díaz-Giménez, José-Victor Ríos Rull, and Andy Glover, "Facts on the Distributions of Earnings, Income, and Wealth in the United States: 2007 Update," *Federal Reserve Bank of Minneapolis Quarterly Review* 34 (2011): 2–31.
24. George Marcus and Peter Hall, *Lives in Trust: The Fortunes of Dynastic Families in Late Twentieth-Century America* (Boulder, CO: Westview Press, 1992).
25. Charles Collier, *Wealth in Families* (Cambridge, MA: Harvard University Alumni Affairs and Development Communications, 2002).
26. C. Wright Mills, *The Power Elite* (New York: Oxford University Press, 1956), 105.
27. Budría et al., "Updated Facts," 6.
28. Díaz-Giménez, Rull, and Glover, Facts.
29. Piketty, *Capital*, 18.

30. Edward Wolff, "The Asset Price Meltdown and the Wealth of the Middle Class," paper presented at the annual meeting of the Association for Public Policy Analysis and Management, Baltimore, MD, November 10, 2012. While estimates of both the income and wealth of this group vary considerably, the magnitude of the difference between income and wealth is surprisingly consistent across estimates.

31. United States Census Bureau, *2009–2013 American Community Survey 5-Year Estimates* (Washington, DC: U.S. Department of Commerce, 2014); Edward Wolff, "Household Wealth Trends in the United States, 1962–2013: What Happened over the Great Recession?" NBER Working Paper 20733, 2014.

32. Wolff, "The Asset Price Meltdown."

33. Christopher Ingraham, "If You Thought Income Inequality Was Bad, Get a Load of Wealth Inequality," *Washington Post*, May 21, 2015.

34. Kennickell, "Ponds and Streams."

35. Jacob Davidson, "Wealth Inequality Doubled over Last 10 years, Study Finds," *Money*, June 25, 2014.

36. Kerri Anne Renzulli, "Household Wealth Is the Highest Ever. Probably Not Your Household's, Though," *Money*, March 13, 2015; Jesse Bricker, Lisa Dettling, Alice Henriques, Joanne Hsu, Kevin Moore, John Sabelhaus, Jeffrey Thompson, and Richard Windle, "Changes in US Family Finances from 2010 to 2013: Evidence from the Survey of Consumer Finances," *Federal Reserve Bulletin* 100 (2014): 1–41. See also Cap-Gemini, *World Wealth Report* (Paris: Cap-Gemini, 2011).

37. Cap-Gemini, *World Wealth Report* (Paris: Cap-Gemini, 2015).

38. Bricker et al., "Changes in US Family Finances from 2010 to 2013."

39. Jill Treanor, "Half of World's Wealth Now in Hands of 1% of Population—Report," *The Guardian*, October 13, 2015.

40. For number of HNWIs and amount of their wealth, see Cap-Gemini, *World Wealth Report*. For GDP figures, see International Monetary Fund, *World Economic Outlook* (Washington, DC: IMF, 2015).

41. Lawrence Friedman, *Dead Hands: A Social History of Wills, Trusts, and Inheritance Law* (Stanford, CA: Stanford University Press, 2009), 4.

42. Edward Wolff and Maury Gittleman, "Inheritances and the Distribution of Wealth: Or Whatever Happened to the Great Inheritance Boom?" Bureau of Labor Statistics, Working Paper 445, 2011.

43. Ibid., Table 7, section B, 35.

44. "Inherited Wealth," *Buttonwood's Notebook* blog, *The Economist*, March 18, 2014.
45. Jens Beckert, "Political and Social Interests in the Transfer of Property," *Archives of European Sociology* 46 (2005): 359–368.
46. Thomas Piketty, "On the Long-Run Evolution of Inheritance: France 1820–2050," Working Paper, Paris School of Economics, 2010.
47. Randall Morck, Daniel Wolfenzon, and Bernard Yeung, "Corporate Governance, Economic Entrenchment, and Growth," *Journal of Economic Literature* 43 (2005): 655–720.
48. Jens Beckert, *Inherited Wealth* (Princeton, NJ: Princeton University Press, 2008), 18.
49. Gabriel Zucman, *The Hidden Wealth of Nations* (Chicago: University of Chicago Press, 2015), 53.
50. Federico Cingano, "Trends in Income Inequality and Its Impact on Economic Growth," OECD Social, Employment and Migration Working Papers 163, 2015.
51. Deborah Hardoon, "Wealth: Having It All and Wanting More," Oxfam Issue Briefing, January 2015.
52. Friedman, *Dead Hands*, 5.
53. Piketty, *Capital*. See also Kennickel, "Ponds and Streams."
54. Alexis de Tocqueville, *Democracy in America* (New York: Knopf, 1945 [1835]), 1:53.
55. Kopczuk and Saez, "Top Wealth Shares in the United States."
56. Jean-Jacques Rousseau, *The Social Contract and Discourses* (London: J. M. Dent and Sons, 1913 [1762]). See also Jens Beckert, "The *Longue Durée* of Inheritance Law: Discourses and Institutional Development in France, Germany and the United States since 1800," *Archives of European Sociology* 48 (2007): 79–120.
57. Karl Marx and Friedrich Engels, "Manifesto of the Communist Party," in Robert Tucker, ed., *The Marx-Engels Reader* (New York: Norton, 1978 [1848]), 499.
58. Friedman, *Dead Hands*.
59. Ibid., 113.
60. Sven Steinmo, "The Evolution of Policy Ideas: Tax Policy in the 20th Century," *The British Journal of Politics and International Relations* 5 (2002): 206–236.
61. John McKinnon, "House Passes Bill to Repeal Estate Tax," *Wall Street Journal*, April 16, 2015.

62. Jonathan Beaverstock, Philip Hubbard, and John Short, "Getting Away with it? Exposing the Geographies of the Super-rich," *Geoforum* 35 (2004): 402.

63. Thomas Volscho and Nathan Kelly, "The Rise of the Super-Rich: Power Resources, Taxes, Financial Markets, and the Dynamics of the Top 1 Percent, 1949 to 2008," *American Sociological Review* 77 (2012): 679–699.

64. Nicholas Confessore, Peter Lattman, and Kevin Roose, "Close Ties to Goldman Enrich Romney's Public and Private Lives," *New York Times*, January 27, 2012.

65. Mayer Zald and Michael Lounsbury, "The Wizards of Oz: Towards an Institutional Approach to Elites, Expertise and Command Posts," *Organization Studies* 31 (2010): 980.

66. Zucman, *The Hidden Wealth of Nations*, 47.

67. Ibid., 46.

68. Ibid.

69. Friedman, *Dead Hands*, 135.

70. Marcus and Hall, *Lives in Trust*, 233.

71. Tocqueville, *Democracy in America*, 1:50–51.

72. Marcus and Hall, *Lives in Trust*, 55, 79, emphasis added.

73. David Cay Johnston, "Costly Questions Arise on Legal Opinions for Tax Shelters," *New York Times*, February 9, 2003.

74. Karen Burke and Grayson McCouch, "COBRA Strikes Back: Anatomy of a Tax Shelter," *Tax Lawyer* 62 (2008): 64–65.

75. Michael Parkinson, *Trustee Investment and Financial Appraisal*, 4th ed. (Birmingham, UK: Central Law Training, 2008). For the seminal work on the "equity risk premium" theory, see Franco Modigliani and Merton Miller, "The Cost of Capital, Corporation Finance and the Theory of Investment," *American Economic Review* 48 (1958): 261–297.

76. Pinçon and Pinçon-Charlot, *Grand Fortunes*.

77. David Golumbia, "High-Frequency Trading: Networks of Wealth and the Concentration of Power," *Social Semiotics* 23 (2013): 1–22. See also Mila Getmansky, "The Life Cycle of Hedge Funds: Fund Flows, Size, Competition, and Performance," *Quarterly Journal of Finance* 2 (2012): 1–53.

78. Jenny Anderson, "For Hedge Funds, Life Just Got a Bit More Complicated," *New York Times*, March 31, 2006.

79. David Rynecki, "How to Profit from Falling Prices," *Fortune*, September 15, 2003.
80. Douglass North, "Economic Performance through Time," Nobel Lecture, December 9, 1993, www.nobelprize.org/nobel_prizes /economic-sciences/laureates/1993/north-lecture.html.
81. Bricker et al., "Changes in US Family Finances," 4.
82. Ibid.
83. Matthew Miller and Duncan Greenberg, "The Richest People in America," *Forbes*, September 30, 2009.
84. Peter Bernstein and Annalyn Swan, *All the Money in the World: How the Forbes 400 Make—and Spend—Their Fortunes* (New York: Knopf, 2007), 14.
85. Marcus and Hall, *Lives in Trust*.
86. James Hughes Jr., *Family Wealth: Keeping It in the Family* (Princeton Junction, NJ: NetWrx, 1997).
87. Piketty, *Capital*, 26.
88. John Dryden, *The Dramatick Works of John Dryden, Esq., Volume the Sixth* (London: Jacob Tonson, 1717), 364.
89. Marcus, "The Fiduciary Role in American Family Dynasties."
90. Pinçon and Pinçon-Charlot, *Grand Fortunes*, 15–16.
91. Collier, *Wealth in Families*.
92. Marcus, "The Fiduciary Role in American Family Dynasties," 233. See also Friedman, *Dead Hands*.
93. Timothy Colclough, "To PTC or Not to PTC," *STEP Journal*, November/December 2009, 51–53.
94. Frederic Stimson, *My United States* (New York: Charles Scribner's Sons, 1931), 76.
95. Alvin Gouldner, "Organizational Analysis," in Robert Merton, Leonard Broom, and Leonard Cottrell, eds., *Sociology Today: Problems and Prospects* (New York: Harper, 1959), 2:405.
96. Pinçon and Pinçon-Charlot, *Grand Fortunes*, 209.
97. Nelson Aldrich, *Old Money: The Mythology of Wealth in America* (New York: Allworth, 1997). See also Peter Collier and David Horowitz, *The Rockefellers: An American Dynasty* (New York: Holt, Rinehart and Winston, 1976).
98. Pinçon and Pinçon-Charlot, *Grand Fortunes*, 100.
99. Max Weber, *Economy and Society* (Berkeley: University of California Press, 2013 [1922]), 2:1096–1097.

100. Timur Kuran, "Why the Middle East Is Economically Underdeveloped: Historical Mechanisms of Institutional Stagnation," *Journal of Economic Perspectives* 18 (2004): 71.

101. Beckert, The *Longue Durée* of Inheritance Law.

102. Piketty, *Capital.*

103. Bashkar Mazumder, "The Apple Falls Even Closer to the Tree than We Thought: New and Revised Estimates of the Intergenerational Transfer of Earnings," in Samuel Bowles, Herbert Gintis, and Melissa Osborne Groves, eds., *Unequal Chances: Family Background and Economic Success* (New York: Russell Sage Foundation, 2005), 96.

104. Stephen McNamee and Robert Miller, "Inheritance of Wealth in America," in Robert Miller and Stephen McNamee, eds., *Inheritance and Wealth in America* (New York: Plenum Press, 1998), 20.

105. *Tax Me if You Can*, transcript of *Frontline* documentary film, 2004, 2, www.pbs.org/wgbh/pages/frontline/shows/tax/etc/script.html. See also Zucman, *The Hidden Wealth of Nations.*

106. Austin Mitchell, Prem Sikka, John Christensen, Philip Morris, and Steven Filling, *No Accounting for Tax Havens* (Basildon, UK: Association for Accountancy & Business Affairs, 2002).

107. Friedrich Schneider, "The Shadow Economy and Shadow Economy Labor Force: What Do We (Not) Know?" Discussion Paper 5769, Institute for the Study of Labor, Bonn, Germany, 2011. See also Alain Parguez, "Modern Austerity Policies (MAP): An Analysis of the Economics of Decadence and Self Destruction," paper presented at the annual meeting of the Eastern Economic Association, Boston, 2012.

108. Palan et al.,*Tax Havens*, 12.

109. Thomas Piketty, "Foreword," in Gabriel Zucman, *The Hidden Wealth Of Nations* (Chicago: University of Chicago Press, 2015), viii.

110. Adam Hofri, "The Stripping of the Trust: A Study in Legal Evolution," *University of Toronto Law Journal* 65 (2015): 27–28.

111. Catherine Dunn, "Widespread Costs of Predatory Lending Limit Economic Mobility: Report," *International Business Times*, June 16, 2015.

112. Iris Goodwin, "How the Rich Stay Rich: Using a Family Trust Company to Secure a Family Fortune," *Seton Hall Law Review* 40 (2010): 515.

113. Simon Gray, "VISTA Trusts Allow BVI to Slough off Past and At-tract Global Businesses," *The Lawyer,* January 17, 2005.

114. Goodwin, "How the Rich Stay Rich," 468.

115. Andrea Campbell, "Self-Interest, Social Security and the Distinc-tive Participation Patterns of Senior Citizens," *American Political Science Review* 96 (2002): 565.

116. Volscho and Kelly, "The Rise of the Super-Rich."

117. Bowie and Lioz, "Billion-Dollar Democracy," 14.

118. Daron Acemoğlu and James Robinson, *Why Nations Fail: The Ori-gins of Power, Prosperity, and Poverty* (New York: Crown, 2012), 365.

119. Brooke Harrington, "Can Small Investors Survive Social Security Privatization?" in David Canon and John Coleman, eds., *Faultlines: Debating the Issues in American Politics,* 308–313 (New York: W. W. Norton, 2007). See also Brooke Harrington, "What Is Social, or Se-cure, about Social Security?" in Dimitri Papadimitriou, ed., *Govern-ment Spending on the Elderly,* 343–346 (New York: Palgrave, 2007).

120. Benjamin Page, Larry Bartels, and Jason Seawright, "Democracy and the Policy Preferences of Wealthy Americans," *Perspectives on Politics* 11 (2013): 51. See also Paul Krugman, "Pension-Cutters and Privatizers, Oh My," *New York Times,* August 19, 2015.

121. Alonso Soto, "Brazil May Tax Inheritances instead of Wealth—Minister," Reuters, March 17, 2015.

122. Tom Phillips, "High above Sao Paulo's Choked Streets, the Rich Cruise a New Highway," *The Guardian,* June 20, 2008.

123. Goodwin, "How the Rich Stay Rich," 516.

124. Graham Moffat, *Trust Law: Text and Materials* (Cambridge, UK: Cambridge University Press, 2009), 60.

125. Michael Norton and Dan Ariely, "Building a Better America—One Wealth Quintile at a Time," *Perspectives on Psychological Science* 6 (2011): 9–12.

126. Michael Parkinson and Dai Jones, *Trust Administration and Ac-counts,* 4th ed. (Birmingham, UK: Central Law Training, 2008).

127. Michael Cadesky, "A Question of Legitimate Tax Policy," *STEP Journal,* March 2010. See also Marshall Langer, *Tax Agreements with Tax Havens and Other Small Countries* (London: STEP, 2005).

128. Parkinson and Jones, *Trust Administration and Accounts,* 267.

129. Jason Sharman, *Havens in a Storm: The Struggle for Global Tax Regulation* (Ithaca, NY: Cornell University Press, 2006).
130. Parkinson and Jones, *Trust Administration and Accounts*, 268, emphasis added.
131. Michael Parkinson, *Trust Creation: Law and Practice*, 3rd ed. (Birmingham, UK: Central Law Training, 2005), 295.
132. Palan et al., *Tax Havens*, 7.
133. Beckert, The *Longue Durée* of Inheritance Law, 6. See also Sighard Neckel, *Flucht nach vorn: Die erfolgskultur der marktgesellschaft* (Frankfurt am Main: Campus, 2008).
134. Roger Cotterrell, "Power, Property and the Law of Trusts: A Partial Agenda for Critical Legal Scholarship," *Journal of Law and Society* 14 (1987): 77–90.
135. Gregory Jackson and Stephen Brammer, "Grey Areas: Irresponsible Corporations and Reputational Dynamics," *Socio-Economic Review* 12 (2014): 153–218.
136. Blake Ashforth and Glen Kreiner, "Dirty Work and Dirtier Work: Differences in Countering Physical, Social and Moral Stigma," *Management and Organization Review* 10 (2014): 81–108.
137. Rémi Clignet, *Death, Deeds and Descendants* (New York: Aldine de Gruyter, 1991), 29.
138. Luc Boltanski and Laurent Thévenot, *On Justification: Economies of Worth* (Princeton, NJ: Princeton University Press, 2006).

6. Wealth Management and the State

1. Gerard Hanlon, "Institutional Forms and Organizational Structures: Homology, Trust and Reputational Capital in Professional Service Firms," *Organization* 11 (2004): 205.
2. Eliot Freidson, *Professionalism: The Third Logic* (London: Polity, 2001), 128.
3. Doreen McBarnet, "After Enron: Corporate Governance, Creative Compliance and the Uses of Corporate Social Responsibility," in Justin O'Brien, ed., *Governing the Corporation: Regulation and Corporate Governance in an Age of Scandal and Global Markets*, 205–222 (New York: John Wiley & Sons, 2005).

4. Tim Bartley, "Institutional Emergence in an Era of Globalization: The Rise of Transnational Private Regulation of Labor and Environmental Conditions," *American Journal of Sociology* 113 (2007): 298.

5. Greta Krippner, "The Financialization of the American Economy," *Socio-Economic Review* 3 (2005): 202.

6. William Robinson, "Social Theory and Globalization: The Rise of a Transnational State," *Theory and Society* 30 (2001): 160.

7. Krippner, "The Financialization of the American Economy."

8. Richard Deeg and Mary O'Sullivan, "The Political Economy of Global Finance Capital," *World Politics* 61 (2009): 731–763.

9. Bill Maurer, "Complex Subjects: Offshore Finance, Complexity Theory, and the Dispersion of the Modern," *Socialist Review* 25 (1995): 113–145.

10. Anthony Giddens, *The Consequences of Modernity* (Stanford, CA: Stanford University Press, 1990), 21.

11. Michael Parkinson, *Certificate in International Trust Management*, 4th ed. (Birmingham, UK: Central Law Training, 2004), 3.

12. George Connor and Christopher Hammons, *The Constitutionalism of American States* (Columbia: University of Missouri Press, 2008).

13. Constitution of the Commonwealth of Massachusetts, Part I, Article VII, www.malegislature.gov/Laws/Constitution.

14. Jack Goldstone, *Revolution and Rebellion in the Early Modern World* (Berkeley: University of California Press, 1991). See also Joseph Schumpeter, *Die Krise des Steuerstaats* (Graz, Austria: Leuschner & Lubensky, 1918).

15. Edmund Burke, *Reflections on the Revolution in France* (Oxford, UK: Oxford University Press, 1999 [1790]).

16. Philipp Genschel, "Globalization and the Transformation of the Tax State," *European Review* 13 (2005): 60.

17. Thomas Piketty, "Foreword," in Gabriel Zucman, *The Hidden Wealth of Nations* (Chicago: University of Chicago Press, 2015), xii.

18. Ibid. See also Ronen Palan, "Trying to Have Your Cake and Eating It: How and Why the State System Has Created Offshore," *International Studies Quarterly* 42 (1998): 625–644.

19. Kim Gittleson, "Where Is the Cheapest Place to Buy Citizenship?" *BBC News*, June 4, 2014.

20. Dan Bilefsky, "Give Malta Your Tired and Huddled, and Rich," *New York Times*, January 31, 2014.

21. Gittleson, "Where Is the Cheapest Place to Buy Citizenship?"

22. Edward Taylor, Matthias Inverardi, and Mark Hosenball, "Special Report: How Germany's Taxman Used Stolen Data to Squeeze Switzerland," Reuters, November 1, 2013. On the United Kingdom, see David Jolly, "Tax-Evasion Case Spreads to U.K. from Germany," *New York Times*, February 24, 2008.

23. Sebastian Fischer, "Stolen Data Prompts Wave of Remorse: German Authorities Expect Tax Evaders to Fess Up," *Der Spiegel*, February 3, 2010.

24. Harry de Quetteville, "Liechtenstein and Europe's Tax Men," *The Telegraph*, February 27, 2008.

25. Robert Sitkoff and Max Schanzenbach, "Jurisdictional Competition for Trust Funds: An Empirical Analysis of Perpetuities and Taxes," *Yale Law Journal* 115 (2005): 356–437.

26. Ronen Palan, "Tax Havens and the Commercialization of State Sovereignty,"*International Organization* 56 (2002): 152.

27. Nicholas Shaxson, "A Tale of Two Londons," *Vanity Fair*, April 2013.

28. Ibid.

29. David Leigh, Harold Frayman, and James Ball, "Offshore Secrets: British Virgin Islands, Land of Sand, Sea and Secrecy," *The Guardian*, November 25, 2012.

30. Hanlon, "Institutional Forms and Organizational Structures."

31. Stephen Moss, "Special Report: An Outsider's Guide to the City of London," *The Guardian*, May 27, 2014.

32. International Monetary Fund, "Report for Selected Country Groups And Subjects," *World Economic Outlook Database, April 2015* (Washington, DC: IMF, 2015).

33. Austin Mitchell, Prem Sikka, John Christensen, Philip Morris, and Steven Filling, *No Accounting for Tax Havens* (Basildon, UK: Association for Accountancy & Business Affairs, 2002).

34. Leah Goodman, "Inside the World's Top Offshore Tax Shelter," *Newsweek*, January 16, 2014.

35. George Monbiot, "Our Economic Ruin Means Freedom for the Super-rich," *The Guardian*, July 30, 2012.

36. Danny Boyle, *The Little Money Book* (Bristol, UK: Alistair Sawday, 2003).

37. Oliver Bullough, "The Fall of Jersey: How a Tax Haven Goes Bust," *The Guardian*, December 8, 2015.

38. Palan, "Commercialization of State Sovereignty," 168.

39. Goodman, "Inside the World's Top Offshore Tax Shelter."

40. Bullough, "The Fall of Jersey."

41. Nicholas Shaxson, *Treasure Islands: Tax Havens and the Men Who Stole the World* (London: Random House, 2011), 5.

42. Robert Wood, "Americans Renouncing Citizenship up 221%, All Aboard the FATCA Express," *Forbes*, February 6, 2014.

43. Palan, "Commercialization of State Sovereignty," 168.

44. John McKinnon and Scott Thurm, "U.S. Firms Move Abroad to Cut Taxes," *Wall Street Journal*, August 28, 2012.

45. George Marcus and Peter Hall, *Lives in Trust: The Fortunes of Dynastic Families in Late Twentieth-Century America* (Boulder, CO: Westview Press, 1992), 78–79.

46. Ibid., 69.

47. Iris Goodwin, "How the Rich Stay Rich: Using a Family Trust Company to Secure a Family Fortune," *Seton Hall Law Review* 40 (2010): 467–516.

48. Data on the Bessemer Trust, accessed September 9, 2015, www .bessemertrust.com/portal/site/bessemernew/menuitem.c4974f7d4e 9b050ed0db70106e730a6c; data on Rockefeller & Co., accessed September 9, 2015, www.rockco.com/our-history.

49. James Hughes Jr., *Family Wealth: Keeping It in the Family* (Princeton Junction, NJ: NetWrx, 1997), 2.

50. See, for example, Charles Collier, *Wealth in Families* (Cambridge, MA: Harvard University Alumni Affairs and Development Communications, 2002).

51. Hughes, *Family Wealth*, 75.

52. Ibid.

53. Marco Albertini, Martin Kohli, and Claudia Vogel, "Intergenerational Transfers of Time and Money in European Families: Common Patterns—Different Regimes?" *Journal of European Social Policy* 17, no. 4 (2007): 320.

54. Marcus and Hall, *Lives in Trust*, 69.

55. Stephanie Strom, "Big Gifts, Tax Breaks and a Debate on Charity," *New York Times,* September 6, 2007.

56. Donald McNeil, "WHO Official Criticizes Gates Foundation 'Cartel' on Malaria Research," *New York Times,* February 18, 2008.

57. Genschel, "Globalization and the Transformation of the Tax State," 58.

58. Colin Riegels, "The BVI IBC Act and the Building of a Nation," *IFC Review,* March 1, 2014.

59. The 40 percent figure is from Emile de Willebois, Emily Halter, Robert Harrison, Ji Won Park, and Jason Sharman, *The Puppet Masters: How the Corrupt Use Legal Structures to Hide Stolen Assets and What to Do about It* (Washington, DC: World Bank, 2011). The valuation is from IMF calculations; see International Monetary Fund, "British Virgin Islands: Financial Sector Assessment Program Update— Financial System Stability Assessment," IMF Country Report No. 10/323, 2010.

60. Natasha van der Zwan, "Making Sense of Financialization," *Socio-Economic Review* 12 (2014): 114–115. See also Deeg and O'Sullivan, "The Political Economy of Global Finance Capital," 738.

61. Robert Lee, "The Civil Law and the Common Law: A World Survey," *Michigan Law Review* 14 (1915): 99–100.

62. Parkinson, *Certificate in International Trust Management.*

63. Emily Erikson and Peter Bearman, "Malfeasance and the Foundation for Global Trade: The Structure of English Trade in the East Indies, 1601–1833," *American Journal of Sociology* 112 (2006): 195–230.

64. Bullough, "The Fall of Jersey."

65. Norman Peagam, "Nine Centres Worth Finding on the Map," *Euromoney* 1989, 4–10.

66. U.S. Bureau of International Narcotics and Law Enforcement Affairs, "International Narcotics Control Strategy Report, Volume II: Money Laundering and Financial Crimes, Turks and Caicos," U.S. Department of State, Washington, DC, 2014.

67. Matthew Shaer, Michael Hudson, and Margot Williams, "Sun and Shadows: How an Island Paradise Became a Haven for Dirty Money," International Consortium of Investigative Journalists, Washington, DC, 2014.

68. Anthony van Fossen, "Money Laundering, Global Financial Insta-
    bility, and Tax Havens in the Pacific Islands," *The Contemporary
    Pacific* 15 (2003): 237–275.
69. Heather Stewart, "Wealth Doesn't Trickle Down—It Just Floods
    Offshore, New Research Reveals," *The Guardian*, July 21, 2012.
70. CNBC Africa, "Nigerian Millionaires on the Rise," February 12, 2015.
71. Anna White, "Is the Luxury London Housing Bubble about to Burst?"
    The Telegraph, November 1, 2014. See also Rosemary Marr, "Jersey:
    Riding the Tides of Change," *STEP Journal*, November 2014, 75.
72. Andrew Sayer, *Why We Can't Afford the Rich* (Bristol, UK: Policy
    Press, 2015), 237.
73. Shaxson, *Treasure Islands*, 10.
74. Sayer, *Why We Can't Afford the Rich*, 256.
75. Ibid., 257.
76. Maurer, "Complex Subjects."
77. Stephane Fitch, "Pritzker vs. Pritzker," *Forbes*, November 24, 2003.
78. Maurer, "Complex Subjects," 117.
79. Ed Pilkington, "Islanders Count Cost of Billionaire's Collapsed Em-
    pire," *The Guardian*, February 21, 2009.
80. Shaxson, *Treasure Islands*, 10.
81. Goodman, "Inside the World's Top Offshore Tax Shelter." See also
    my experience in the BVI, as recounted in the appendix to Chapter 1
    of this book.
82. Jason Sharman, *Havens in a Storm: The Struggle for Global Tax
    Regulation* (Ithaca, NY: Cornell University Press, 2006).
83. Robinson, "Social Theory and Globalization," 173.
84. Riegels, "The BVI IBC Act and the Building of a Nation."
85. Harneys, "Harneys Marks BVI's Landmark IBC Act's Anniversary
    with New Video," press release, July 15, 2014.
86. Kris Devasabai, "Crisis Legislation Leads to Thriving Industry,"
    Hedge Funds Review, BVI Supplement, Risk.net, May 4, 2009.
87. Ibid.
88. Jonathan Dunlop, "Healthy Competition," *STEP Journal*, April
    2008, 29.
89. Riegels, "The BVI IBC Act and the Building of a Nation."
90. Ben Judah, "London's Laundry Business," *New York Times*, March 8,
    2014.

91. Anne Michel, "Inside the British Virgin Islands: A Forbidden City," International Consortium of Investigative Journalists, Washington, DC, 2014.
92. Ibid.
93. Ibid.
94. The 40 percent figure is from de Willebois et al., *The Puppet Masters.* The valuation is from IMF calculations; see International Monetary Fund, "British Virgin Islands: Financial Sector Assessment Program Update."
95. Harneys, "Harneys Marks BVI's Landmark IBC Act's Anniversary."
96. Michel, "Inside the British Virgin Islands."
97. Ibid.
98. Palan, "Trying to Have Your Cake and Eating It," 635.
99. Werner Conze and Jürgen Kocka, "Einleitung," in Werner Conze and Jürgen Kocka, eds., *Bildungsburgertum im 19. jahrhundert*, vol. 1, *Bildungssystem und professionalisierung in internationalen vergleichen* (Stuttgart, Germany: Klett-Cotta, 1985), 18.
100. Stephen Brenkley, "England Tour of West Indies: Dark Shadow of Allen Stanford Grips Antigua," *The Independent*, February 28, 2014.
101. Bullough, "The Fall of Jersey."
102. Palan, "Trying to Have Your Cake and Eating It," 630.
103. Sayer, *Why We Can't Afford the Rich*, 239.
104. Charles Tilly, *From Mobilization to Revolution* (Reading, MA: Addison-Wesley, 1978).
105. Adam Hofri, "Professionals' Contribution to the Legislative Process: Between Self, Client, and the Public," *Law & Social Inquiry* 39 (2014): 117.
106. Tamar Hermann, Ella Heller, Chanan Cohen, Gilad Be'ery, and Yuval Lebe, "The Israeli Democracy Index 2014," Israeli Democracy Institute, Jerusalem, 2014.

7. Conclusion

1. Joan Didion, "7000 Romaine, Los Angeles 38," *Slouching towards Bethlehem*, 67–72 (New York: Farrar, Straus, and Giroux, 1968).
2. Ibid.

3. Ronen Shamir, *Managing Legal Uncertainty: Elite Lawyers in the New Deal* (Durham, NC: Duke University Press, 1995).

4. Jeffrey Winters, *Oligarchy* (New York: Cambridge University Press, 2011), 219.

5. Jens Beckert, *Inherited Wealth* (Princeton, NJ: Princeton University Press, 2009).

6. Arthur Kennickell, "Ponds and Streams: Wealth and Income in the US, 1989 to 2007,"Finance and Economics Discussion Series, Federal Reserve Board, Washington, DC, 2009.

7. Thomas Piketty, "On the Long-Run Evolution of Inheritance: France 1820–2050," Working Paper, Paris School of Economics, 2010.

8. Santiago Budría, Javier Díaz-Giménez, José-Victor Ríos-Rull, and Vincenzo Quadrini, "Updated Facts on the US Distributions of Earnings, Income, and Wealth," *Federal Reserve Bank of Minneapolis Quarterly Review* 26 (2002): 2–35.

9. John Langbein, "The Secret Life of the Trust: The Trust as an Instrument of Commerce," *Yale Law Journal* 107 (1997): 165–189.

10. Thomas Piketty, *Capital in the Twenty-First Century* (Cambridge, MA: Harvard University Press, 2014).

11. Holly Brewer, "Entailing Aristocracy in Colonial Virginia: 'Ancient Feudal Restraints' and Revolutionary Reform," *William and Mary Quarterly* 54 (1997): 307–346.

12. Jens Beckert, "The *Longue Durée* of Inheritance Law: Discourses and Institutional Development in France, Germany and the United States since 1800," *Archives of European Sociology* 48 (2007): 79–120.

13. Michael Parkinson, *Trust Creation: Law and Practice*, 3rd ed. (Birmingham, UK: Central Law Training, 2005).

14. Michel Pinçon and Monique Pinçon-Charlot, *Grand Fortunes: Dynasties of Wealth in France,* trans. Andrea Lyn Secara (New York: Algora, 1998), 10.

15. Annette Weiner, *Inalienable Possessions: The Paradox of Keeping-while-Giving* (Berkeley: University of California Press, 1992). See also Ian Hodder, *Çatalhöyük: The Leopard's Tale* (London: Thames & Hudson, 2006).

16. Rogers Brubaker, *The Limits of Rationality: An Essay on the Social and Moral Thought of Max Weber* (Abingdon, UK: Routledge, 2006).

17. George Marcus and Peter Hall, *Lives in Trust: The Fortunes of Dynastic Families in Late Twentieth-Century America* (Boulder, CO: Westview Press, 1992), 242.

18. Alison Wylie, "The Promise and Perils of an Ethic of Stewardship," in Lynn Meskell and Peter Pells, eds., *Embedding Ethics*, 47–68 (London: Berg Press, 2005).

19. Helen Berry and Elizabeth Foyster, "Introduction," in Helen Berry and Elizabeth Foyster, eds., *The Family in Early Modern England*, 1–17 (New York: Cambridge University Press, 2007).

20. Brian Powell, Laura Hamilton, Bianca Manago, and Simon Cheng, "Implications of Changing Family Forms for Children," *Annual Review of Sociology* 42 (2016).

21. Marcus and Hall, *Lives in Trust*, 4.

22. Ibid., 15.

23. Daniel Muzio, David Brock, and Roy Suddaby, "Professions and Institutional Change: Towards an Institutionalist Sociology of the Professions," *Journal of Management Studies* 50 (2013): 699–721.

24. Tamar Frankel, "Cross-Border Securitization: Without Law, but Not Lawless," *Duke Journal of Comparative and International Law* 8 (1998): 255–282.

25. Peer Fiss and Paul Hirsch, "The Discourse of Globalization: Framing and Sensemaking of an Emerging Concept," *American Sociological Review* 70 (2005): 29–52.

26. Bertrand Malsch and Yves Gendron, "Re-theorizing Change: Institutional Experimentation and the Struggle for Domination in the Field of Public Accounting," *Journal of Management Studies* 50 (2013): 872.

27. Marion Fourcade and Joachim Savelsberg, "Introduction: Global Processes, National Institutions, Local Bricolage: Shaping Law in an Era of Globalization," *Law & Social Inquiry* 31 (2006): 514.

28. Quotation is from ibid., 516. On the neglect of the interpersonal level, see Bruce Carruthers and Terence Halliday, "Negotiating Globalization: Global Scripts and Intermediation in the Construction of Asian Insolvency Regimes," *Law & Social Inquiry* 31 (2006): 521–584.

29. Muzio, Brock, and Suddaby, "Professions and Institutional Change."

30. Ibid., 702.

31. Carruthers and Halliday, "Negotiating Globalization."

32. Paul Boreham, "Indetermination: Professional Knowledge, Organization and Control," *Sociological Review* 31 (1983): 693–718.

33. Eliot Freidson, *Professionalism: The Third Logic* (Chicago: University of Chicago Press, 2001). See also Andrew Abbott, "The Order of the Professions: An Empirical Analysis," *Work and Occupations* 18 (1991): 355–384.

34. Michael Smets, Tim Morris, and Royston Greenwood, "From Practice to Field: A Multilevel Model of Practice-Driven Institutional Change," *Academy of Management Journal* 55 (2012): 899.

35. Mustafa Emirbayer, "Manifesto for a Relational Sociology," *American Journal of Sociology* 103 (1997): 281–317.

36. On interactional analysis: Andrew Abbott, *The System of the Professions: An Essay on the Division of Expert Labor* (Chicago: University of Chicago Press, 1988). On network analysis: Peter Dicken, Philip Kelly, Kris Olds, and Henry Yeung, "Chains and Networks, Territories and Scales: Towards a Relational Framework for Analyzing the Global Economy," *Global Networks* 1 (2001): 89–112.

37. Boreham, "Indetermination."

38. Eugene McCann and Kevin Ward, "Relationality/Territoriality: Toward a Conceptualization of Cities in the World," *Geoforum* 41 (2010): 175–184.

39. On globalized local solutions, see Boaventura Santos, *Toward a New Legal Common Sense: Law, Globalization and Emancipation* (London: Butterworths, 2002). On the Wall Street legal firm, see Yves Dezalay, "The Big Bang and the Law," in Mike Featherstone, ed., *Global Culture: Nationalism, Globalization and Modernity*, 279–294 (London: Sage, 1990). On Anglo-Saxon financial models, see Frankel, "Cross-Border Securitization."

40. James Faulconbridge, "Relational Networks of Knowledge Production in Transnational Law Firms," *Geoforum* 38 (2007): 926.

41. Thomas Lawrence and Roy Suddaby, "Institutions and Institutional Work," in Stewart Clegg, Cynthia Hardy, Thomas Lawrence, and Walter Nord, eds., *The Sage Handbook of Organization Studies*, 2nd ed., 215–254 (London: Sage, 2006).

42. Michael Smets and Paula Jarzabkowski, "Reconstructing Institutional Complexity in Practice: A Relational Model of Institutional Work and Complexity," *Human Relations* 66 (2013): 1282–1283.

43. Patricia Thornton, William Ocasio, and Michael Lounsbury, *The Institutional Logics Perspective: A New Approach to Culture, Structure and Process* (Oxford, UK: Oxford University Press, 2012). See also Giuseppe Delmestri, "Streams of Inconsistent Institutional Influences: Middle Managers as Carriers of Multiple Identities," *Human Relations* 59 (2006): 1515–1541.

44. Ronald Jepperson, "Institutions, Institutional Effects and Institutionalism," in Walter Powell and Paul DiMaggio, eds., *The New Institutionalism in Organizational Analysis* (Chicago: University of Chicago Press, 1991), 143.

45. Norbert Elias, *The Genesis of the Naval Profession* (Dublin: University College Dublin Press, 2007), 28.

46. Ibid., 27, emphasis added.

47. On the legal profession, see Abbott, *The System of the Professions*; on accountancy, see Hugh Willmott, "Organising the Profession: A Theoretical and Historical Examination of the Development of the Major Accountancy Bodies in the U.K.," *Accounting, Organizations and Society* 11 (1986): 555–580.

48. Giovanni Arrighi, *The Long Twentieth Century* (London: Verso, 1994). See also Greta Krippner, "The Financialization of the American Economy," *Socio-Economic Review* 3 (2005): 173–208.

49. Brooke Harrington, "Going Global: Professionals and the Microfoundations of Institutional Change," *Journal of Professions and Organization* 2 (2015): 1–19.

50. Grace Lees-Maffei, "Introduction: Professionalization as a Focus in Interior Design History," *Journal of Design History* 21 (2008): 1–18.

51. Francis Sanders, *An Essay on the Nature and Laws of Uses and Trusts, Including a Treatise on Conveyances at Common Law and Those Deriving Their Effect from the Statute of Uses* (London: E. & R. Brooke, 1791), 194, emphasis and spelling in original text.

52. Peter Hall, "Family Structure and Class Consolidation among the Boston Brahmins," Ph.D. diss., State University of New York at Stony Brook, 1973, 282.

53. For relevant text from the U.S. Uniform Trust Code, see Section 708 of the law: www.cobar.org/index.cfm/ID/593/subID/2551/TRUST/SECTION-708.-COMPENSATION-OF-TRUSTEE. For relevant text from the U.K. Trustee Act of 2000, see Part V, Section 28, www.legislation.gov.uk/ukpga/2000/29/section/28.

54. Eugene Glader, *Amateurism and Athletics* (West Point, NY: Leisure Press 1978), 158.

55. Christoph Bertling, "The Loss of Profit? The Rise of Professionalism in the Olympic Movement and the Consequences That Arise for National Sport Systems," *Journal of Olympic History* 2 (2007): 50–59.

56. Ibid.

57. Mathew Dowling, Jonathon Edwards, and Marvin Washington, "Understanding the Concept of Professionalisation in Sport Management Research," *Sport Management Review* 17 (2014): 520–529.

58. Robert McGraw, "The Road to Sustainable Growth in Wealth Management: Transformation through New Operating and Service Models," KPMG, New York, 2014.

59. Keith Macdonald, *The Sociology of the Professions* (London: Sage, 1995), 31.

60. Elias, *The Genesis of the Naval Profession*, 31.

61. Ibid.

62. Talcott Parsons, *The Social System* (London: Routledge and Kegan Paul, 1951). See also Alvin Gouldner, *The Future of Intellectuals and the Rise of a New Class* (New York: Seabury Press, 1979).

63. Ronan Palan, "Trying to Have Your Cake and Eating It: How and Why the State System Has Created Offshore," *International Studies Quarterly* 42 (1998): 630.

64. Elizabeth Paton, "Sexy Fish Caters to London's Stateless Superrich," *New York Times*, December 11, 2015.

65. G. K. Chesterton, *The Man Who Was Thursday: A Nightmare* (Eastford, CT: Martino, 2011 [1909]), 104.

66. Stephen Moss, "Special Report: An Outsider's Guide to the City of London," *The Guardian*, May 27, 2014.

67. James March, "Bounded Rationality, Ambiguity and the Engineering of Choice," *Bell Journal of Economics* 9 (1978): 595.

68. Nelson Aldrich, *Old Money: The Mythology of America's Upper Class* (New York: Vintage Books, 1988).

69. Eduardo Porter, "The Case for Raising Top Tax Rates," *New York Times*, March 27, 2012.

70. Robert Wood, "Citizenship Renunciation Fee Hiked 442% and You Can't Come Back,"*Forbes*, January 13, 2015.

71. Richard Bellamy, review of *The Cosmopolites: The Coming of the Global Citizen*, by Atossa Araxia Abrahamian, *New York Times*, January 11, 2016.

72. Gabriel Zucman, *The Hidden Wealth of Nations* (Chicago: University of Chicago Press, 2015), 79.

73. Ibid., 91.

74. Oliver Bullough, "The Fall of Jersey: How a Tax Haven Goes Bust," *The Guardian*, December 8, 2015.

75. Ibid.

76. Zucman, *The Hidden Wealth of Nations*, 89.

77. Bullough, "The Fall of Jersey."

78. Ibid.

79. Manish Bhansali, Deepti Sharma, and Vijay Raina, "Epigastric Heteropagus Twins: 3 Case Reports with Review of Literature," *Journal of Pediatric Surgery* 40 (2015): 1204–1208.

80. Zucman, *The Hidden Wealth of Nations*, 34.

81. Ibid., 30.

82. Doreen McBarnet, "After Enron: Corporate Governance, Creative Compliance and the Uses of Corporate Social Responsibility," in Justin O'Brien, ed., *Governing the Corporation: Regulation and Corporate Governance in an Age of Scandal and Global Markets*, 205–222 (New York: John Wiley & Sons, 2005).

83. Zucman, *The Hidden Wealth of Nations*, 73.

84. Adam Hofri, "Professionals' Contribution to the Legislative Process: Between Self, Client, and the Public," *Law & Social Inquiry* 39 (2014): 96–126.

85. Zucman, *The Hidden Wealth of Nations*.

86. David Campbell, "Mining the African Frontier of Wealth Management with Aston," *Wealth Manager*, May 16, 2013.

87. Finaccord, *Global Expatriates: Size, Segmentation and Forecast for the Worldwide Market* (London: Finaccord, 2014).

88. Jason Sharman, *Havens in a Storm: The Struggle for Global Tax Regulation* (Ithaca, NY: Cornell University Press, 2006).

89. Hofri, "Professionals' Contribution."

Acknowledgments

This book is the product of an unconventional study. Not only did it involve an unusual approach to data-gathering, but it was funded from a patchwork of sources rather than the more usual (and respectable) large grant from a major institution. When I started this research in 2007, inequality was not nearly as big an issue among scholars or in the media as it is now. That made it difficult to convince academic funding agencies to front large sums to study the subject over the course of years. Moreover, my plan to gather data about the secretive world of wealth managers by training in the profession myself—a strategy detailed in the Appendix to Chapter 1—seemed very risky to some. Even people who supported my project in theory thought it would founder on the shoals of professional resistance to disclosure. "Why on earth would they agree to talk with you?" was the common response.

So the hundreds of thousands of dollars it took to complete the training program, and then to "follow the money" of the ultra-rich to eighteen countries, had to be pulled together from a wide variety of sources, including my own pocket. Ultimately, it took eight years—a process drawn out in part by the necessity of writing many grant applications—to gather the sixty-five in-depth interviews with wealth managers that form the basis for this study. For keeping the process rolling along financially, I am very grateful to the following individuals and institutions (listed in chronological order):

> Jens Beckert and the Max Planck Institute for the Study of Societies in Cologne, Germany
> The University of Michigan's Panel Study of Income Dynamics
> The American Sociological Association's Fund for the Advancement of the Discipline
> The Alexander von Humboldt Foundation's Research Fellowship
> Leonard Seabrooke, who put me on two of his grants: the European Research Council project Professionals in the International Political Economy, and the FP7 project Global Re-ordering: Evolution Through European Networks
> My mother, whose frequent flier miles made the Cook Islands trip possible

I am also indebted to Jens, Len, Eleni Tsingou (my colleague at CBS), John Campbell (my former professor at Harvard and now part-time colleague at CBS), Sigrid Quack (formerly my colleague at the Max Planck Institute), and Adam Hofri (law professor at the Hebrew University of Jerusalem) for excellent feedback on previous drafts and presentations of this work, leading to major insights on my part. Finally, I would like to thank Charles Denby, formerly my student at Brown University, for acting as my research assistant fifteen years ago, when I first conceived this project.

Many dear friends and loved ones have made it possible for me to do this research by providing moral and practical support. Pipaluk and Peri gave me extra time to write by hosting playdates at their house; *qujanarsuaq* to you both. Kerstin, alias Homeskillet, helped me create a nurturing bubble of American culture and friendship in the middle of Copenhagen; plus, she threw in many meals and kid sleepovers to boot. Sara and Thomas have been the best neighbors ever, providing a bit of the Midwest here on this side of the Atlantic. Without Luann's help, the trip to Argentina and Uruguay would not have been possible. Mom and Kerem were the pillars of the support system, and for that they have my eternal gratitude. Panda gamely endured thirteen-hour flights and sometimes hairraising adventure as I dragged him from Buenos Aires to Shanghai, and from Johannesburg to Rarotonga. He also embodied the passage of time over the course of this project. I just barely finished the wealth management training program before he was born; then, as I was reviewing the production edits for this manuscript, he sat nearby and began writing his very first story ("The cat was driving . . ."). This book is dedicated to him.

Index

accountants: in asset-holding-structure creation, 13, 53; in offshore financial centers, 131; opinion letters by, 210; of Persian shah, 2, 23, 80; professionalization of, 283; the rich can afford the best, 208, 274; trustees not allowed to delegate to, 49; wealth managers as, 3, 205, 234; wealth managers as part, 7, 26

advertising: by wealth managers, 98; for wealth managers, 60, 76–78

Africa: corruption as concern in, 143; EMEA (Europe, Middle East, and Africa), 243; growth of private fortunes in, 203; land ownership in, 4; Nigeria, 259; taboos in, 117–18; wealth moved to Switzerland from, 130. *See also* South Africa

African National Congress, 142

agency: in economic inequality, 205–8, 273, 274–76; in globalization, 279, 280; in institutional theory, 282; in professional settings, 281; relational theory for, 281–82; in undermining Westphalian state system, 294

Alan (banker and trustee), 123, 124

Alex (Singapore-based wealth manager), 98

alimony, 295

Alistair (Cayman Islands–based wealth manager), 66, 83, 85, 88, 125, 141, 162–63

amana, 111

amateurs, 36, 42, 54, 284, 285

Amelia (Cayman Islands–based wealth manager), 64–65, 99–100

American Academy of Financial Management, 30

American College of Trust and Estate Counsel (ACTEC), 30

American Medical Association, 58

America's Cup races, 104

anarchists, 150, 290, 295

Antigua, 260–61, 268

apprenticeship, accidental, 103–5

Arabian Peninsula, 88, 110–12, 116–17, 166

Arjun (Mauritius-based wealth manager), 117–18, 145, 258

art, 160, 211, 291

Asians: British Virgin Islands used by, 146–47, 177; Cayman I slands used by, 177; cultural preferences of, 114–15; India, 145–46, 258. *See also* China; Singapore

Dickens, Charles, 1–2
Didion, Joan, 271
Dieter (German wealth manager),
    69–70, 91, 97, 100–102, 103–4, 234
discretionary trusts, 155–56, 162–63
dispositions, 94, 103, 105, 109, 119, 121
diversification, 211
"divide-and-conquer" strategy, 135, 153
divorce, 162–64
Donovan, Jim, 206
double taxation avoidance agreements
    (DTAAs), 145–46
Drew (London-based wealth manager),
    66–67, 136–37, 138–39, 143, 241–43
Dryden, John, 215
due process, 141, 147
Durkheim, Émile, 277
dynastic trusts, 170, 229
dynastic wealth: as challenge to state
    authority, 243–52, 268–69;
    creating, 208–17; defining
    characteristic of, 208; destabilizes
    governments and markets, 203;
    economic impact of, 217–21;
    *Family Wealth: Keeping It in the
    Family*, 250–51; impact of, 217–25;
    institutions developed to preserve,
    249–52; laws that threaten to
    dissipate, 42; passing on strategic
    positions in apparatus of appropria-
    tion, 15–16; political economy
    affected by, 246–49; political
    impact of, 221–25; wealth
    management's historical connec-
    tions to, 10. *See also* family
    fortunes

e-commerce, 297
economic inequality: agency in,
    205–8, 273, 274–76; contributions
    to theory and research of this study,
    273–76; democracy threatened by,
    220; in income, 11, 195, 199, 200,
    203–4, 273; inequality defined,

197; inheritance in, 201–5, 207,
    218; offshore finance in, 194, 196,
    219–20; the problem of inequality,
    197–208; in recovery from financial
    crisis of 2008, 201, 211–13; renewed
    interest in, 195–96, 273; rising levels
    of, 194, 220; STEP and changing
    views of, 225–30; tax avoidance in,
    194, 207; in wealth, 11, 12, 195,
    200–201, 203, 205–8, 273; wealth
    management in, 10–12, 20–21, 172,
    193–232, 272, 297–98
economic mobility: decline in, 218–19;
    inheritance reduces, 217; upward
    mobility, 219, 221, 265
education: family institutions take on
    functions of, 250; philanthropic
    trusts address problems of, 252;
    wealth managers' educational
    background, 102–3; wealth
    provides basis for long-term
    investments in, 273; wealth unduly
    influences, 266, 268
Elaine (Dubai-based wealth manager),
    83, 86, 104–5, 117, 166, 287
Eleanor (Swiss-based wealth manager),
    69, 79–80, 89
Elias (Panama-based wealth manager),
    114, 177, 229–30, 232, 298–99
Elias, Norbert, 282–83, 286–87, 288
elites: alliances among, 17–18; assert
    their autonomy from government,
    43, 128, 314n29; change disliked by,
    89; as class that inherits, 203;
    dynastic wealth and political power
    of, 15–16, 223; essential sameness
    of, 81–82; family institutions
    opened to the public, 250; gaining
    trust of high-net-worth individuals,
    92–105; getting them to submit to
    rule of law, 303; habitus of, 95, 103;
    hypermobile international, 236;
    imperial, 254–55; landed, 43, 46–47,
    124; local, 260, 261; noblesse oblige

finance: complexity of international
financial markets, 272; continuing
crises in, 298; defined, 6; deregula-
tion of, 126; dirty work of, 132–33;
divorce financial analysis, 162,
331n101; each jurisdiction creates
its own legal system for, 237;
fiduciary responsibility absent in,
82; as global, 56–57, 60, 128,
253–59; lack of organization at
international level, 235; little
infrastructure needed for, 255;
long-term relationships with
clients in financial services, 320n1;
payment and privilege in, 59–67;
professional innovation in, 279;
wealth management as at core of,
6. *See also* bankers; financial
(subprime mortgage) crisis of 2008;
offshore finance
Financial Action Task Force, 158
financial (subprime mortgage)
crisis of 2008: conflict over tax
avoidance after, 239; Goldman
Sachs in, 63; inequality of
subsequent recovery, 201, 211–13;
interest in 1 percent renewed by,
195; wealth management in, 19;
the wealthy as able to buy when
everyone else was selling, 211, 214;
world financial crisis nearly
destroyed by, 295
financialization, 126, 253, 283, 287, 288
flee clauses, 175, 176, 177
Forbes magazine: *Forbes* billionaire
class, 126; Forbes 400, 195–96, 201,
213–14; on Pritzker family, 13
foundations, 177–81; beneficiaries on
managing council, 179; control as
characteristic of, 151–52;
corporations compared with, 180,
186–87; in defining bounds of
family, 277; downsides of, 180–81;
in economic inequality, 275;

family, 151; in financial architecture created by wealth managers, 6,
271; in Latin America, 178; legal
status as persons, 179; modifying to
increase their appeal, 185; in
Panama, 148, 149, 185; perpetual,
176, 179, 187; privacy and, 152, 153,
180; Roman law origins of, 178;
salaries of officers of, 152; for tax
avoidance, 150–53; tax risks for,
178, 180, 186; transaction costs of,
180; trusts compared with, 152,
178–80, 186–87. *See also* charitable
(philanthropic) foundations
fragmentation, 133–35
Frank (Cyrus-based wealth manager),
114, 147
free trade, 239, 254, 293
"friction," 9
"full immersion" approach, 25, 274

Gabrielle (Seychelles-based fiduciary),
65
Gates, Bill, 123–24
Gates, Bill and Melinda, Foundation,
252
Gayatri (Mauritius-based wealth
manager), 142–43
Geertz, Clifford, 106
gender: demographic composition of
interview sample, 34, 35; gendering
of fiduciary role, 64–65; social
identity and trust, 119–20;
transformation in gender roles,
165–67. *See also* women
George (New Jersey–based wealth
manager), 137
gift, logic of, 49–50
Gilded Age, 126, 203, 276, 313n6
globalization: agency in, 279, 280;
contributions to theory and research
of this study, 278–82; dominant
perspectives on, 28–29; global
capital flows, 21, 22, 219, 235, 248,

Nick (Panama-based wealth manager), 104, 136, 234, 257, 287
Nigel (Singapore-based wealth manager), 92
Nigeria, 259
noblesse oblige, 275, 292
nominee shareholders, 183–84, 185
North, Douglass, 212
Northern Trust Company, 52, 52, 127, 191
notaries, 57–58
oaths, 40–41

Occupy Wall Street, 224–25
OECD (Organisation for Economic Co-operation and Development): elites seek autonomy from institutions such as, 43; financial secrecy and opacity opposed by, 298; hypocrisy regarding tax avoidance, 239; Seoul Declaration on tax avoidance, 12–13; on slowing economic inequality, 202–3; tax havens opposed by, 55, 256, 257, 261; wealth managers seen as under attack by, 23
offshore finance, 128–35; characteristic features of offshore financial centers, 129–33; competition between jurisdictions, 134–35; corporations, 12, 182–84, 185; counterlegislation by offshore financial centers, 171; for debt avoidance, 156–58; in defining bounds of family, 277; diverse characters involved in, 136; "divide-and-conquer" strategy for, 135; divorce-protection trusts, 162–64; economic development reduced by, 219–20; in economic inequality, 194, 196, 219–20, 275; economic prosperity results from, 268; for family-business protection, 168–71; as Faustian bargain for

offshore financial centers, 268; "feudal remnants" in, 37–38; the finance curse for offshore financial centers, 247; flee clauses in trusts, 175, 176, 177; foundations, 180–81; Gates' failure to use, 123–24; in global capital flows, 21; increase in wealth held offshore, 207; lawless zones created by, 295–97; as parasitic on traditional state system, 296–97; as permissive environment for financial-legal creativity, 173; political climate of offshore financial centers, 261; political instability and corruption as reason for using, 140–49; private investment opportunities, 212; scattering assets in, 133–35; in secrecy jurisdictions, 260; seen as scam, 131–32; sovereignty of offshore nations, 296–97; special-purpose vehicles in, 19; states in development of, 239; for tax avoidance, 133, 134, 135, 136, 174–75, 219; for tax sheltering, 47; for trade-restriction avoidance, 159–60; transporting cash to offshore banks, 138–40; trusts, 75, 125, 167–68, 176–77, 185, 191; ultra-freedom in offshore financial centers, 259; wealth management and development of, 5–6; Westphalian state system threatened by, 293–97
Olympic Games, 285
1 percent, 200–201; average annual income of, 200; growth in wealth of, 200; renewed interest in, 195–96; wealth of global, 201
opinion letters, 210
Organisation for Economic Co-operation and Development. See OECD (Organisation for Economic Co-operation and Development)

corporation configuration, 9; on trusts, 174–76, 186; trusts shift burdens to taxpayers, 220; wealth managers' professional subversion of, 17; wealth managers relocate to low-tax jurisdictions, 66; wealthy families shop around for most favorable conditions, 6. *See also* inheritance taxes; tax avoidance; tax evasion; tax havens; tax shelters

tax evasion: British Virgin Islands refuses to respond to evasions of, 264; European Union's Savings Tax Directive for combating, 299; Israel co-opts wealth managers in crack down on, 270; tax avoidance distinguished from, 150; wealth managers associated with, 12, 23

tax havens: African and Russian wealth held in, 203; British Virgin Islands as, 262; client-facing jobs in, 265–66; economic effects on former colonies, 258–59; in former British empire, 264; Jersey as, 24; OECD opposition to, 55, 256, 257, 261; sovereignty in, 256–57, 259–62; the wealthy move to, 137. *See also* offshore finance

tax shelters: colonies as, 254; complexity of, 53; corporate, 151; offshore financial centers as, 47; trust-corporation configuration as, 188; in United Kingdom, 241–42

TEP (Trust and Estate Planning) certification, 26; in advertisement for wealth manager, 60; as industry standard, 30, 55–56; on offshore financial centers, 129, 130; on the state, 236–37; on taxes, 226

testamentary freedom, 166

Thyssen-Bornemisza, Baroness Carmen, 160

tiered entities, 189–92

Tocqueville, Alexis de, 204, 209

trade: free, 239, 254, 293; sanctions, 295; trade-restriction avoidance, 159–60; wealth from global, 5, 51

training programs, 97–98, 103

transaction costs: continuity of wealth reduces, 214; for corporations, 181, 182; for foundations, 180; increased cost of borrowing, 221; minimizing, 209, 212; for private investment opportunities, 212; succession planning reduces, 215

treaties, 133, 256, 264

Treaty of Westphalia (1684), 133, 234, 235, 290, 293–97

Trevor (Panama-based wealth manager), 83, 229, 255

Trudeau, Kevin, 157–58

trust: in client relations, 20, 81–105, 120–21, 287; culture and, 108–16; in institutions, 75; pricing related to, 107, 108; rule of law as basis of, 109; similarity as basis for, 95; social identity and, 119–20

trust and estate planning: American College of Trust and Estate Counsel, 30; bar association special-interest groups for, 29; becomes an industry, 126; Chartered Trust and Estate Planner certification, 30; disparate professions in, 55; professionalization of, 4, 5–6; transformation of capitalism and emergence of, 51; university degrees in, 56. *See also* STEP (Society of Trust and Estate Practitioners); wealth management

Trust and Estate Planning (TEP) certification. *See* TEP (Trust and Estate Planning) certification

trust companies, 3, 77, 190, 191–92, 250

trust-corporation configuration, 185–92; asset transfer in, 8–9; as best-of-both-worlds, 188–89; relationship among substructures

170, 191; regulation of, 174–75;
as relationships, 50, 176, 179;
Romney's, 206; secrecy of, 13,
173–74; social status bestowed on
beneficiaries, 215; spendthrift, 155,
157, 215–16; spreads with expansion
of British Empire, 253–54; stacked,
153–54, *154*; for tax avoidance,
150–51, 153–54, 155, 173; taxing,
174–76, 186; for trade-restriction
avoidance, 159–60; trust companies, 3, 77, 190, 191–92, 250; trust
instruments, 7, 48. *See also* trust
and estate planning; trust-
corporation configuration; trustees
Trusts & Estates (magazine), 51, 54
Turks and Caicos, 167, 255

UNESCO Convention on the Means
of Prohibiting and Preventing the
Illegal Import, Export and Transfer
of Ownership of Cultural Property
(1970), 160
Uniform Prudent Investor Act, 45
United Arab Emirates, 128, 174
United Kingdom: Bubble Act, 48, 181,
314n44; lost revenues due to tax
avoidance, 219; Nigerian
investment in, 259; offshore
finance encouraged by, 239, 255;
Parliamentary Agents, 242–43;
reduced redistributive ambition in,
205; Statute of Elizabeth, 155, 156,
157; stolen client data in, 240;
taxation in, 150; tax shelters in,
241–42; Trustee Act, 49, 284;
Trustee Investment Act, 48–49;
trusts and fiduciary role spread
with expansion of British Empire,
253–54; wealth management's
origins in, 234. *See also* London
university degrees in wealth management, 39, 56
upward mobility, 219, 221, 265

Van Maanen, John, 25–26, 27
vaqf (waqf), 111–12, 218, 324n55
vassalage, 40
Veblen, Thorstein, 125–26, 127
VISTA (Virgin Islands Special Trusts
Act) trusts, 57, 114–15, 168, 169–70,
177, 185, 222

wealth: balance of power between the
state and the wealthy, 244, 291;
breaking link between clients and
their fortunes, 138–39, 174;
changing methods of accumulating, 126; changing nature of,
4–6, 47, 48, 73, 125, 298–99;
circulating, 18, 75; corporate, 19,
74, 130, 238; difficulty in studying,
195–96; distrustfulness among the
wealthy, 85; diversity of the
wealthy, 137; economic and
political privileges resulting from,
198–99; fungible, 38, 47, 48, 74,
126, 238, 288; as global, 11; from
global trade, 5, 51; government
seizure of, 146; hazards of, 135–40;
increase in amount held offshore,
207; increasing world, 11;
inequality, 11, 12, 195, 200–201,
203, 205–8, 273; international
complexity of modern, 125;
international mobility of, 236;
lends special dynamic to families,
84–85; loosening legal restrictions
on deployment of, 48–49, 74;
median household net worth, 200;
mobility of, 11, 218, 236, 238, 248,
290, 303; money makes money,
208, 274; multigenerational
concentrations of, 153, 191, 194,
201–5, 209, 214–17, 275; new
political economy of, 248, 289;
outside of client's control, 75;
paranoia in the wealthy, 137;

clients, 67–68; legal background of managers, 35; managers as indispensable and difficult to replace, 80; methods as disruptive, 18–19; naming the practitioners of, 3–4; negative public image of, *14*, 14–15, 231–32, 258; "neutrality to world of interests" ethic of, 64; new direction for policy regarding, 302–3; new opportunities for growth in, 299–302; origins of the profession, 2–6, 15, 214; in other cultures, 105–20; penalties for divulging client information, 196; personalized service in, 61–62, 92, 93; political impact of, 14, 22, 36, 56, 221–25, 231, 237, 272, 291; prestige of, 61–65, 73; pricing structure in, 106–7, 286; professionalization of, 2–6, 48–53, 194, 207, 283–89; profit margins in, 61, 62; recruiting new clients, 98–100; recruitment of managers, 86, 103–5; resistance to professionalization in, 284–86; salaries for, 59–64, 73, 105, 106–7, 286; societal role of, 12–15; sole practitioners, 70–72, 73; symbolic terrain of, 59; tactics and techniques of, 20, 123–92; traditional point of entry into, 97; training programs in, 97–98, 103; as transnational, 234, 236; trusts as dominant tool in, 185; unique

character of, 76; university degrees in, 39, 56; wealth managers see themselves as protecting clients' assets, 62–63, 67; Westphalian state system hobbled by, 293–97; what wealth managers do, 6–9; women in, 64, 65, 287. *See also* trust and estate planning

Weber, Max: on court accountants of Persian shah, 2, 80, 217–18; on expert authority, 276; sociology defined, 28; on traditional authority wrapped in rational-legal structure, 113; on value spheres, 277; on *vaqf*, 112

Westphalian system, 133, 234, 235, 290, 293–97

Whyte, William, 25, 27

wills: British limitations on writing of, 57, 58; in financial architecture, 7; land transference by, 46–47; written by amateurs, 54, 58

women: couverture doctrine, 165; gendering of fiduciary role, 64–65; mistresses, 125, 165; under shar'ia law, 166; trusts originate to protect daughters, 164–65; as wealth managers, 64, 65, 287

Wyly brothers, 159–60, 196, 300

Zucker, Lynne, 74–75
Zucman, Gabriel, 293–94, 295, 296